Tenants and the
Urban Housing Crisis

Edited by
Stephen Burghardt

THE NEW PRESS
Dexter, Michigan

Grateful acknowledgment is hereby made to the publishers and authors specified for permission to use the following copyright or proprietary materials:

Mark D. Naison and Peacock Press, Chapter 1; Thomas Jennings and the Michigan Law Review, Chapter 3; Ted R. Vaughan and The Society for the Study of Social Problems, Chapter 5; Thomas M. Quinn, Earl Phillips and Fordham University Press, Chapter 6; Myron Moskovitz, National Housing and Economic Development Law Project, Earl Warren Legal Institute, University of California, and Prentice-Hall, Chapter 15.

This book is also available in a less expensive paperbound edition, complete and unabridged, photographed from the same masters used in this edition.

International Standard Book Number: 0-913-23600-4
Library of Congress Catalog Card Number: 72-85329
The New Press, Dexter, Michigan 48130
© 1972 Stephen Burghardt, Ann Arbor, Michigan
First Edition, July 1972
Printed by Litho-Crafters, Ann Arbor
Composition and Keylines by CompType, Ann Arbor
Designed by Bill Haney
Dust jacket photo by Bruce Davidson, Magnum, New York

To
Nancy Romer Burghardt, with love
My closest friend and most trusted critic

A house she hath, 'tis made of such good fashion
The tenant ne'er shall pay for reparation
Nor will the landlord ever raise her rent
Or turn her out of doors for non-payment;
From chimney-tax this cell is free,
To such a house who would not tenant be?

Epitaph from the tombstone of
Rebecca Bogess
Folkestone, England
August 22, 1688

CONTENTS

Acknowledgements

I owe a great deal to a great many people in the preparation of this book. Probably the greatest debt of appreciation and thanks go to Bill Haney, editor and founder of The New Press. If it were not for his original interest in the manuscript, his encouragement and enthusiasm in the laborious process of preparing it, and, to top everything else off, his considerable talent in making stylistic sense out of my sometimes garbled prose, this book would never have been printed. I owe him a debt that will take years to repay—if he'll only let me.

Others at The New Press can't be forgotten either. Doug Truax and his editing, Marcy Haney and Cherie Trudell and their thorough proofreading, were all indispensable. Furthermore, members of The University of Michigan School of Social Work were quick to help me throughout the early stages of this book. Among many, Fred Cox, John Erlich, Rosemary C. Sarri, and Robert Vinter all shared their time and experience in helping me prepare a publishable manuscript.

Wayne Alber and his skilled staff at Comptype were patient and careful with a less than crystal-clear manuscript and their excellent composition and key-lining is much admired and appreciated.

Some of my closest friends were also some of my most helpful critics. David Black, Stuart Katz, and Carol Steiner—all activists experienced in tenant organizing—gave valuable comments and criticisms on the various introductions in the book.

On top of all these people, three others stand out as clearly the greatest aid to me in my work; indeed without all of them, whatever worth the book has would be severely diminished. Michael Beckman did as much in setting the parameters and organizing the structure of the book as I did. Nancy Romer Burghardt was able to give me better direction in both my writing and my analysis than anyone else. Her insistence on tight organization and a coherent thematic structure corrected more than an occasional problem. Finally, Bob Ross's trenchant criticism, both stylistically and analytically, was of tremendous value. While all three people made life more than a little painful on occasion, I owe them each a tremendous debt.

There is one final debt—to the tenants and activists of the Tenants' Rights Movement. Without them, there would be no movement, no attempt to rectify the problems of our housing community. Without them, people like me couldn't write and edit books. My respect for them goes beyond a few token words of appreciation. To make certain of that, sixty percent of whatever royalties received will be going to the National Tenants' Organization in Washington, D.C. Since these people deserve credit for the movement, they should share in its profits as well.

July 1972

Stephen Burghardt
Ann Arbor, Michigan

Foreword

In the Greek myth, Sisyphus must spend his eternity in Hades pushing a boulder up a mountain slope. When he nears the crest, the great stone rolls back down and he must begin again . . . and again.

One senses—in these demoralized times—that efforts of common men and women to wrest control of their conditions from the seemingly faceless forces of urban decay and stagnation are condemned to a similar fate. Great bursts of popular energy build and explode only to be suffocated under a cloud of hopelessness, a funk of cynicism.

These pulsations of energy and despair present a stark contrast to as recent a time as 1967, when mayors of every major city in this country kept fire-watch through long summer nights of anger and pride. Yet these are not repetitive cycles. Make no mistake, the ups and downs of popular revolt are each influenced—one way or another—by what came before. It requires, one admits, something like faith to say this, but there is also some evidence that the revolutionary spirit is cumulative. And if so, it is here that we must discard the Myth of Sisyphus as a useless metaphor to the current situation in America. The Greek scenario was unequivocal, explicit—Sisyphus wasn't going to make it, not ever.

In this volume of cases and documents from the tenants' movement one sometimes gets a sense of the size of that boulder, and the immense frustration of endlessly rolling it. After all, the "housing crisis" of the cities is very much with us; no sudden, massive, life-changing victories which effect thousands of families are recorded in these pages. But before one succumbs to creeping fatalism, one needs to broaden the focus of vision, to understand the context in which these documents speak to us.

The challenge, while examining the record of a social movement such as this one (which is less than world-shaking) is to discern in it what it may become. Even if it appears limited in the nature of the issues it engages and the kinds of people it appeals to in its present form, it makes an indirect contribution by the experience which its participants may later bring to other issues and groups. This challenge forces us to think historically about the future. What is it about the present from which men and women will learn and gain in a few years' time? (Of course, unpredictable events and yet-to-emerge social forces may prevent the transference of experience from one period to another; especially is this so in social movements of common people acting for their own collective interests.) When the formal historical writing, the newspapers and the libraries are all filled with markings of the Great upon history, it is easy to lose the record of the struggles of Everyman. And because it is easy to lose them, today's activists sometimes view each task as if it were an entirely new one, without precedent or tradition to help guide one's work. This may lead to arrogance, an overweening refusal to learn from others, or to needless duplication of avoidable errors.

Because popular struggles are not well-served by formal media of communication or history, they depend greatly on person-to-person communication. Older workers teach younger ones about how the union was formed; fathers teach children about the great marches in which they participated.

Recently, a student at the University of Michigan interviewed a veteran of the Detroit automobile factories about the organization of the UAW-CIO. Here is a passage from the interview with Jim C. who discussed the early union meetings of workers at Ford's Dearborn plant. The time is the late Thirties:

> "We may have maybe 20 people at the meeting, and the leader, if you want to call him a conference leader, may come from the coal mines down in Pennsylvania. He would be introduced as Mr. Smith, and he would have been in the United Mine Workers' organization for so many years. He would be an older man than we would be . . . . I remember Michael Woodman who was the first organizer for us and he came from the coal mines. But he was a member of the United Mine Workers. He was an organizer sent out by John L. Lewis to organize other industries. And John L. Lewis believed in the CIO because he had a running feud with the AF of L because AF of L thought it was above them. He sent out those leaders, lieutenants of his, and those are the people who addressed us in the meetings, and told us the things we would get and the things we needed for a better living: security, better wages, better conditions. Because we had been abused . . ."

"He would be an older man than we would be . . ." So saying, Jim C. is telling us that the organization of the CIO did not pop out of the Depression on land innocent of the plow. Right there, at 1188 Michigan Avenue, says Jim C., one generation made, face-to-face, the link to the next. (The struggles of the miners paid off in Detroit as well.) This is an example of historical continuity that worked. Our more recent experience is less successful—though certainly not devoid of the same general relations. One aspect of the experience of the New Left is an example of this.

In 1964 Students for a Democratic Society was two years old, still small. Its view of both the Communist and nonCommunist Left was compressed into the notion that both were "Old Left", both preoccupied with issues which were irrelevant, practices which were obsolete, theories which had failed. Based on the experience of one of the chapters (at Swarthmore College) which had engaged in an alliance with blacks in Chester, Pennsylvania, the organization judged that mass radical politics could be organized amongst the poor people of America—both blacks and whites alike. Community organizing of poor people became the strategic thrust of large and influential parts of the SDS leadership.

The resulting series of projects had originally been funded by a grant from the UAW for "economic research and action." This was part of the continuity: younger sons and daughters of UAW leaders were members of SDS, and through them there was access to and some support from this sector of the labor movement. But the lack of militance of the contemporary trade union leadership led the members of SDS to look elsewhere than labor, elsewhere than the traditional working class in its analysis of potential radicalism. Yet, as we embarked on community organizing in order to achieve, in the words of a working paper of that time, "an interracial movement of the poor," we were warned that it is very hard, if not impossible, to organize for political action the most desperately poor members of the society. And we were further warned by older leftists and trade unionists, that students on a summer vacation, or middle class graduates making an indefinite, but still temporary commitment to such organizing work would not be effective. And finally, we were told that our spartan style of life, with little or no money to support ourselves, crowded living conditions, and intense, totalistic preoccupation with the organizing projects would burn us out, exhaust and disillusion us.

Nevertheless, in the summer of 1964, even as thousands of white students were working with SNCC in the Mississippi Freedom Summer, SDS members were working in a number of Northern cities to organize what later became community unions.

It was a momentous time in the history of our republic. Goodman, Chaney and Schwerner, three civil rights workers, were killed in Mississippi; in August, the Gulf of Tonkin nonincident occassioned a Congressional Resolution which Lyndon Johnson used to authorize war in Vietnam; and LBJ himself ran a peace campaign against Barry Goldwater. At the Democratic Convention the Mississippi Freedom Democratic Party, made up of integrated civil rights challengers to the Dixiecratic regulars, was refused seating at the meeting. Never again were youthful civil rights militants to work so closely with establishment politics.

Through that summer, students in SDS laboriously made contacts in the poor neighborhoods in which they had taken up residence. In Chicago an effort was made to organize unemployed Appalachian migrants. Names were painstakingly gathered by leafletting at the office of the unemployment compensation bureau. Then one of the project members would visit the person, trying to convince him or her that through a united organization something could be done to provide decent jobs at decent pay for everyone. A small meeting would be called, and the student organizers would pick people up and bring them to it; the meeting would be long and frustrating. As the hot months wore on, the self-blame of the people emerged as one of the largest obstacles to organizing. Too often, the organizers thought, collective political action was made impossible by the peoples' feeling that they themselves were responsible for their plight. To counteract this, the slogan was adopted: In Unity There is Strength.

As the summer ended most of the project members went back to their colleges; the one or two who stayed on felt that a different strategy was needed. The transition, which was successfully managed only with tremendous effort, resulted in the formation of JOIN Community Union, based in Chicago's Uptown area. Even then, it was only years later that the participants began to understand some of the truth in the criticisms which had been given to them prior to their effort. The consuming and spartan existence *was* conducive to burning people out; transient students do *not* make good or even adequate organizers; the most desperately poor people *are* frequently too disorganized personally to sustain political leadership. The gap between the last generation of organizers and the present one had been so sharp that we could not take their knowledge and use it. And this discontinuity made our efforts fragile; five years later none of the seven or eight projects were left.

Those were different, less mobilized times: but another part of the lesson still holds. Outside of the gleaming corporate world, where office furniture magically appears out of overhead budgets and duplication machinery blinks and hums like figments of Buck Rogers' imagination, the work of organizing and sustaining organization is painfully slow and hard. But even when the right moment and competent political work and a deeply felt issue do mobilize people, as is frequently the case, the work is just begun.

Consider the tenants' movement of the Sixties and Seventies. Such a prodigious amount of energy of hundreds of people: passing out petitions, learning the intricacies of housing and legal codes, fighting off eviction notices, demonstrating at slumlords homes, contacting the mass media to get a "mention" of the struggle, running out at midnight to find a magic marker to finish the poster announcing tomorrow's meeting, and, after a while realizing that very little has been won, that life in the slum is still precarious, dangerous, dirty, and depressing and that many poor people are resistant to organizing efforts. So much work, so little to show for it.

Yet, wherever people are working seriously at the grass roots in or for a peoples' movement, there is much to be learned from their experience and much that needs to be thoughtfully analyzed, recorded, and transmitted. When we look at the tenants' movement, a number of "lessons" emerge. Here are some examples.

First, as Stephen Burghardt emphasizes, the requirements of unity and the complexity of the legal situation facing tenants require vast amounts of work before a rent strike can be undertaken. This is important to notice because the experience of many activists in the struggle for Black Liberation and against the War in Vietnam has been somewhat different. These have very frequently involved symbolic targets in which the activists did not risk everyday things—like eviction from their homes. (This should not be interpreted to mean that they do not run high risks: they do.) And they have tended to be open for voluntary participation in contrast to the specific need for tenants of a given structure to be unified. Thus, not only the most militant, informed, enthusiastic people need be recruited—but the least likely tenant must be too. This requires intensive political work.

Second, the tenants' movement is filled with classic reminders of the pitfalls into which organizing can fall. Excessive legalism can kill enthusiasm; excessive rigidity around one tactic—the strike—can deprive the tenants' group of some extremely potent auxiliary tactics. Utopianism, too, is forbidden by a careful reading of the economic situation in slum housing: taking over ownership of even an abandoned building requires great effort and the mastery of complex programs to gain the capital necessary to run the building. Study of this movement, then, is another reminder that change sought on a small scale may, despite both liberal and conservative claims, be harder than change sought on a larger scale. For many tenants, gaining victory over the landlord in a struggle for power is confounded or even useless because the real villain is the system to which even the landlord is enthralled.

Third, the tenants' movement, as in Muskegon Heights, described by Neagu in Chapter 2, reminds us that ordinary people can organize themselves, can devise winning strategies, can advance their own cause. As we move into the decade of the Seventies this lesson is perhaps the most important. The temptation to depend on experts, social planners, or government action to initiate social reform will be and has been very great. There is a fear of the mass of people in America, especially among the educated and affluent. Solid work in such movements as these makes such fear foolish, even mean.

Many people of goodwill note the problems involved in these lessons, and they turn their efforts into more orthodox—that is, routinized and conventional—channels of work. They work for this piece of legislation or that; they take up employment with this public agency or that political liberal's administration; they try to wring from the "system"—which they claim they are "within"—the meliorating action which action-oriented popular movements have only partially won. They turn to the State: they work for reform.

But our post-war history shows, especially in housing and the attendant urban quagmire, that from Washington to Manhattan the governmental structure is incompetent. I do not mean that individuals are stupid or venal—although surely many are; rather, that urban reform has failed and is failing to solve problems. Name the program, and the dismal record can be produced: public housing; urban renewal; community action; model cities: where are the results now that we need them?

In twenty-three years the public housing program has failed to construct the number of units projected for its first five; those it has constructed are some of the greatest disasters of social policy of the century. Pruitt-Igol in St. Louis, Robert Taylor homes in Chicago, these fortresses of horror would be bad even if they housed enough people.

Urban renewal has redistributed amenities from low income residents to middle and upper middle income residents of the city; it has redistributed tax benefits from workers to the middle class; it has torn down more housing than it has built; it has failed in its own goals to attract middle class whites back to the city despite the costs of the attempt; it has contributed to crowding and the spread of ghetto neighborhoods even as it claimed to deter them.

The community action programs have been stripped of funds and freedom, leaving some new black leadership, but little in the way of service, or help. Its successors, model cities, invite residents to participate in the deployment of funds too small to make a difference.

In the meantime, as the tenants' movement is sharply aware, the economics of slum real estate and the soaring property taxes in the cities lead to abandonment of buildings, and make the profit in cheap housing dependent on the neglect of maintenance. Increasingly, the cities become economic dependencies of the federal government, collecting points of too many people with too few of the skills which the economy is willing to compensate adequately.

There are those who will attribute these failures to technical matters; but this writer's judgment is different. Planning and reform efforts fail because they are subject to the same dreary parade of power and privilege which caused the problems to begin with. They do not represent the victories or the establishment of popularly based power: They are the results of reform which redistributes *nothing to the poor but symbols and slogans.* Even while the federal government, for example, is spending money on public housing, it is spending far more on subsidizing middle and upper income housing through tax laws. Consciously or not, the reforms of the era of Big Government have yielded free enterprise for the poor, but a welfare state for the rich.

Now it is an event of no small social importance that liberal democracy has become institutionalized as an ideology appending to the large public bureaucracies in Western Capitalism. Since the New Deal in this country, there have been relatively clear "parties" in regard to the future of capitalism. One—the unreconstructed "royalists"—has defended, and continues to defend the rights of capital in the face of all social need. The other, which has been ascendant since Roosevelt, is "enlightened" and understands that reform for preservation is in the long-run interest of the royalists, as well as in the short-run interests of various affected constituencies who must seek the power of the state to compensate for the skewed justice of the market. Those with this second perspective, but without the personal ties or history in the large institutions of corporate capitalism, have tended to cluster around public bureaucracies: social welfare, education, public health, etc. But somewhere during the Second World War the reforming zeal of their constituency melted. There is no social movement of reforming liberalism. Left stranded, historically, in charge of social welfare institutions, many of these administrators have "displaced goals" that is, they have come to see the survival of their institutions, and the possibilities for careers like theirs, as the definition of the (incrementally) good society. So, increasingly, this sort of liberalism is bureaucratic in base, and oriented to orderly institutional functioning as content. How far have we come from the more or less humane genesis of this ideology? Consider how retrospectively sympathetic we are with the big auto sit-ins of the Thirties, and how presently disturbed are the urban managers at welfare sit-ins and tenants' squat-ins.

Despite the pitfalls, the uncertainty of results, the difficulty and slowness of progress, the route to social justice and better life in the cities requires change that is initiated from the bottom, and that embodies the power of masses of people, organized. This preference for the rougher path of social movements for positive changes is not a product of tantrum or derangement, or even, as some commentators say, of "bitter alienation." It is a choice based on experience.

Glancing over the tenants' movement, then, we have seen some of the things to be learned from it; a sort of learning that can be critical to future movements which neglect past experience at their peril; and we suggested that despite the problems encountered by the movement, activity like it which is based on popular organization and struggle by the people affected is, in the long run, the better path to take. But the reader may wonder at the tone, the use of conditional terms, qualifiers, and the somewhat defensive style of these comments. And the defense of the value of the movement has been somewhat abstract, as if retreating into generality protects from an admission of concrete failure. The reasons for this can be stated clearly, though: We get no guarantees when we undertake this kind of work. The tenants' movement is most probably both reformist—in the sense that it struggles for changes which turn out to be relatively minor—and a potent resource—in that it trains people for the use of their own power. For the sake of the latter, we engage in the former.

When we act in the present, we make tomorrow's history. Not the history of History—the Big Decisions, the Finland Stations, the Gulf of Tonkin—rather we create the experience from which we and our successors can sift and sort, and from which the material of that Bigger History is made. We do small tasks so that greater ones will be possible. In his recent essay on the New Left, a veteran Communist organizer, Gil Green expresses a part of the dilemma this represents for a radical: "The fight for reforms, whether economic or political opens the door to reformist thinking: but to fail to fight for them closes the door to a mass movement." (Gil Green, *The New Left; Anarchist or Marxist?* International Publishers N.Y., 1971.) The small tasks may be merely the raw material for another Senator's presidential boomlet; but they may, too, train the organizers of next year's upsurge of potent rebellion.

The big city newspapers record a steady percolation of tenants' activity; it is a movement at the grass roots. It is not what one would comfortably call a mass movement as yet, or a revolutionary one. Indeed, one wonders whether we are straining reality by isolating tenants' struggles, analyzing them separately from the great movement for black liberation in the cities. It is, perhaps, best seen as a manifestation of black and minority and poor white restiveness within these new reservations called cities. Yet there is enough working class and lower middle class participation in it, and enough focal concern around the problem of housing itself, for it to be discussed in its own right. This is especially true if we keep the larger context of the advance and retreat of the broader social movements in view.

Because so many of the tenants' unions have been organized by young leftists, it is critical to note that for a few years there have been large groups of student and former student leftists who understand the institutional and class isolation of their campus-based movements. Most successful on elite campuses, the student Left has been basically middle class in background, and also in its style and concern. One does not condemn it by observing, however, that a broader social base is needed for change; moreover, the requirements of justice demand it. For many leftist students, the organizing of tenants remains a strategy which puts these radicals in touch with people with whom they would not otherwise work; it builds, they feel, a solid base for organization, rather than the "sentimental" or "symbolic" nature of much leftist student agitation.

The danger, of course, is that a larger vision, or a fundamental challenge to existing power, will be lost in the complex minutia of everyday work. Many former radicals in the labor movement, for example, seem to have traded in their radicalism in return for a sense of concrete accomplishment. Yet, if Green is right, and I believe he is, the risk must be taken.

The protections available to avoid the trivialization of tenant organizing—as any other area of social struggle—are easier stated than implemented. For example, leftists say, usually to one another, "keep politics up front;" "build consciousness about capitalism;" "avoid overly technical, non-struggle strategies." These are all even harder to heed when there is a pause or a retreat in popular militancy. Then, it seems, all one can do is hang on, wait for a more propitious moment.

In modern America especially, holding to a vision of popular democracy and economic justice is made ever so much more difficult by the saturation of the culture with images of bogus freedom. When human freedom is defined as the choice of auto color, style, or vinyl top, the political organizer is faced with not only the power of the economically privileged and the politically entrenched; he faces, too, a culture which divides his constituency and weakens its will. Tom Hayden's new book on the Indochina war, for example, is called *The Love of Possession Is a Disease With Them.*

Given this situation, the veterans of the New Left, the younger organizers involved in the tenants' movement, indeed, any radical or peoples' advocate must do his or her work with great care and forethought. In the current period, especially, the temptations for different kinds of strategic excess are many. The problems of reformism have been mentioned. The other temptation involves a kind of flight from the present reality through what is sometimes called the "new culture". Escaping from the oppressive present, fleeing from the historical "now", many former activists see the future of the new culture as the future of the revolution. Through orgasmic music, uninhabited styles of dress and personal relationships, and a refusal to be taken up in the mundane concerns of "straight" society, these cultural revolutionaries symbolically choose to live in their version of an exotic new society, rather than transform the old one.

But the flamboyance of rock music and the new culture just doesn't speak to the needs of the poor or the hard-pressed lower middle class residents of the big cities. On the other hand, strict enforcement of housing codes, or a five-dollar reduction in rent will not affect the general conditions of urban life. The radicalism of the Seventies, for which the experience of the tenants' movement can be a fertile resource, must be balanced somewhere between avant-garde and exotic culture, and petty meliorism. This will not be easy, a point editor Burghardt has made abundantly clear. The two poles seem to be related: in desperate rejection of reformism, the American Left repeatedly flirts with exoticism. Combining vision with steady work: that is the task before us. Ten years ago, when SDS wrote its Port Huron Statement, it ended with these lines: "If we appear to seek the unattainable, as it has been said, then let it be known that we do so to avoid the unimaginable."

In the decade that followed, despite the rebirth of American radicalism and the growth of popular struggles, the unimaginable happened. America has, in Vietnam, committed barbarous act after barbarous act under three governments and in the face of the most active domestic opposition to a modern foreign policy. Ten years from now it will be 1982. This book is about and by those who work for what seems to be the unattainable. By then, if it has not become more real, who knows what bestiality the unimaginable will hold.

July 1972   *Robert Ross*
                                          Ann Arbor, Michigan

Introduction

The growing tenants' rights movement has already experienced vast changes. It began in the 1930s as an expression against general economic conditions; later on, its rent strikes played a secondary role in the struggles for civil rights and Black Power. Today, it is diverse enough to be considered by some as potentially "the largest grass roots movement in the country."[1]

This book is a product of the tenants' rights movement. It does not attempt to be its definitive statement. Instead, the articles have been chosen for two primary purposes. The first is to analyze the reasons why the tenants' rights movement has developed and to describe the wide variety of activities within it. The second is to give interested tenants and professionals a thorough review of the kinds of work available to them—community and tenant organizing, legal advocacy, planning—if they wish to help further the development of that movement.

There is a more general purpose to the book as well. Social movements are often discussed but seldom understood by either participants, students, or professionals. Social movements are so amorphous and ever-changing that it is difficult to discern their definitions, why they developed, the organizing that goes on within them, the stages of growth, and the kinds of people who give them substance. It is of course beyond the domain of this book to expand an analysis to all social movements. However, it is hoped that the articles within it, and the short introductions linking the various sections together, will make the tenants' rights movement a concrete, comparative example to draw upon for understanding the dynamics of other social movements.

The book has been divided into five sections. The first presents an overview of the tenants' rights movement itself. Some case histories of well-known tenant groups are included for specific information relevant to other tenant groups and those interested in setting up their own organizations. Part II examines the legal and economic background of tenants and their rights. It is designed to aid legal advocates in their own preparations and to explain why the movement has developed. Part III looks at the involved process of tenant organizing, starting with the investigatory research of a neighborhood's housing and proceeding through the formation of a tenant union itself. Part IV is divided into two sections. The first, shorter section looks at the immediate strategies and tactics of a new tenant organization as it attempts to get a foot-

---

NOTE: Numbered references are collected at the end of each chapter.

hold in the community as an established, legitimate tenant advocate. The remainder of Part IV presents some of the longer range strategies which a tenant group must consider if it is to remain effective in working for tenants' rights. Part V presents some concluding observations.

Most of the authors have been participants in tenant activities; so has the editor. Personal involvement always shapes one's attitudes, and it would be dishonest not to admit to the biases that helped form the content and scope of this book. There is not a great deal of material that is kind to landlords, or to the property law which has, as two legal scholars carefully document, remained basically unchanged since feudal times.

However, because one's attitudes may be biased, one's perceptions need not necessarily be. There has been no attempt to distort the present realities in our housing community; indeed, part of the movement's rapid growth may be attributable to its long and careful look at our nation's housing problem. The observations that follow in this introductory section are one person's perceptions of just how serious that problem is. By focusing on some of the inherent tensions in the landlord-tenant relationship, and by looking at some comparable tenant problems within public housing, hopefully it will become clear that our urban housing crisis is far more serious than past references to a housing shortage have implied.

The housing problem is most commonly thought of in terms of a housing shortage, even by our experts. The prestigious Kaiser Commission, whose national study in 1968 was to serve as this decade's major prod for ending our housing ills, consistently placed the problem under the rubrics of construction, rehabilitation, and financing. Its major conclusion was a not unworthy goal of 26 million new and rehabilitated units by 1978, all to be completed through combined public and private means.[2]

Presently their target will be missed by over 10 million units, and that is a conservative estimate. As the Kaiser study admitted, its census statistics on units needing rehabilitation could have been off by more than a third the actual number.[3] Even excluding that possibility, the number of units being built or rehabilitated has averaged little more than 1.6 million a year—and the vast majority of that, while placed in urban areas, is outside our major cities.[4] With multi-unit construction in our cities at an ebb between 1968-1971, a realistic appraisal would see our central cities in the year 1978 in much worse condition than today. Some experts have already predicted as much.[5]

How could a presidential commission, with a vast mandate and high expertise, so quickly prove inadequate to its tasks of first analyzing and then finding solutions for our housing ills? The reason is rather simple. The Kaiser Commission, for all its firm conclusions and future growth charts, spent no time considering the *causes* behind constant housing shortages or perpetually inadequate rehabilitation programs. The group looked at what the present was physically lacking—enough housing—and from there proceeded to develop quick, future methods aimed at correcting that part of the problem:

more construction, easier financing, more public aid.

One begins to understand why the narrow vision when looking at the composition of the commission. Over half the group were either executive officers or directors of major construction, real estate, or home management corporations.[6] Most of the consultants and advisors were representatives of various housing and real estate firms.[7] Such individuals, regardless of their good intentions, represented narrow interests within the housing community; indeed, if any group stood to immediately gain from increased construction and rehabilitation, it was their own firms. There were no tenant representatives, and other than Whitney Young and Walter Reuther, no known advocates of the urban poor. To read their report, one would see the housing situation as a picture with no underlying causes, just a flat surface of past and present conditions. For all the report's depth, not once was the question "why?" asked.

This is not the place to speculate on easy answers as to why the report avoids a discussion of causality; whether they avoided or overlooked the actual causes of our housing problem is at present insignificant. But if they missed the answers, others cannot, not if our continual urban housing crisis is to end. Luckily, tenants—those people rarely mentioned by any commission as part of the housing community—are beginning to grope toward some important answers. At first discomforted, and later organized and angry at their housing conditions, poor and middle class tenants have started agitating around problems previously ignored by other housing experts. In the process of building their own movement—the tenants' rights movement—they are also beginning to point to some of the deep-rooted causes of our housing problem.

Tenants, working for better housing, soon learn that poor tenancy conditions are not merely caused by a tight market. It is often a direct educational process. Most tenants begin organizing in one way or another as a response to faulty wiring, garbage in the halls, or inadequate maintenance in general. Their education comes after they find that their justifiable and logical activities are either ignored or insufficient. They discover that new problems replace corrected ones, while the effort to solve all of them remains expensive and time-consuming for the tenant. An introductory lesson on the complexity of the housing problem is learned; maintenance problems continually reoccur because they are manifestations of the problematic relationship between tenant and landlord.

A tenant enters the relationship to secure a home. He expects comfort, privacy, and safety. Most (but not all) landlords, on the other hand, enter the relationship expecting to make money. The organized tenant learns that these expectations are not merely dissimilar; in today's urban and congested world, they are conflicting. A tenant needs a place to live. When he pays for an apartment, the tenant not only expects that the product (or more precisely, the conglomerate of services) will be delivered but that it will be maintained. As the price of the unchanged product increases (which it does, sometimes as much as 40 percent a year), the tenant increases his expectations for more and better maintenance. If not fulfilled, these expectations often find themselves progressing into demands.

On the other side of the lease, the landlord is often faced with increasing maintenance costs and an often unstable land market. He discovers that he can achieve his expectations by first doing one or both of the following: (1) continually increasing his rents; (2) neglecting his maintenance. The former alternative cannot be repeated too often; tax assessment is partially based on earned revenues of the property, and a too-steep increase may prove to be too much of a good thing. This makes the second alternative a much more attractive choice. Grievance procedures for tenants in such matters are all but nonexistent, housing code enforcement is cursory, and, if fines are levied, they are insignificantly small.[8] If pressed, most large landlords who use their buildings for income will admit that the difference between profit margins in the housing market and those in the stock market will depend on the amount of adequate maintenance offered their tenants; the more the maintenance, the less the difference. If landlords are going to contend with the problems of leases, insurance, or tenant grievances (or if they are going to hire a management company to handle such inconveniences), it is not surprising why they choose to overlook tenant interests to achieve their own.

The above is only the first level of the problem. Initially such differences cause strain; over time, they lead to antipathy between the parties involved. There are few present methods to resolve the dissension. If tenants receive their due maintenance, the landlord's profits decrease significantly. Thus, he will raise rents. If rents increase, the tenant will understandably expect that maintenance and other services improve. If there is neither improvement in product nor an increase in services, then the justification for high rent becomes strained and the tenant's own responsibility to the apartment less apparent. The result: negligence on both sides.

As the antagonism continues, the tenant, if he is unorganized, may go to court over housing code conditions, but this has proven to be a notoriously slow and expensive process, one open only to the well-to-do or those with legal resources.[9] In most states, he will have to continue paying rent even while he is going to court, so the costs become prohibitive.[10] The landlord, on the other hand, has a series of options. If no lease exists, he can legally evict the tenant.[11] He can also refuse to renew his lease, or in extreme cases, hire drunks and derelicts to harrass an entire building of tenants into leaving. Both can and have been done without fear of legal reprisal.[12]

If these alternatives prove neither to silence the tenant nor satisfy the landlord, the latter has the option of selling his building. Over time, there are three likely buyers of urban housing; each is either unable to or disinterested in bettering the property.[13] The first type buys the property for speculation, that is, buying as cheaply as possible to sell quickly for a higher profit or to improve quickly the income from the building. Neither alternative can be achieved by helping present occupants improve their own conditions. Either the new landlord forces out the tenants and charges higher rents to new tenants, or he removes tenants so that he can remodel the building for richer tenants.

The second type of buyer purchases a building deliberately to lose money. He (or a corporate group of investors) needs the building for tax write-offs. This investor has an interest in not improving conditions—either the income or land value. To improve maintenance or the building itself would be in direct conflict with his economic interests. The tenant, meanwhile, sits and suffers. He has the alternative of moving, but this is a possibility available to few.

The third type of buyer is the poor or working class individual (or group) who, either out of misguided dreams or with no other alternatives for income, buys the run-down building in which he is living. Finding that mortgage payments sap the income from rents, and with no alternatives for loans, he is left without resources to make all the repairs he and his neighbors would desire. Maintenance is at best patchwork. The result is continued decay of the premises.

But any landlord still has one more alternative: abandonment. Abandonment is a drastic possibility, but at least it does end the tension between himself and his tenants. Furthermore, it is being used more and more often by landlords with property in our urban ghettoes; over one thousand buildings have been abandoned in one neighborhood of New York City alone.[14] Believing that investments are more lucrative elsewhere and refusing to make the alterations necessary to bring their buildings up to code, they are walking away from their holdings, letting the tenants fend for themselves.

But now that the landlord has left, what about the tenant? He is still in the apartment building, still trying to make into a comfortable home whatever the landlord left behind. And, on top of all the problems with keeping the heat and electricity on, what exactly *is* he? He is no longer a tenant, for there is no longer a landlord; it is rather difficult to define oneself through a relationship that no longer exists. Before the law, he is now a non-entity. Since he is not a landlord, he has none of the rights given to those with property; having no contract with anyone, there is no way even to sue for maintenance or to insure that services will be received.

The continual tension of the tenant-landlord relationship, as well as the tenant's inherent legal inability to better his conditions, however poor, clearly illustrates why the nature of the "housing problem" is far more complex than popular discussion of the "housing shortage" would imply.

Besides, as Jane Jacobs, Herbert Gans, and others have repeatedly tried to point out, there are numerous buildings already available which could be used for urban housing—not enough to alleviate the shortage, but certainly enough to lessen it. Furthermore, the use of older buildings would help maintain the variegated structural qualities so necessary for a city's own vitality. Such variety is impossible with massive amounts of new housing, no matter how attractive, merely because they are new. By rehabilitating present facilities, the financial cost may be cheaper than building anew, the psychic and monetary costs of relocation less, and the irregular and highly attractive patterns of our cities' present housing would be kept. If such housing is available, it is a partial solution to housing shortages far more appealing than any massive housing project.

Recent stories in the *New York Times* concretely describe why our shortage is not all that it appears to be.[15] Perhaps even more importantly here, they also suggest why the housing problem in the private sector is far from being either understood or resolved. Odyssey House, a rehabilitation center and home for drug addicts located in New York City, was forced to locate at least two times in the past two years due to complaints from fearful tenants in the various buildings. That such a progressive program has been unable to find a permanent home is unfortunate, but what is of interest here is that the group has been able to find tenancy at all. The reformed addicts successfully found adequate housing for forty members of their group every time they were forced to relocate. And, each time they moved into the various buildings, Odyssey House found a few other tenants still in occupancy. As it sadly turns out, the landlords had "given" them the buildings for less than magnanimous reasons. By "giving" them the apartments, the former owners received a large tax write-off for the coming year. At the same time, the drug addicts' presence unknowingly served the purposes of harassing the remaining tenants to leave the premises—which then ended the landlords' financial and legal responsibilities bound up in the rent-controlled lease.

Our nation's experts decry the housing shortage in our cities, and yet a large group of tenants are tossed in and out of near-empty buildings in one of our nation's most crowded cities. Most surprising of all is that these buildings were so easily available for so many tenants in the first place—and still they and the others in the building could not be guaranteed a safe and comfortable home. The Odyssey House story is merely a more dramatic example of a trend more common than we realize. Apartments are unfilled and buildings remain empty because some landlords believe they stand more to lose by continuing their relationship with tenants than they do by ending it.

This is not to say that making use of all our available housing in our cities will totally eradicate the shortage. What is important here is that at present there are few ways in which one can better the tenant-landlord relationship or, for that matter, force landlords to rent available housing units. Perhaps that is why planners prefer to describe the housing problem solely in terms of the numbers of units needed to end the shortage. Activists in the tenants' rights movement know that the mere addition of new units will not change the relationship of tenant and landlord. While it would allow tenants more leverage in their apartment hunting, it will not lessen their interest in both an inexpensive product and adequate maintenance or a landlord's concern for profit.

Tenant advocates also realize that even with an increased market supply the tenant still has no leverage in ensuring that repairs are made or that safety is adequate. Once a person rents an apartment he has become a tenant, and before the law tenants are powerless to receive quick and inexpensive adjudication of their grievances. An end to our housing shortage may slightly increase one's choice, but it doesn't end his problems as a tenant.

Quite realistically, until service rights—or the right to a safe and healthy home—are equated with property rights, there is little reason for tenants to receive the same degree of justice as received by landlords. And, until justice in the housing community is balanced in favor of equity between tenant and landlord, it is equally realistic to hold little hope for an end of our housing crisis.

Discussion so far has only centered on the private market. However, the situation in the public sector is equally negative. One can quickly see that government-financed housing has been an abysmal failure in almost every respect: health, safety, attractiveness, tenant satisfaction, human dignity. To repeat past performances would clearly be ineffective.

To make certain that past failures do not reoccur, tenant advocates are searching for a redefinition of "public housing" itself. When one thinks of public housing, the image conjured up is a mixture of height, cement, and greyness. Such stale qualities are void of the bright, warm images necessary to turn any house into a home. The second set of images one thinks of are poverty, rats, and fear. Like the first set, they are not formed without real justification. The now-infamous Pruitt-Igol housing project in St. Louis is a singularly disgusting example of all those qualities. When it was first built, words of praise flew as easily in St. Louis as cement mixture had a few months before. Today, Pruitt-Igol is nearly barren. Built to house 12,000 people, the St. Louis project is now virtually abandoned. It stands as a sad and dirty example of why, once again, the housing problem doesn't mean just a housing shortage.

And as long as they maintain their seedy images, Pruitt-Igols will be built, praised, and abandoned. Thousands of units will remain empty because people will be unwilling or afraid to live in them.* The stigma attached to public housing must end. The easiest way to help eradicate that stigma would be to stop building those ugly, vertical swamps that poor people are relocated into and out of. Government planners must recognize that housing, like the people in them, must have varied qualities to remain exciting and interesting.

Public housing must be redefined in such a way that it will be neither stigmatized nor run down and abandoned. Some of the architectural and placement problems have been touched on by countless planners and analysts; more diverse, attractive and "scattered site" projects are obviously needed. However, the final, crucial issue in public housing involves a redefinition of the role of the public housing tenant himself. Any tenant feels somewhat distant from property over which he has no control; for the public housing ten-

---

*Even housing projects with long waiting lists are often found to be merely more subtle wastelands than a Pruitt-Igol. People waiting for this housing do not always do so because they choose it but because the alternatives before them have been bulldozed out of existence. If public housing can only serve a negative function: taking people because they are poor or because they have no other choice—then they will never be more than large wayside stations of unhappy and alienated individuals.

ant this alienation is increased for all the above reasons of community separation and stigmatization.

A further problem is the hovering presence of the public housing staff. The staff members, originally hired for maintenance and administrative functions, often appear to resemble welfare workers in disguise—summarily evicting tenants for abusive noise, watching to see how many people live in an apartment, etc. This often overzealous attention to tenants' personal activities does little to decrease the tenants' alienation from their surroundings. Part of the problem would be eased if income levels for scattered site projects were removed, but it is of paramount importance that urban tenants feel responsibility for the property on which they and others are living. If that sense of responsibility is missing, no housing project, no matter how attractively designed and placed, will remain unblighted.

The real tragedy of most of our housing projects is not that some, like Pruitt-Igol, are ugly and cold, but that too many have an atmosphere which reeks of anomie. If tenants do not eventually move to public housing because they want to, there is little hope of any new program succeeding. Tenants—the people who turn houses into homes and projects into communities—must have real power in the planning and administering of their housing. So far, such an idea is given slight rhetoric in working papers or in presentations to urban groups. To continue to provide only a false sense of participation would be disastrous, and our public housing ills will remain unchanged.

The effort needed to correct a problem of such scope would be cause for despair if it were not for the hopeful paradox imbedded within it. By being so vastly difficult, our housing probelm's chances for amelioration may actually increase. When a situation reaches such crisis proportions that it is indifferent to class, race, or sex, it is a safe assumption that group action will more easily focus on causal factors related to the overall problem than on just manifestations of that problem. It is a rare sight to see the poor and middle class or the black and the white working together in close harmony. It is a sad irony that because the problem is so immense they must. Happily, the tenants' rights movement has shown that such alliances, while perhaps formed out of common desperation, work rather well.[16]

The tenants' rights movement will not prove attractive to professionals with heavy investments in the status quo. However, for those community practitioners and planners interested in social change, yet no longer able to work with many urban groups, the widespread activity of the movement can prove highly rewarding. Tenants' rights, as an issue for social change, involves all groups—middle class and poor, white and black, urban and rural, and all gradations in between. More importantly, tenant inequity is not based on one tenant group's prerogatives over those of another. To work with a middle class group is not to "cop out," not if the group is involved with issues of equal interest to all tenants, such issues as the legal right to collective bargaining and better housing codes. This is not to say that all tenants have the same problems; rats and cockroaches in a coldwater flat are much more discomforting than sharply increased rents. However, if tenant advocates remain cognizant of their common inability to correct any of these difficulties, they can aid each other in their work. The recent formation of city-wide tenant councils in Chicago and Boston (composed of representatives from tenant unions throughout each city) suggests that the underlying interests are becoming well recognized.

Furthermore, because present landlord-tenant law is, to quote two authors in this book, "just plain bad," it is an obviously potent arena in which advocate lawyers can work. The unharrassed right to be a member in a tenant union, to bargain collectively, and the right of due process are still only dreams for most tenants. With obvious legislative parallels forged out of previous labor struggles to aid them, tenants and their lawyers can eventually expect beneficial tenant reform. It will be tedious and long work, with battles fought and refought in many court rooms, but organized labor's precedents are large ones.

Tenant law has other subtle advantages that are not often realized. For example, rent strikers in Ann Arbor found that jury trials usually ended with unexpected and pleasant results. The juries themselves were little different from those found throughout the country: middle class housewives, retired military men, small businessmen. The rent strikers bore them little resemblance. Many of the tenant union members were well-known university students, radicals, and some long-haired ones at that. A few of them had been recently tried and convicted for previous sit-ins protesting inadequate welfare allotments. In the case of the sit-ins, the juries had not taken long in reaching their verdicts and their recommendations for sentencing were hardly lenient. And yet, the rent strike settlements handed down by the juries were uniformly fair to the strikers.

The rent strike, due to its longevity and large size, had more notoriety attached to it than the sit-in. The juries were comprised of the same kinds of people as before, people not known for their sympathy to student causes. Tenant union members, using the rent strike as a political platform for radical analyses of other political and economic issues, made no attempt to present the evidence in a manner less hostile to the landlords' interests. What had changed?

The difference was that the rent strikers, unlike the welfare protestors, unquestionably had a trial by peers. Student radical or crew-cut ex-marine; they may have looked different, had different politics, and danced to very different drums, but all of them had been tenants at one time or another. Now, when facing each other across the court room, the commonality of that experience cut through the maze of political and personal dissimilarities to link the middle-aged jury with the student activists. They all knew what it was like to obsequiously sign a lease with a landlord or to wait through the winter for a little more heat. This identity is a powerful weapon, and tenant union members representing the poor and minority groups would be wise to exploit it both in and outside the court room.

But the equity of juries reflects the commonality of the tenants' rights movement, not the progressiveness of our legal system. The long battles taking place in our court rooms are necessary ones, but legalism means very little to tenants with no worthwhile place to live.

It seems that a lot of tenants already know that they will need more than legal suits if their struggle is to succeed. Legal advocacy usually begins only if enough people have first shown sufficient courage and conviction to challenge the present social order. Walter Reuther broke a lot of old laws organizing the United Auto Workers. Mrs. Rosa Parks didn't just have tired feet that day she sat in the front of the bus; she had enough courage to challenge a system that viewed racial discrimination as proper and just.

And some tenants are challenging our present social order that still views housing as a prerogative of the propertied, rather than as a right for everyone. They are taking over unused buildings, cleaning up abandoned apartments,[17] withholding their rent from indifferent landlords. They are often militant, often extra-legal. There is little question that they can be offensive to others. Behind their militancy lies a conviction in their cause that goes far beyond questions of propriety. It is the same kind of conviction that has marked the beginnings of every successful social movement, be it labor, civil rights, or common suffrage: a belief in their struggles, however militant, because they see no other effective alternatives for change.

The excitement that this belief creates, and the momentum that it builds, suggest even further growth of the tenants' rights movement. The movement has grown rapidly in less than seven years of intense activity. It is one of the few movements to have survived the Sixties unsplintered and still directed towards its original goals of both better housing and increased tenant equity. America is becoming a nation with more and more tenants, and its leaders will soon have to pay close attention to their interests.

---

1. New York *Times,* November 7, 1971, p. 33.

2. The Report of the President's Commission on Urban Housing, *A Decent Home,* Government Printing Office, Washington, D.C., 1969, p. 8.

3. *Ibid.*

4. In 1969, 1.4 million units; in 1970, 1.5; projected figures for 1971 are 1.9 million units (Housing and Urban Development statistics).

5. George Drucker, as reported in the Detroit *Free Press,* June 24, 1971, p. 7-D.

6. President's Commission on Urban Housing, *op. cit.,* Appendix C, pp. 225-27.

7. *Ibid.,* Appendices E & F, pp. 231-234.

8. For a wide-ranging discussion of these and other problems, see Myron Moskovitz & Peter Honigsberg, "A Model Landlord-Tenant Act," *Georgetown Law Review,* June 1970, pp. 1013-64.

9. *Ibid.,* p. 1015.

10. See Thomas Quinn & Earl Phillipps, "The Law of Landlord-Tenant," within this book, pp. 89-108.

11. Quinn & Phillips, *op. cit.,* p. 95.

12. See New York *Times,* January 31, 1970, p. 1 for an example of this unpunished harassment.

13. For the best discussion to date on the types of landlords present in urban housing, see George Sternlieb's *The Tenement Landlord,* Rutgers University Press, East Brunswick, N.J., 1965.

14. New York *Times,* March 28, 1971, VI, p. 30.

15. New York *Times,* January 25, 1970, p. 29, and *Times,* March 7, 1971, p. 52.

16. The New York *Times* reported that the National Tenants' Organization's 1971 national convention, while predominantly black, had "sizable groups of Chicanos, Indians, and whites." November 7, 1971, p. 33.

17. Building takeovers are increasing in every major city. The New York *Times,* for example, reported three such squat-ins in less than a week early in 1971. (February 22, February 25, and March 1). Each involved different groups and different buildings.

Part I

CASE HISTORIES OF THE MOVEMENT

The Development of the Movement

A social movement does not arise spontaneously. It grows out of two sources: first, the accumulated experiences, skills and perceptions of people; and second, the historical moment that crystallizes an issue once unformed or unnoticed. Its sustained growth depends on the continued regeneration of these same sources: new and better skills, more sophisticated experiences, and periods of activity which more clearly and powerfully refine issues for others to understand and support.

Tenant activity itself is not new. In the 1890's, the Ladies Anti-Beef Association made rent strikes an annual affair on New York's Lower East Side. Fed by the labor unrest of that period, these strikes were a common expression of tenant dissatisfaction for over ten years. They subsided only after the passage of the New York Tenement Law of 1901. Again, in the depression of the 1930's, workers in New York City hard hit by unemployment and threatened by eviction from their housing formed one of the first city-wide tenant councils. They too began massive rent strikes to protest their living conditions.

But these first tenant experiences, while militant, soon subsided after general economic conditions improved. In the 1940's housing experts developed a more specialized and legalistic approach to ameliorating housing problems. Efforts were focused on zoning problems, better housing codes, and, of course, more housing. Left to professionals and middle class groups interested in issues of "good government," the "housing problem" became so streamlined in definition that the interests of tenants were forgotten.

Ironically, it was this inattention to tenant interests which catalyzed tenants into action again. This time their anger was not generated from general economic conditions but from problems inherent in urban renewal. Urban renewal, as Herbert Gans has cogently pointed out, had been designed with one basic error: it was a method to eliminate the slums in order to renew the city, not a program to properly rehouse slum dwellers. It was a costly error.

In the 1950's, tenants, upset and embittered at their forced relocation, started organizing their own interest groups to fight further upheavel. They became skilled in undercutting all the prerogatives of expertise, legitimacy, and planning belonging to urban renewal experts. As their activities increased, urban renewal became more and more unpopular with the public. Too many housing units had been torn down and not enough replaced. Too many tenants had been uprooted at too high an economic, social, and psychological cost. Plans that had looked so stylishly finished on the drawing boards looked colorless and incomplete in our cities. And, while some planners were among the first critics of urban renewal, tenants, after a lapse of twenty years, were beginning to lead the attack against poor housing conditions and inadequate housing policy.

Furthermore, the civil rights movement was starting to grow rapidly. The organizing and leadership skills developed within that movement were not lost on poor urban tenants—especially on urban black tenants, the group with the least leverage in finding adequate housing. The potent combination of increased organizing skills, legitimacy in their protests, and, certainly not least of all, an increased sense of self-sufficiency, was to lead this group into the forefront of the tenants' rights movement.

Skills, perceptions, and experiences were being formed, but that catalyzing historical moment was still missing. That moment was to come during the middle 1960's, a time when the causes of civil rights, the Great Society, and Black Pride all mingled together in heady alliances within our cities. At that time, people were trying to do what few people had ever tried before: to eradicate the slums and all their fellow travellers: unemployment, illiteracy, poor health.

Such lofty aims were destined for failure. But urban tenants, while active in these struggles, were beginning to organize their own separate groups as well. Housing was no longer just another urban problem: it was perceived as a right denied to some and abused by others. Led by men like Jesse Gray and Tony Henry, two skilled tenant union organizers in New York City and Chicago, and women like Mary Daniels, the courageous leader of the successful Muskegon (Mich.) Tenants Organization, tenants in every major city were beginning to demand an end to poor *and* inequitable housing conditions. More importantly, they were not just agitating for help. These people were developing their own particular organizations—tenant unions—to help them achieve their demands for better housing and increased tenant equity. Unlike members of the student movement, who primarily organized quickly dissipating demonstrations, tenant leaders were building strength through organized, collective action within numerous local communities. As unions sprang up around the country—in St. Louis, Boston, Washington, D.C., and elsewhere—the issue became clear. These tenant groups were formed to aid tenants and the inequities to correct were those in the housing community; other problems, while not forgotten, were now complementary issues. At last, the tenants' rights movement had been born.

The movement today is perhaps best understood by looking at the National Tenants' Organization. The N.T.O., formed in 1969 by tenant union organizers with the aid of the American Friends Service, now has local affiliates in over forty cities. With four regional offices and a monthly newsletter to local affiliates and other tenant organizations around the country, the group has been able to keep abreast of and help coordinate local developments as they occur. In turn, they disseminate timely information on recent activities in other states, legal decisions of possible use elsewhere, and other information of importance to local tenant groups.

The N.T.O. has been most active in public housing. Its most recent success was also its greatest. Through a combination of localized militant rent strike activity (such as the widely publicized public housing rent strike in St. Louis during 1969-70) and effective advocacy to H.U.D. officials, the N.T.O. was able in early 1971 to establish grievance procedures and a "model lease" in all federally-funded public housing projects. These two achievements, long sought by tenants everywhere, are now being used by legal advocates as precedents for comparable application in the private sector.

But this growth and achievement has not been accomplished easily. Behind every new tenant organization lies many failed rent strikes. The N.T.O. had over one thousand members at its 1971 national conference: for every person in attendance there were numerous others who had formed tenant organizations, only to see them dissolve through membership disinterest or intimidation. In Boston, a new municipal court has been formed to hear only housing complaints; earlier in the year, Nebraska's legislature killed an elementary housing code for the remainder of 1971.

As the above contrasts suggest, the paradox which any successful political social movement must maintain is its ability to grow and learn from defeat. The tenants' rights movement is still too young to consider itself fully successful. It now must continue achieving victory even when the social forces around it—decaying cities, inadequate housing starts, piecemeal legislation from indifferent public officials—spell short range defeat for many of its members. The N.T.O.'s ability to blend strategies of localized social action with sound national and statewide planning, and its awareness of the very real contextual differences within every state which expedite or impede social change, suggests that many of the movement's members recognize the importance of this task.

Part of a social movement's growth also lies in its ability to examine continually its own strengths and weaknesses. Perhaps the easiest and most effective way for constant examination to occur is through the use of case histories. While far from prophetic in their content, their analyses may help others avoid the mistakes (and apply the successes) of past groups.

The tenants' rights movement, while young, has within it a number of lively and relevant experiences which can help illuminate the dynamics of tenant unionism. However, there is no single, pre-packaged strategic design for groups to heat and serve at the local level. When such inclusive adaptations are made (as they unfortunately have been), the results are almost always disastrous. For example, the tenant organizations blanketly patterned on a labor union model have proven to be remarkably alike in their ineffective responses to their memberships' distinct tenancy needs. Situational factors such as varying personnel, financial resources, complexity of the economic relationship between tenant and landlord, etc., make it unlikely that a strategy developed from another social movement could be applied to the tenants' situation.

The following case studies present varied experiences and reflect distinctive analytical approaches to each situation. They include examples from the three major arenas in which tenant unions are now forming: public housing, private housing of the urban poor, and housing in the student community. Failures and successes are examined within these situations; analytical viewpoints range from the thoughtfully radical to the more detached and professional interest in intergroup processes.

One of the most exciting and encouraging analyses of tenant union development has been written by George V. Neagu. Two points become clear in the article: first, concerned professionals can be active participants for social change when they choose to be. The second and even more important point is that there are no substitutes for the often-unknown members of a social movement dedicated to widespread reform. The story of the Muskegon Heights Tenant Union is the story of what community organizing is really all about: that combination of people's courage, determination, and skills which serves as the catalyst for social change.

Any discussion of the tenant movement which excluded mention of Jesse Gray and his rent strike activities in New York during the early 1960's would be incomplete. Gray initiated some of the largest and most well-known rent strikes to date, and those efforts have had far-reaching importance in motivating other tenants throughout the country to begin group activity. However, as Mark Naison points out in "Rent Strikes in New York", it would be difficult to call the New York tenant activity a marked success in aiding tenants to better their housing conditions. The author, in analyzing the reasons behind much of the failure of these first forays into tenant militancy, presents a variety of organizational constraints for tenants in the private housing market to consider before initiating their own rent strike.

University students have also become active in the tenants' rights movement. Many student housing communities are far from comfortable. High transiency rates and an increasingly large student population have together created some housing situations far less enticing than they may have once appeared. With more and more students demanding the right to live outside college dormitories, many now find themselves looking for housing in strictly a seller's market.

The results have been, to use the slogan of one student group, a proliferation of "luxury slum" apartments. Quickly built and furnished with cheap, modern furniture, the apartments often rent for the "luxury prices" of $250 to $350 a month for two-bedroom quarters. With their tenants constrained by the limitations of the school year and involved in a variety of academic and extracurricular interests, landlords are able to avoid the costly maintenance demands of less transient tenants and their families.

Such situations, when combined with the high political interest of some portions of student bodies, make tenant union activity an increasingly familiar process around university campuses. However, as Thomas Jennings notes in his article on the Ann Arbor Tenants' Union, there are also certain factors within the student community which limit effective tenant action. Coupled with his longitudinal analysis of the union is the most thorough discussion of applied legal tactics yet to appear in the literature, making the piece of interest to students, professionals, and active tenants as well.

CHAPTER 1

The Rent Strikes in New York

Mark D. Naison*

In the fall of 1963, when rent strikes began to make their appearance in New York City on a massive scale, housing conditions in the city's slums were much the same as they had been for the past 60 years. In the old neighborhoods which the European migrants once inhabited—Brownsville, Williamsburg, Harlem, the East Bronx and the Lower East Side—Negroes and Puerto Ricans now resided, crowding tenements which had been regarded as substandard in the Progressive Era. Nine hundred thousand people still lived in houses built before 1900,[1] when the Tenement House Law had established the city's first set of health standards for residential construction.

Despite the continued decay of the slum areas, only partially offset by the construction of low-income public housing, it required the impetus of the Civil Rights Movement to transform passive resentment into active protest. Inspired by the mood of growing militancy which the March on Washington both reflected and negated, several CORE chapters had begun, in the summer of 1963, to apply the tactics of nonviolent direct action to the field of housing. Brooklyn CORE started with a campaign to pressure the city into enforcing the existing housing code. It taught tenants how to file forms with the building department to set the code enforcement machinery into operation, and it picketed the homes and businesses of landlords who refused to yield to tenant demands. Two college chapters, NYU CORE and Columbia CORE, also formed "housing committees" and began to organize slum tenants in Harlem and the Lower East Side. The Columbia chapter, like the Brooklyn group, tried to teach tenants to work through the city agencies to improve conditions, but NYU CORE and a small organization called the Northern Students Movement convinced tenants in six buildings on the lower East Side to fight their landlords by withholding rent.

These rent strikes won the approval of James Farmer, the national director of CORE. On November 9, in a statement to the *Amsterdam News* he declared that "the rent strike had proved an effective weapon," and urged that

*From Mark D. Naison, "The Rent Strikes in New York," *Radical America,* Nov.-Dec., 1967 and in Cox, et al. *Strategies of Community Organization* (Peacock Press, 1970), pp. 227-238.

"more of them be employed by tenants having problems with indifferent slumlords."[2] A week later, he warned of a "citywide rent strike with up to ten thousand tenants on strike if slum conditions are not cleared up," and predicted that the civil rights drive in the city would be stepped up on all fronts after the first of the year.

Enter Jesse Gray

Although Farmer's prediction of a citywide rent strike proved to be accurate, the initiative for it did not come from CORE but from a 38-year-old Harlem tenants' leader named Jesse Gray. For 10 years, Gray had been trying to do what CORE chapters had only now begun to think about: organize a mass movement in the ghetto around the issues which mattered most to the lower class Negro—poor housing, unemployment, police brutality. A long-time radical expelled from the National Maritime Union for his left-wing associations, he had begun his work in Harlem with a revolutionary dream. But the response to his agitation was unenthusiastic, and instead of a mass movement, he was able to develop only a small tenants' organization on a few blocks in Central Harlem called the "Community Council on Housing." In October of 1963, at the head of a protest march on city hall which he had organized, Gray threatened to lead a political rebellion of Harlem tenants unless the city acted to take over buildings with longstanding violations and meted out stiffer punishments to landlords.

Immediately after this protest march, which drew 200 tenants, Gray decided to organize a rent strike in the Central Harlem buildings he had been working in. The stimulus for this decision, made, apparently, with little preparation (there had been no mention of a rent strike at the protest parade), was the growing militancy that Gray's followers had been showing at meetings and protest rallies since the end of the summer. Tenants who had once meekly accepted Gray's aid with their buildings department forms, were now demanding dramatic action to get repairs. "The people," Gray told the Amsterdam News, "are much more conscious than ever of the slum conditions in which they are ready to listen to an agitator who tells them not to be frightened by eviction notices."[3] After one week of organizing, Gray claimed, he was able to place 16 buildings on strike.

The Community Council on Housing, when it began the strike, was a small, informally run operation that teetered on the edge of bankruptcy. It depended for its support on a combination of membership dues, which were rare in coming, and private contributions from wealthy radicals. Aside from Gray, who managed to eke out a meager salary from its treasury, there were four men who served as organizers, only one of whom, Major Williams, worked full time. Gray, moreover, could expect very little help from the tenant members of the council in organizing the strike. Most of them . . . would join a picket line or give a small contribution to the Council's treasury, but they were also content to leave the formation of strategy and the organization of buildings to Gray and his aides. Despite these disadvantages, Gray was able to almost triple the number of buildings on strike during the month of November. In the few blocks that he had organized before, the response to his message was enthusiastic, and the only limit on the speed of organization seemed to be the time that was required to explain the mechanics of the strike. There were buildings in Central Harlem where the name "Jesse Gray" would open any door. In the neighborhood where he had lived and worked for 10 years, Gray, by countless hours of unpaid service, had built up a remarkable reserve of trust. Like the Democratic district leaders in the old immigrant quarters, Gray was the man people called upon when they were in trouble with the welfare department, the police, or any of the other huge and confusing bureaucracies with which they were dependent for their survival.

In early December, at a mass rally held at the Milbank Community Center near Mount Morris Park, Gray announced the results of November's organizing. Tenants in 34 tenements, he declared, had joined the strike, raising the number of buildings participating to 52. The rent strike, he proclaimed jubilantly, had become a mass movement, "with almost 3,000 persons ready to participate in the action."[4]

The political implications of a mass movement under Gray's leadership were not lost to Harlem's established political leaders. Men like Adam Clayton Powell, Huelan Jack, and Lloyd Dickens, who had never shown much zeal in demanding housing reform, quickly announced their support of the rent strike. Fifteen church and civic groups pledged their support to the rent strikers and informed a coordinating committee to help extend the strike to other parts of Harlem. The voices were angry and the spirits were high. "The bells toll, the drums roll," Adam Powell exulted, "Harlem is on the march again."[5]

Gray seemed almost intoxicated by the community solidarity that had been manifested at the rally. "If our plans materialize," he told a *Times* reporter two days after the rally, "we will have 1,000 buildings on strike by the first of the year. We hope, by means of a citywide rent strike, to force a mass rehabilitation of the slums."[6]

"Mass Movement" Stumbles

In early December, when the Community Council was beginning to make plans to turn the rent strike into a "mass movement," it was counting on extensive cooperation from civil rights groups and civic organizations within the Harlem community. The initial response of such groups had been enthusiastic; 15 Harlem organizations, including block associations, church groups, Democratic clubs, and a labor union (Local 1199 of the Drug and Hospital Workers) had joined a coordinating committee set up by Gray to extend the strike. Gray's expectations of support, however, proved to be over-optimistic. As December came to a close, and the rent strike began to make the front pages of the daily newspapers, the Community Council's organizers were struggling to extend the strike in Harlem almost entirely unaided. The 15 Harlem civic groups who supported the strike gave Gray some money and helped publicize the movement in the community, but did not provide what the rent strike needed most to become a mass movement—manpower—to organize buildings, to run the office, to keep up contact with the striking tenants and advise them on legal matters. In the beginning of January, the bulk of the organization was still being done by the same 7 to 10 workers from the Community Council and the Northern Students Movement. The strike expanded to involve 100 buildings, far short of the 1,000 which Gray had predicted.

The major national offices of the civil rights groups, moreover, did not reply at all to the Harlem rent strike's pleas for assistance. James Farmer of CORE refused to comment on the tactic as soon as it became publicly identified with the work of Jesse Gray,[7] and the Community Council received neither organizational help nor financial aid from CORE. The NAACP's Central Harlem chapter, under Reverend Hildebrand, told its members to participate in the strike, and contributed money to the Community Council's treasury, but its national office remained cold to the movement. Roy Wilkins refused to answer calls from Gray's press agent, and made no reference to the rent strike in his public statements.

But the Activists Respond

The hostility of the established civil rights leaders to the rent strike, however, did not accurately mirror the feeling of the rank and file of the city's civil rights groups. Jesse Gray's initial successes in organizing the people of Harlem, exaggerated and glorified by a "muckraking" press, captured the imagination of young civil rights activists around the city, activists who were unacquainted with Gray's radical background. One after another, local CORE groups in the city dropped their other activities and began to organize rent strikes in their districts. The Brooklyn chapter, which had been organizing tenants since the summer, placed its first buildings on strike on December 1, and had a number of cases in court before the end of the month. Downtown CORE and Columbia CORE, which had been operating small housing programs which worked through city agencies, dropped their reformist approach and began to organize rent strikes early in January. And Bronx CORE and East River CORE, which had been devoting most of their time to "employment" campaigns, began rent strikes of their own in February.

With the possible exception of the Brooklyn groups, these CORE chapters entered the rent strike with only the vaguest notions of what they were trying to accomplish and the most limited experience with tenants organization and housing law. The young activists who composed the bulk of these organizations were responding more to the general sense of excitement which surrounded the rent strike than to the appeal of a well-thought-out strategy of action. The headlines in the press, the radio broadcasts, the mass meetings, and the leafleting campaigns created what those who experienced it called a "rent strike fever," an extraordinary sense of exhilaration and even of historic destiny that drew people to the movement as the initiator of a new stage in the civil rights movement. The excitement reached its height at a mass meeting held in Harlem on January 11.

A crowd of 800 people, composed of Harlem tenants and representatives of almost every civil rights group and tenants' organization in the city, heard a group of prominent speakers, including James Baldwin, William Fitts Ryan, Jesse Gray, and John Lewis tell them to spread the rent strike to other parts of the city. "At this meeting," one leader of a student CORE group told me, "everyone caught the fever—Rent Strike. No one knew about the legal consequences, or the amount of work involved. It seemed like the thing to do . . . the only way to beat the landlord."

In addition, Mobilization for Youth, a federally sponsored social work project trying to encourage social action among low-income people on the Lower East Side, saw in the mass movement that Gray seemed to be developing a model well worth imitating. Throughout December, MFY's directorate worked to advise a way to sponsor a successful rent strike on the Lower East Side without offending the political interests upon which it depended for its funds. To be successful, they believed, a rent strike on the Lower East Side would have to be as militant and vocal as the strike in Harlem, it would have to attack the city government as well as the landlords. But if MFY organized such a rent strike, it might jeopardize its existence, for the use of government funds to organize protests against the government was then hardly an officially sanctioned mode of "community organization." They decided to organize the rent strike behind a "smokescreen" of small community groups set up by MFY and provided with paid "organizers." In late December and early January, MFY officials organized groups of tenants, gave them storefronts and operating expenses and assigned to them paid community workers— neighborhood people on MFY's payroll who had experience in the civil rights movement—who were to do most of the work connected with the strike. In addition, they contacted tenants' organizations, civil rights groups and social fraternal organizations (such as the Congress of Puerto Rican Organizations) which had organized rent strikes or expressed interest in them, and asked them to join with the newly formed "tenants" groups in a coordinated rent strike on the Lower East Side that would be partially subsidized by MFY's funds. The invitations were accepted, and on January 11, eleven organizations, representing the most diverse social and political perspectives one could imagine,[8] met at MFY headquarters and agreed to work together to create a massive rent strike on the Lower East Side.

Gray and Coordination

The task of coordinating these local rent strikes and giving them a unified political impact proved to be a difficult one. While there was considerable sharing of information about methods of organization and an effective coordination of legal services, there was no successful attempt to define the goals of the movement on a citywide level and to devise tactics in which members of the participating organizations could effectively combine their energies. Much of the movement's potential for coordinated action was debilitated in power struggles between leaders of the various rent-striking groups. Perhaps the main axis of conflict was between Jesse Gray and the Metropolitan Council on Housing, a federation of housing organizations formed in the middle 1950's to protect rent control and organize support for the construction of low-income housing. Early in the strike, the Met Council, whose leaders regarded themselves as "experts" on the political dimensions of housing problems, made tentative efforts to set itself up as a clearinghouse for rent strike information and to incorporate the rent strike into its own legislative campaigns. It invited Jesse Gray to become the leader of a citywide rent strike coordinating committee, which it proposed to establish. Gray, however, rejected their offer. He did not want his leadership of the movement diluted by what he called a "white middle-class organization." After 10 years of organizing without recognition, he was not willing to share his newly won prestige with an organization that he regarded as being out of touch with the rising spirit of race consciousness and nationalism in the black ghettos.

He decided, thus, to coordinate the movement himself. He spoke at rallies in behalf of groups organizing rent strikes in all parts of the city, and had numerous private conferencs with rent strike leaders to discuss with them techniques of tenants organization and related problems of housing law. And in the press conferencs and news broadcasts which his press agent arranged for him, he dramatized the slum conditions which gave rise to the strike and the movement's immediate aims in a forceful and ominous way, setting off a wave of short-term reforms by the city before the strike had even approached its projected strength. On February 12, rent strike leaders were invited to a mass meeting in Harlem to form a Citywide Committee for Decent Housing, which would coordinate protest to force the city and state governments to act against the slums.

But when the speeches ended, only two proposals for direct action, and rather mild ones at that, were ratified by the delegates—to join the March on Albany for a $1.50 minimum wage with a tenants parade to demand code enforcement and the construction of more public housing, and to begin a "Rats to Rockefeller Campaign," which consisted of a drive to send rubber rats to the Governor along with form letters from tenants urging the Governor to support legislation to provide emergency repairs in slum housing.

The hopes voiced by the strike's leaders a few months before, that the movement would mobilize the population of the ghettos for mass action to force a comprehensive rehabilitation of the slums, seemed strangely remote from the debate now taking place—the proposals ratified were an extension of the "responsible" methods that tenant organization had engaged in for years without bringing basic changes in the conditions of the homes. There was no initiative (from Gray or anyone else) for a drive to force public authorities to commit themselves to a systematic program of slum rehabilitation that would make use of the disruptive powers of the black masses. Gray was the man everyone looked to for leadership, but he seemed unable to visualize a way of maintaining the militancy of the Harlem movement within the context of a coalition of groups. His rejection of the Metropolitan Council on Housing as comfortable and middle class seemed ironic indeed, for the new "militant" coordinating group that he had formed began by appropriating its methods. The irony was apparent even to Gray. At future meetings of the "citywide committee for decent housing," Gray himself, involved in a campaign against the police in Harlem, rarely showed up.

In the last week of February, the aura of cataclysmic power that had surrounded the rent strike in its early days had largely faded away. The press seemed to lose interest in the movement. Reporters no longer anxiously kept track of Gray's predictions of how large the strike was going to get, and muckraking articles about slum conditions and inefficiencies of the buildings department seemed to go out of fashion. From February 11 onward, no article dealing with the strike appeared on the front page of the *Times*. The city government ceased issuing promises to appease the movement's leaders and the aroused conscience of the public. The Mayor's last dramatic gesture to the strike came on February 8, when he announced the beginning of a one million dollar anti-rat campaign to help rid the slums of pestilence.

While the public authorities resumed their habitual complacence toward slum conditions, the rent strike leaders found their attention pulled further and further away from political questions. There was a clear shift in perspective of the rent strikes from citywide to a local level in this period, and a growing concern with legal and technical problems that had been ignored in the beginning of the strike. The mass meetings in Harlem which had confirmed and inspired the high aspirations of the movement were now held infrequently and had poor attendance. In many parts of the city, indeed, the rent strike began to resemble a social service operation rather than a militant protest.

The Courts and the Movement

The Community Council on Housing had entered the strike without clearly defining its attitude toward the legal system. It did not have much confidence in the legal process through which striking tenants could get repairs (section 755 of the buildings code) but it was unwilling to boycott the courts entirely, for it had promised tenants that there would be no evictions. In the early stages of the strike, the organizers had paid only perfunctory attention to the legal procedures required to win a "755"—which included filing forms for inspections with the buildings department; checking that violations were actually recorded after inspections; and subpoenaing records for the court—they were trying to get buildings on strike quickly to give the movement political leverage. In many cases, observers noted, organizers simply called a meeting of tenants, told them to stop paying rent and left, reminding them to call the Community Council's office when they received a dispossess.

The confusion of the organizers about the role court action would play in the movement was increased by two favorable but conflicting decisions handed down by lower court magistrates in late December. On December 30, in the first court decision affecting the Harlem rent strikes,[9] Judge Guy Gilbert Ribaudo ordered 13 striking tenants in two Harlem tenements to pay rent into court until the landlord repaired outstanding violations, asserting that conditions in the buildings were "shocking, and should be repaired as soon as possible."[10]

This reaffirmation of the applicability of 755 was accompanied by a statement declaring that the court did not condone rent strikes; it was illegal for the tenants to withhold rent except in cases involving "real and so-called constructive eviction and where hazardous violations exist."[11] One week later, however, a decision was handed down in a Brooklyn court which went far beyond Judge Ribaudo's dictum and broke down many of the guidelines which the organizers had set after the earlier decision. Judge Fred Moritt, after hearing the case of five striking tenants who argued that their living quarters were not fit for human habitation ruled that "any act or default on the part of the landlord which deprives the tenant of the beneficial enjoyment of his premises, constitutes, in the eyes of the law, an eviction. A wrongful eviction, by the landlord, whether partial or total, has an effect of terminating the tenant's liability for rent."[12] This meant, he later explained, that in "extreme cases, the landlord is not entitled to any rent until the conditions are remedied . . . . If it takes the landlord two years to make the repairs, he gets no rent for two years. Period."[13] This decision, which was not based upon section 755, differed from Judge Ribaudo's in two significant respects; it did not require the tenants to pay their rent into court, and it did not entitle the landlord to back rents for the period that the violations were in existence.

Both the Ribaudo and Moritt decisions seemed to suggest that the movement could get repairs for individual tenants through court action. But neither decision, as it turned out, was representative of the kind of treatment the strike was to receive in the housing courts. Once cases began to appear in large enough numbers to be free of publicity, the housing court judges, a breed notorious for their subservience to the party machines, showed strong resistance to the use of the court as an agency to supervise repairs. In some cases, judges made no attempt to hide their contempt for the tenants and their opposition to the rent strike, and didn't try to separate their legal arguments from their personal biases. But more common was a strict adherence to legal technicalities on the part of "objective" judges, which, given the nature of the housing laws and the peculiar problems of the low-income person in a court situation, proved to be a frustrating and confusing barrier to effective action.

In the housing courts, it was common, for example, to grant parties in the case adjournments, when their cases were not sufficiently prepared or relevant witnesses such as buildings department inspectors were absent. When low-income people were a party to the case, the seemingly innocent power of adjournment took on new importance—the power to adjourn was the power to destroy. For most of the striking tenants, living on the edge of subsistence burdened by economic and familial responsibilities, a court appearance was a major sacrifice which had to be arranged far in advance by the organizer. If, after extensive planning and preparation, and the loss of a day's salary on the part of the tenants, the result was only adjournment, the tenants, generally anxious and fearful to begin with, might begin to question whether the yet to be achieved gains of the strike were worth the price of the disruption it wrought in their personal lives.

Landlords, fully aware of the subversive effects of adjournments on the morale of a tenants' committee, would often purposely leave their cases unprepared, or demand that new witnesses be called in who were not present at the first hearing. Many judges, insensitive to the differential impact of the adjournment on landlord and tenants, would grant the landlord's request and become an unconscious party to his harassment—others, no doubt, less innocent in their intentions saw in this an inconspicuous and "safe" way of frustrating a movement they despised.

In addition, the civil court judges interpreted 755 in a way that made it difficult for all but the most carefully briefed tenants' committee to win a case. Virtually without exception, they rejected the procedures of the Moritt decision; they would only accept as evidence "violations of record" subpoenaed from the buildings department. When tenants offered verbal testimony about conditions in the building or photographs of violations, they were told that such information would not affect the outcome of the case. This meant, in effect, that the strikers were dependent on the cumbersome and quite fallible machinery of the buildings department at every point in the strike; they had to get an early inspection, make sure that the inspector took down relevant violations, see whether they were actually recorded at the Hall of Records (which cost two dollars and required a trip downtown) and subpoena the inspection sheet from the Hall of Records on the day of the trial.

The organizations sponsoring the rent strike soon learned that the only way to get inspections on a workable basis was to put pressure on high officials of the buildings department for an arrangement that entirely bypassed bureaucratic channels. Gray had done that early in the strike, and was able to get on-the-spot inspections in Harlem buildings merely by making a telephone call. But even so, there were problems in arranging the mechanics of an inspection. At the time of day when the inspector arrived, most of the tenants in the building could be out, and only a fraction of the violations would be recorded. It was necessary to arrange a time for inspection mutually agreeable to inspector and tenant, but city laws didn't make room for such an arrangement. The inspector would often arrive unannounced and find most of the tenants absent or unwilling to let him in. Moreover, there was no guarantee that the violations would be recorded once the inspection was made. Inspectors were notoriously corrupt and amenable to bribes, and would often slant their inspection reports to favor the landlord. Finally, there were huge delays in recording the violations once they were reported by the inspector. At the buildings department computer which processed inspection reports, information was held up for 13 working days by backlog.[14]

The Failure of Legalism

It was common, thus, for striking tenants to appear in court without buildings department records to back up their cases, or with records which did not truly reflect the nature of the conditions in their building. Judges, using a "strict construction" of the doctrine of constructive eviction, would declare that the evidence presented was insufficient to warrant issuing a 755, and would order the tenants to give back rents to the landlords and resume regular payment. Such a decision, the "final order," greeted a large number of the striking tenants whose cases appeared in court. The Lower East Side Rent Strike was losing three-fifths of its cases during March and April and improved its performance only slightly later on. None of the other rent-striking organizations seem to have done much better. The one exception was Brooklyn CORE, which found the Brooklyn courts more responsive to tenants' interests than those in other boroughs.

Even when the judges actually granted a 755, it was by no means certain that conditions in the building would be significantly improved. As the law was interpreted, the landlord was only required to correct violations recorded on Buildings Department forms. Since these records were often incomplete because of inefficient or corrupt inspections, some of the worst violations in the struck buildings were declared outside of the court's jurisdiction. In addition, the procedures which the court used to enforce its order were often unreliable. To receive his rent, the landlord had to establish to the judge's satisfaction that he had removed, or would remove, all violations of record.

But most judges were reluctant to assume the responsibility of acting as a full-time administrator of repairs, and tried to get the parties to settle out of court as quickly as possible. In cases where a building required extensive remodeling to meet the standards of the court, they were prone to grant the landlord a trial period after which he would receive his rent if he made a reasonable percentage of the repairs. But all too often, such trial periods served as an excuse to end jurisdiction, and landlords were able to stop repairs with impunity when they came to a halt.

There were many instances where a "court victory" for the rent strike resulted in token repairs. Even if administered by men with the best of intentions —which it was not—the court system was poorly designed to supervise a massive program of repairs in slum housing. For the rent strike groups, taking a case to court was like piloting a ship through a minefield: at any moment, a hidden obstacle could appear and destroy the whole effort.

The organizers, led by the early course of the movement to expect a "revolutionary" transformation of the slum environment, found their energies absorbed in legal preparations which yielded intermittent and unsatisfying results. When they were busy arranging court appearances, supervising inspections, filling out Buildings Department forms, subpoenaing records and conferring with lawyers, there was little time for the street rallies, the leafleting, and the building organization which seemed to shake the slum population out of its apathy, and which made the rent strike such an exciting thing to be a part of in its early stages.

In Central Harlem, where buildings had been organized most hastily and hopes of creating a mass movement had been highest, the emotional letdown evoked by the advent of litigation was particularly marked. The Community Council's attempt to perform simultaneously the functions of a militant political movement, designed to force major reforms from the power structure, and of a traditional housing clinic, working to improve conditions for individual tenants, began to falter badly once legal perspectives and legal problems became prominent. But even those groups which had committed themselves to a legal perspective from the start, such as Brooklyn CORE and Ted Velez' East Harlem Tenants Council, eventually discovered that they could achieve their aims more effectively by organizing tenants to use the city agencies to achieve repairs.

Regardless of whether court cases were won or lost, there was a huge disproportion between the amount of time and energy which they consumed and the limited results obtainable. Exhausted by the endless routine of court appearances, frustrated by the impossibility of actively involving slum tenants in complex legal procedures, unable to sustain the militant atmosphere of the early days, one group after another abandoned the rent strike. While Jesse Gray became involved in a campaign against police brutality and corruption, Brooklyn CORE—which had organized 400 tenant councils and 200 rent strikes—abandoned tenant organization entirely and applied its energies to the formation of an independent political movement known as the Brooklyn Freedom Democratic Party. By the fall of 1964, little or nothing was left of the rent strike movement in New York.

Conclusion: Rent Strikes in Perspective

Most of the groups which had participated in this movement did so both in order to improve housing conditions in the slums and also to create the basis for lasting changes in the political attitudes and behavior of slum tenants. To what extent were either of these goals achieved?

On the first count, the rent strike had a mixed record. Its short-term gains were fairly impressive. Most of the buildings which were on rent strike won a number of minor improvements as a result of court victories or informal agreements with landlords who wished to avoid litigation. The strike was particularly effective in dealing with "emergency" situations such as leaks, gaping ratholes, and lack of heat and hot water. Such complaints were not too difficult to deal with on a temporary basis, and landlords were often willing to bear the small expense of patching up a wall or fixing a boiler, in order to avoid public exposure as a slumlord, or a court appearance which involved the risk, however small, of "having the book thrown at him" and being forced to make major repairs. In areas where the rent strike attained massive proportions and attracted the attention of the media, even unorganized buildings experienced a temporary improvement in services.

But though the immediate grievances often were dealt with, the rent strike in the vast majority of cases did not change the basic conditions in the buildings which continually created emergencies—thin and flimsy walls, archaic plumbing and wiring systems, lack of adequate building service. What good did it do to patch up ratholes in a wall that could be gnawed through in a few hours by the rats that made their home in the garbage-ridden foundation of the building? Or to fix a single leak in a pipe system that was rusty and decayed?

To be made livable, these buildings required substantial rehabilitation—at the very minimum, new walls, a new boiler and new wiring system, and a floor-to-roof cleaning and extermination. But the cost of such repairs was staggering. In five buildings which the city took into receivership, Real Estate Commissioner Lazarus told the *Times,* the total sum required to remove all violations was $97,139.28. At an operating profit of $6,401 a year which the buildings yielded with their present level of rents, "it would take about 24 years to amortize the $97,139.28 investment with 4 percent interest." The city, he concluded, could not deal with the worst slums unless it was ready to operate by a policy in which "humanity comes before economics." If the rent strike did not achieve major political reforms, its effect on slum conditions would be entirely transitory.

The political achievements of the rent strike, however, were not substantial. There were three main formal improvements in housing procedures which the rent strike brought about: (a) the initiation of a million-dollar rat extermination program; (b) the addition of 50 inspectors to the buildings department; (c) and the passage of three new laws legalizing rent strikes. These programs were hastily devised by Mayor Wagner in the early months of the strike to meet the insistent clamor of the movement's leaders and the press for "action against the slumlords."

The first two were slight improvements in a system of administrating slum properties that was clearly inadequate; but the third, the new rent strike laws, seemed to offer the hope of a dramatic change in the structure of landlord—tenant relations. Drafted under the supervision of Bruce Gould, the head lawyer for the Harlem rent strikes, they seemed to define a procedure through which rent withholding could be made a controlled and standardized process for the rehabilitation of slum buildings. Among the major improvements made over Section 755 were provisions enabling the tenant to initiate action in the courts, rather than waiting for the landlord to sue for eviction; allowing the court to appoint a third party to administer repairs, rather than entrusting the job to the landlord; and enabling tenants to buy fuel with the rent money three days after the strike had been initiated.

The laws, thus, removed the danger of eviction from the rent strike procedure, and assured tenants that repairs would be comprehensive if a favorable decision were issued. They were regarded by housing experts as the Mayor's one meaningful concession to the rent strike, designed to remove the radical extralegal dimension from the tactic while making it a sure and effective device for achieving repairs.

Once the bill was passed, however (in the summer of 1965), tenants' organizations discovered that it was extremely difficult to use—cumbersome, expensive, and far from foolproof. There were far more documents to serve under the new laws than under 755, which made the landlord the initiator of the suit. The minimum cost of a "new law" rent strike for the tenants was $500, at standard legal rates. Unless sponsored by a wealthy organization or provided with free legal aid, no slum building could initiate such action. The new law, thus has been used quite sparingly, only in fact by groups receiving large grants from the poverty program or from private foundations. For the unorganized, unsubsidized poor who compose the vast majority of the slums' inhabitants, the new law did nothing, illustrating once again the depths of the chasm separating the poor from the democratic process.

The greatest gains made by the rent strike were not in the form of new laws, but in changes in the administrative procedures of the city housing agencies. During the rent strike, the organizations such as the Department of Buildings, the Department of Health, and the Rent and Rehabilitation Administration, were subjected to extraordinary pressures to improve the quality of Code enforcement. To preserve their reputation, and perhaps their jobs, officials of these agencies were forced to make radical innovations in their procedures, which enabled them to meet the rent strike's demands for more efficient service. Tenant groups involved in the rent strike were granted "hot lines" to the heads of agencies which enabled them to get on-the-spot convictions and quick rent reductions—special phone numbers were set up for tenants who lacked heat and hot water, and a study was begun by the city to devise a plan to streamline and unify city agencies dealing with housing complaints. Lower level officials were instructed to keep close contact with militant tenants organizations and to aid them in every possible way.

The rent strike movement thus had a salutary effect on slum housing conditions in the short run, but did not change the basic economic relationships which made for decay and poor service. The major changes wrought by the strike were a general improvement in building code enforcement machinery and an increased interest in reform and innovation in housing in the community at large, but it did not bring the kind of massive rehabilitation programs that were needed to give the poor real protection from the dangers of tenement existence. This failure was crucial. The earliest organized tenants' groups in New York had understood that there could be no justice for slum tenants as long as low-income housing was operated by the private enterprise system. But these groups, like the Harlem rent strike, won improved public regulation of housing rather than changes in ownership or massive rehabilitation programs, and did not change the fundamental conditions of life in the thousands of old-law tenements which stood then, and stand today, as a blight on the face of the city.

As regards the strike's effect on the level of social action in the communities where it took place, its results were even less substantial. The rent strike did not convert large numbers of slum tenants to social activism, it did not "radicalize the ghetto." Organizers in all parts of the city were struck by the extreme difficulty of getting tenants to participate in any of the movement's activities outside of the strike itself. At rallies, street meetings, and demonstrations, there were usually fewer tenants than organizers and curious students—this was particularly true of Gray's famed "mass meetings," which drew extraordinary numbers of middle-class "activists," but few tenants.

The tenants' committees formed by the organizers to administer the strike in individual buildings proved to be highly unstable units. Although the strike had raised hopes of developing a permanent matrix of tenants' committees to keep up the buildings after the movement had subsided and to serve as reserve units of organizational strength to be mobilized for other protests, none of the groups was able to maintain these committees as functioning units beyond the duration of the strike. Their failure mirrored that of major tenants' groups in the past, who had tried to apply principles of labor organizations to housing and "unionize" tenants in individual buildings. Both the Tenants Defense Union of 1919-1920 and the Citywide Tenants Union of the 1930's had declared it their goal to organize into permanent organization "every renter in the city," but had fallen absurdly short of this goal. Even among the most "organizable" ethnic and socio-economic groups, tenants' house committees were a most difficult form of organization to maintain on a stable basis.

Errors of the Movement

Whether or not a different kind of rent strike movement could have produced more stable organizational forms remains an open question. What is certain is that, both in terms of organizational involvement and political impact, the rent strike movement made a serious error of judgment in attempting to secure immediate improvement through the agency of the courts. For the courts did not, by and large, deal with the tenants' grievances. Many cases were lost entirely and cases that were won usually resulted in token repairs. But more importantly, involvement in court action put strains on the organization of the rent strike movement which prevented it from attaining the size, flexibility, or internal solidarity required to force government action to rehabilitate slum buildings. The city, state, and federal governments were the only bodies which had the financial resources to subsidize comprehensive repairs in slum housing—they were the ones whom the rent strike had to force to act, not the slumlord. The rent strike movement should have given priority to those of its attributes which had the most influence on political authority.

There were three main qualities of the rent strike that contributed to its political effectiveness. First, its *size*. The larger the rent strike grew, the more politicians perceived in it a threat to the public order, or the danger of a broadly based radical movement arising to undermine established political relationships. Second, *militancy*. The more the rent strike broke laws, or massed large numbers of people together in volatile situations, the more politicians felt the danger of a contagion of civil disorder to other groups and other issues—a breakdown of the peaceful "rules of the game" in which they were used to operating. Third, *rapport between leaders and followers.* The more stable the movement's organization was, and the more closely its participants were linked to its leaders, the more politicians grew afraid that agitation would be lengthy and would spread to other issues when the rent strike ended.

Court action, however, hindered the rent strike movement severely in each of these areas. It prevented the rent strike from attaining optimum size because it absorbed so much of the organizers' energy in paper work and mechanical problems relating to court appearances such as arranging transportation for tenants and subpoenaing records. The time spent filling out forms, conferring with lawyers, and arranging transportation for the day in court could have been spent on activities which expanded the strike. In addition, when the organizers got involved in court action they were unable to devote as much time to the organization of demonstration and rallies which had given the rent strike the aura of mass movement in its early days.

Involvement in court action seemed to impose a nonmilitant psychology on the rent strike's leaders and subtly steered them away from mass action or civil disobedience. The kind of massive resistance to evictions that characterized the strikes of the 1920's and 1930's did not take place in the Harlem rent strike. The most publicized instance of a resisted eviction involved only 10 people—a far cry from the 4,000 people who massed before an Olinville Avenue Building on rent strike in 1933. Finally, the technical responsibilities associated with court action prevented the organizers from using their time with the tenants for political education or activities which strengthened tenants organization. Some preliminary surveys by the Columbia School of Social Work of tenants involved in the rent strike show that there was very little contact between organizers and tenants and that very little of the rent strike's meaning was communicated to the tenants. The organizers, moreover, had very little success in getting tenants to participate in related protest activities, and this was an important reason why government officials felt they could safely stop making concessions after the first few months of the strike.

The rent strike, thus, by getting involved in court action, severely compromised its strength as a political protest, but it did so in large part because it did not have a clear conception of itself as a political protest. The rent strike began suddenly and spread haphazardly—it had an epidemic quality. Many organizations rushed into it without knowing anything about housing or without previous experience in organizing low-income people. Without a clear strategy to guide them, and without real confidence in their ability to stay with the movement, they were pushed into the safe and legitimate style of organizing, which would not put themselves, or the tenants, in danger. They did not know enough about housing work, or perhaps about American society in general, to realize that major economic changes could not be effected by the courts.

A certain naive and totally unjustified confidence in established institutions characterized the organizers, many of whom were white college students and professionals. Unsure of their own commitment, at once afraid of and patronizing to the people they were organizing, and subtly beholden to the bourgeois notion that reason prevails in the chambers of power—they made of the rent strike an elaborate form of social work.

---

1. *New York Times*, January 13, 1964, p. 34.

2. *Amsterdam News*, November 9, 1963, p. 12.

3. *Amsterdam News*, December 7, 1963, p. 1.

4. *New York Times*, December 2, 1963, p. 30.

5. *Newsweek*, December 30, 1963, pp. 17-18.

6. *New York Times*, December 23, 1963, p. 30.

7. From the middle of December on, James Farmer did not make a single statement on the subject of the rent strike, although he had himself advocated a citywide rent strike earlier in the year. In February, moreover, when interviewed by *The Saturday Evening Post* about problems of the civil rights movement, he declared at the outset that he would answer no questions relating to the rent strike and to Jesse Gray.

8. The groups participating were The University Settlement Housing Clinic, the East Side Tenants Council (these two were Metropolitan Council on Housing affiliates), the Educational Alliance Housing Clinic, the Presbyterian Church of the Crossroads Housing Clinic, the Downtown CORE Housing Committee, the Integrated Workers (Progressive Labor Party) Housing Clinic, The Housing Clinic of the Council of Puerto Rican Organizations, the Stanton Housing Clinic, The Community House Tenants Association Housing Clinic, and the Negro Action Group (the last three were groups set up by MFY).

9. Under New York City Housing Law, tenants cannot initiate action in court against a landlord for grievances constituting a "constructive eviction"; they must wait for the landlord to send a dispossess and then contest the dispossess in court.

10. *New York Times*, December 31, 1963, p. 7.

11. *Ibid.*, p. 16.

12. *Ibid.*, p. 7.

13. *Ibid.*, p. 25.

14. *New York Times*, January 21, 1964, p. 1.

CHAPTER 2

Tenant Power in Public Housing — The East Park Manor Rent Strike

George Neagu*

The successful struggle of the East Park Manor Tenant's Organization against the City of Muskegon Heights, Michigan Public Housing Authority has received considerable attention, as it marked the first time in the U.S. that tenants of a low-income public housing project gained control over policy affecting their lives.

Most important, however, has been the inspiration it provided to tenant advocates and tenant unions. In June, 1969, *Tenant's Outlook,* the official newsletter of the National Tenant's Organization (NTO), in a feature article on the East Park Manor rent strike stated, "The case study of East Park Manor rent strike . . . shows that tenants organizing can force landlords and housing authorities to improve housing conditions." A review of the East Park Manor rent strike and the conditions leading up to it, as well as the historic agreement subsequently reached, may prove beneficial to tenants who find themselves in a similar situation and who want greater self-determination.

There were actually two rent strikes—the strike from July 2, 1967, to August 21, 1967, and the strike from July 2, 1968 to October 3, 1968. The first rent strike, while unsuccessful in its own demands, provided useful insights for the strategies developed during the second rent strike. Whatever success was achieved in the second strike was based upon the work in the first one.

The Community

Muskegon Heights is a residential community of about 25,000 people, 52 percent of whom are black. Civil rights leaders often refer to it as the "Missis-

---

*Mr. Neagu, former District Executive of the Michigan Civil Rights Commission in Muskegon, presently works for the Illinois Department of Welfare.

sippi of the North." It has had active local chapters of the John Birch Society, Minutemen, K.K.K., and National States Rights Party. In addition to apathy created by a chronically depressed economy, active discrimination often proved a formidable force against black self-determination.

Available housing for blacks was limited throughout the Muskegon area as a result of both low income and entrenched patterns of housing discrimination. Housing which was available was old and substandard. It had one low-income public housing project—East Park Manor—which was built in the early 1960's. There were two hundred units in East Park Manor proper and seventeen in Fairview Homes nearby, both of which were managed by the Federal Housing Authority (F.H.A.). Fairview Homes was rapidly deteriorating war housing scheduled for demolition whenever all the tenants moved out. The populations of both projects were almost entirely black.

Many of the residents of the "Heights," as it is called locally, worked in a nearby foundry. Culturally, the were severely limited in their outlets—at the time of the second rent strike Muskegon Heights did not even have a movie theater.

East Park Manor Tenants' Organization

The East Park Manor Tenants' Organization was organized by a tenant, Rheava Brooks, who was an aide with the Community Action Against Poverty Program. She knew there was widespread frustration and dissatisfaction with the physical conditions in East Park Manor and the management of it. It was not unusual for basements to become flooded after each rain and for sewage to back up. Whenever police were called to a unit it was reported to management and, regardless of reasons or proof of guilt, if the police came a third time to the same unit, the tenant had to move. Repairs were slow and garbage disposal was a problem. There was no recreational area for the children. To many, the list of problems appeared endless.

Efforts to remedy the problems through the project director, who was white, not only were fruitless but led to a feeling on the part of the tenants that he was unconcerned about them. Efforts to involve the councilmen were unsuccessful. Letters to the mayor were unanswered. The tenants clearly perceived that they were faced with institutional indifference.

Out of this frustration, several tenants called a meeting at the Catholic Information Center. Nine persons attended. The director of the Center, a Catholic priest, provided the place because the group could not meet at the project's Administration Building. The basic organizational plan that developed out of the group was quite simple. The tenant organization would hold a meeting on each block in East Park. Only those blocks with more than half of the block in attendance could elect a Block Captain and be eligible for membership in the Tenants' Organization.

On November 16, 1965, the first large organizational meeting was held and officers were elected. This time the meeting was held at the Administration Building—a small but significant step forward in itself. In addition to the

Executive Committee, each Block Captain was a member of the Steering Committee.

One of their first acts was to draw up formally a list of fifteen grievances to present to the Public Housing Commission. A request to meet with the Commissioners was denied and so they contacted HUD's Chicago Regional Office. The Chicago Regional Office representative was sent to meet with the group. He stated he could not commit himself to any particular course of action but promised something would be done in thirty days. The fledgling tenants' organization was cautiously elated about the prospect that something would soon be done. After all, was this not a federal department representative?

After six months of waiting, without any remedial action evidenced, the tenants were through waiting for administrative action. Soon after, the East Park Manor Tenants' Organization Steering Committee made a private decision to have a rent strike in the future. However, they did not know whether they could gain widespread support for it. They recognized that apathy, dependence, and fear would not be easy to overcome. Proceeding carefully, they felt their first goal was to achieve formal official recognition from the Housing Commission as the sole representative group of the tenants. This action was viewed as necessary to legitimize the group as genuinely voicing the concerns of the entire project as well as inspiring trust in the non-member tenants to join it. The rent strike, they recognized, would never be successful if their organization did not have the full support of East Park Manor.

Early in January, 1967, a meeting was called at the Administration Building by the Tenants' Organization. The tenant group, excited by their progress, made certain all block captains contacted their tenants. The F.H.A. director also sent out notices of the meeting. The meeting was held to determine by vote of the Commissioners whether the Tenant Organization would be recognized officially as the tenants' representative group. The meeting, which was relatively short, contained only one minor surprise for the tenants. A recognition petition was presented by a rival group, allegedly organized by the Muskegon Area Development Council (local Chamber of Commerce), to neutralize the Tenants' Organization. The organization, which had been active for months with the majority of tenants in the project, were infuriated by this attempt to discredit them as the project's official tenant representatives. They believed that the director was in collusion with this activity as well. Angered by what they perceived to be "back-room politics," they viewed the Commissioner's eventual vote of recognition as little more than an attempt to placate both them and their plans for the rent strike. (Three of the five Public Housing Commissioners, including the only black member, voted for recognizing the Tenants' Organization.) The Tenants' Organization, however, was pleased with the recognition and the legitimacy it gave them; work proceeded apace on organizing the rent strike.

Following this meeting, the Tenants' Organization Steering Committee divided responsibility for "selling" the rent strike to tenants. They went door-to-door, day after day, and held innumerable small home meetings. They encountered fear of eviction and even suspicion. Slowly the patience, sincerity, and dedication of the Steering Committee members won the tenants' confidence. At last, in the latter part of January, 1967, a meeting was called at the Administration Building. The meeting place bulged with enthusiastic tenants —at least two-thirds of the project were in attendance. The time had come for tenants to exert their new-found power. A strike vote was taken; the decision was unanimous—strike.

First Tenants' Strike

The first tenants' strike began February 3, 1967. This was the date the monies collected were placed in escrow with the National Lumberman's Bank Company. It was also the date on which the first pickets appeared around the Housing Administration Building. They stood from 9 a.m. to 5 p.m. on that date—the temperature was eight degrees below zero! The group picketed every Friday for the length of the strike. A local attorney, Ron Riosti, served freely as legal advisor to the tenants and the Michigan Civil Rights Commission (MCRC) Muskegon District Executive served as consultant. The F.H.A. Director reacted almost immediately by announcing on television that the tenants on strike would be evicted on February 21.

The tenants increased their demands to include the ouster of the five commissioners. The more oppressive the F.H.A. Director reacted, the more the tenants discovered "togetherness" in the group. The greatest difficulty for the Tenants' Organization was convincing some members that they should not simply withhold rental payments but put them in escrow. One hundred and fifty-five tenants—over seventy percent of all tenants in the project— placed money in escrow.

A judgment of eviction was ordered by the Circuit Court Commissioner against the 155 tenants. On February 14, 1967, a meeting was called by the Mayor of Muskegon Heights, Kenneth Heineman, which was attended by over 150 tenants, three city councilmen, and the Public Housing Commission. A resolution was passed calling for a moratorium until March 21, 1967; in the interim, grievances were to be discussed. During this time, tenants who withheld rent payments were immune from eviction. At this point the Mayor's role was that of a liaison person. He carefully avoided becoming centrally involved by not committing himself on the Public Housing Commission's jurisdiction. When the moratorium deadline arrived, grievances still were unsettled. The F.H.A. Director announced that if rents were not paid in seven days, tenants would face eviction.

The tenants' legal advisor decided to appeal the evictions. At a hearing in Circuit Court on April 11, 1967, the judge announced, after conferring privately with attorneys for the tenants and City of Muskegon Heights, that he would mediate the dispute. Both sides agreed to this, pending approval by the city's Public Housing Commission. This approval was subsequently given. The tenants, many of whom were worried about the possibility of eviction, were hoping the mediation would help end the increasing tension felt throughout the project. In May, 1967, the judge announced that an agreement was approved by the Public Housing Commission and tenants' representatives and that a special meeting would be held in the courtroom at which time a vote would be taken by the East Park Manor Tenants' Organization to accept or reject the agreement. The Tenants' Organization accepted the agreement which was molded into a new lease for tenants and the Commission and then sent to federal authorities for sanction. The lease included the aforementioned recognition clause and an altered rent schedule, specified a four-step grievance procedure, delineated orders to repair defects in structures and included a clause which kept the lease in effect until January 31, 1968. The latter was included because tenants planned to test the lease for six months; they stressed another rent strike could develop if the lease failed to work properly.

However, HUD did not approve the historic agreement until several weeks later but on August 21, 1967, more than $50,000 (which included late fees and court costs), was turned over to the Housing Commission by the East Park Tenants' Organization, thus concluding the first strike.

Not included in the officially publicized agreement between tenants and Housing Commission was a compromise to the demand that the Commissioners be ousted. According to the tenants an agreement was reached in January, 1968, whereby a black director would replace the white man who had held the job. This agreement was subsequently honored.

It is interesting to note that, despite the prior institutional indifference of the courts and other groups, there was an apparent readiness on the part of the tenants to trust the judge's conciliatory efforts. Also, at this point, the Tenants' Organization appeared not to have a heavy investment in the removal of the commissioners. They were willing to settle for the replacement of the F.H.A. director; this meant that the Mayor, who appoints commissioners, was not seen at this time as central in pursuit of their goals.

However, a year following the resolution of the first strike, very few of the physical repairs agreed upon were completed. The patience and good will of the tenants had been sorely tested. In early April, 1968, the tenants took a strike vote to begin withholding rent on May 1, 1968. The President of the Muskegon Branch of the N.A.A.C.P. contacted the Tenants' Organization on April 17, 1968, and asked that the new F.H.A. director be given sixty days without a strike to produce a new contract and remedy problems. The Tenants' Organization agreed that they did not want to embarrass the new director (who was black) if at all possible. They complied with the N.A.A.C.P. request.

At the end of the sixty days, the director presented a list of fifteen Modernization Work Items which constituted a proposal he wanted to submit to HUD for the Tenants' Organization approval. As this was essentially the same list included in the grievances presented by the tenants a year earlier, the dismayed tenants decided to pursue the strike.

Many factors were the same in the second rent strike as in the first one: (a) The same tenants' organization versus the same five member housing commissioners; (b) the same law firm rendering legal aid to the tenants and the same city attorney advising the F.H.A.; (c) Michigan Civil Rights Commission involvement; and (d) the same mayor in office. What had changed was the president of the Tenants' Organization since the first rent strike. The new President, Mary Daniels, was involved in the first rent strike as a member. The legal advisor to the group, Vern Kortering, had been involved "behind the scenes" in the first strike while another firm member was in the public eye as the advisor. There was a new District Executive (George Neagu, the author of this chapter) of the Michigan Civil Rights Commission who had arrived in Muskegon about four weeks after the second rent strike began.

Another important factor was the increased legitimacy of the Tenants' Organization among East Park Manor residents. The group had organized a large youth activities program centered around football as well as sponsoring banquets in the community which raised funds for emergencies. It also sponsored holiday activities and helped tenant families with their personal problems, often serving as a referral agent to social service agencies. When new tenants moved into the project, the Tenants' Organization representatives would visit soon after arrival to orient them to the project and assist them in getting settled. All these activities helped to develop a feeling of neighborliness and maintained an atmosphere that the Tenants' Organization's concern was not housing alone. Their efforts had solidified their legitimacy with their neighbors. The entire group was well-trusted.

The Second Tenants' Strike

No longer willing to listen to institutional pleas for more time, the Tenants' Organization began the rent strike on July 2, 1968. But in this second strike there was a significant difference from the first—the East Park Manor Tenants' Organization stood virtually alone.

The pattern of picketing was the same as in the first strike. By now, however, the tenants' distrust of governmental institutions was very deep. From the outset it was the strategy of the East Park Manor Tenants' Organization to demand the ouster of all five Commissioners. Toward the end of July, the Tenants' Organization leadership began to hold daily meetings with the M.C.R.C. Muskegon District Executive. It was clear that the situation was at an impasse as the Public Housing Commission had not initiated any meetings and the Mayor was maintaining a policy of non-involvement. Confronted with this dilemma, Mary Daniels, as President of the Tenants' group, had turned to the new M.C.R.C. officials. Daniels could not assume that the new District Executive could be trusted as was his predecessor. Rapport, at the outset, with tenant leadership was maintained by providing the group information received through the M.C.R.C. Housing Division and by checking with this Division on strategic decisions.

The mere fact of M.C.R.C.'s lending its resources to aid the tenants cannot be underestimated in the re-establishment of institutional trust. Much information regarding HUD's stated policy toward greater tenant involvement in the decision-making process, as well as other useful data, had obviously not been conveyed by the F.H.A. to the tenants. At a quickening pace, a mutually respectful and trusting relationship developed between the tenant leadership and the Muskegon District Executive.

Interestingly enough, from the outset, M.C.R.C.'s contact with HUD's Chicago Regional Office was similar to that of the tenants. For example, when the Muskegon District Executive called Chicago to introduce himself and interpret the gravity of the East Park Manor situation, the HUD representative asked, "What business is it of yours?" The Executive had to explain that the crisis involved racial tension. The HUD representative stated the project "was beautiful and I saw nothing wrong for tenants to complain about." Such attitudes, when conveyed to others in the community, did little to increase the respect of HUD's position with the strikers.

The tenant leadership, on the other hand, was viewed with great trust by most tenants. None of them wealthy, they all sacrificed personal and material resource for the good of the strike. Mrs. Daniels was a remarkably courageous person with a sense of mission. At no time did she ever hope to gain anything for herself. Leroy Hughes, the Organization's secretary, was equally dedicated and provided his car, time, and money, as well as his home where most of the early meetings were held. There was the foresight and wisdom of Rheava Brooks, the tenant whose idea of a tenants' union became a reality largely through her efforts. There was Joel McDaniel whose knowledge of parliamentary procedure kept meetings on an even keel. There was the respected senior citizen member, Erley McKinney and Mrs. Evelyn Sims, who became the President of the Organization following the second strike; she was also the head of the Welfare Rights Chapter she organized. These were individuals worth knowing and there were many others like them.

By now these people, once trusting in institutional authority, had decided after much discussion that the basic issue should be the removal of the Commissioners. They related paternalistic and racist comments allegedly made by Commissioners to the tenants. They realized how much influence such men had over their housing lives. It was apparent that the communications problem between the Public Housing Commission and the tenants was beyond repair.

In the early part of August, the Tenants' Organization sent letters to the Mayor and the F.H.A. Director, formally requesting the removal of all five Commissioners. At this point, although the Tenants' Organization had about 117 members, monthly escrow deposits had dropped. In the meantime the M.C.R.C. official had trained the tenant leadership in using the news media. Such activities as drafting and issuing a press release, appearances on television, contacting the newspaper for photographs to be taken, using the wire services—all these public relations skills were taught and effectively used by the Tenants' Organization as it pressed its course.

Despite the widespread public interpretation of the strike, the tenant leadership knew a serious situation was at hand in the drop of money in escrow. In an evaluation of the situation, an important strategic decision was made to involve the Mayor and, hopefully, bring him into a central position in the dispute.

On August 23, 1968, at the request of the Tenants' Organization, the M.C.R.C. District Executive held a lengthy meeting with the Mayor, carefully interpreting his role as concern for the potentially explosive racial situation in East Park Manor and a desire to be of assistance to all sides to resolve the situation. One of the major points stressed with the Mayor was the growing emphasis upon tenant participation, especially in the context of the desire for more voice in fate control on the part of black people and the poor. The Mayor showed an understanding of this desire and asked for assistance in resolving this matter. The District Executive indicated that the Mayor's role and understanding was crucial in opening the way for communication, as he seemed to have a sensitivity the Commissioners were alleged to lack. The Mayor indicated he absolutely refused to remove five Commissioners because he felt that someone with experience must remain on the Commission for continuity of experience. However, he agreed to meet with the Tenants' Organization leadership the following Monday at a luncheon meeting. He stated he had already called for a public airing of the East Park Manor situation for Monday night at the regular Council meeting when all sides could be heard: he wanted the Councilmen to hear the facts directly, and to dispel rumors. The M.C.R.C. District Executive, however, suggested that such a public meeting could only be injurious and cause great unpleasantness. However, it was too late to cancel it.

A weekend strategy meeting was held at Kortering's home. (This was just one of many similar late night meetings held with the legal advisor.) Kortering's counsel went beyond legal advice. In many ways his relationship to the Tenants' Organization was as integral a part of the eventual outcome of the strike as that of the tenant leaders. At the weekend meeting ground rules were agreed upon for the discussion with the Mayor. Certain ground rules were set for all participants: (1) Parties involved would not publicize whatever was said, and (2) no commitments would be made by anyone. The latter point amounted to a basic principle with Daniels and Hughes as they never made a commitment for the Tenants' Organization without its approval. During this exploratory meeting, several distinct suggestions emerged. Some of these suggestions were: (1) an end to the rent strike for four to six months during which time the Mayor would "moderate" or work closely with F.H.A. to insure better human relations. If the Public Housing Commission failed to improve following the Mayor's personal appeal to them to shape up in the vital area of attitudes, he would remove them instantly; (2) two tenants would be named as Commissioners when openings occurred; (3) a HUD Training Program would be embarked upon in the near future which would include F.H.A.-tenant participation aimed toward improving tenant relations and decision making; (4) a five-member group composed of tenants would meet in an adivsory committee with F.H.A. at its meetings. Other important ideas were discussed, but it was obvious that the flow of communication was opening up and the Mayor was committing himself to a more central role in the dispute. Before the meeting ended, all had agreed not to allow the Council meeting that evening to become too abrasive in order to enhance the opportunity for resolution of the controversy. It was the first time the Tenants' Organization had shown optimism in over a year.

Unfortunately, at the very time that the Mayor was meeting with the tenants' leadership, the F.H.A. Director had issued 94 seven-day eviction notices. The tenants were furious and their leadership was puzzled, angry, and hurt. The promising liaison between the Mayor, the tenants, and the M.C.R.C official seemed scuttled.

The Mayor moved quickly to revitalize a spirit of cooperation. He issued a public statement claiming that he had found out about the eviction notices after the meeting with the leadership. He stressed that the timing was indeed bad in issuing them. A regular meeting of the Tenants' Organization was called at which time the Mayor, the Public Housing Commission, and the F.H.A. Director would be present. A hearing before the Circuit Court Commissioner the day after the issuance of the notices temporarily blocked until the next Friday the processing of further action on the eviction notices pending the possibility of ironing out differences at the Thursday night meeting. By now, the press was playing up the central role the Mayor had assumed to settle the strike as well. He was finally not only involved in all the private negotiations, but publicly as well.

Prior to the Thursday night meeting, the M.C.R.C. District Executive was able to persuade the Tenants' Organization to modify the demand for ouster of the Commission from all five to three. The tenants decided to compromise on the ouster of all five Housing Commissioners. Talking late into the night, they agreed to demand the removal of only three. They recognized that the Mayor would never accede to the demand for the removal of all five for two reasons: (1) he was firmly convinced that continuity of experience had to be maintained; (2) the demand had been given him in a way which had racial overtones and, politically, with an eye on the next year's election, he felt such a complete concession would destroy him. After careful consideration, they decided to allow the retention of one black person and one white person and to demand the removal of the other three white members.

At the Thursday night meeting, grievances were discussed point by point. The Mayor was sincere in his efforts to respond fully and accurately to each question but also quick to admit what he did not know. Finally, the tenants stated their charges that the three Commissioners were paternalistic and racist. They recounted remark after remark made by each Commissioner to them to substantiate their accusations. One of the accused Commissioners began to laugh out loud in what appeared to be blatant mockery of the tenants. It only lent weight to the charges. The Mayor made no effort to defend the Commissioners but he did urge settlement and gave a "let's go on from here" type speech. The Mayor suggested that certain steps be taken to improve communication and resolve problems between the two major parties. The tenants were unmoved, and narrowed their demands to one—the removal of the three Commissioners. Efforts to reach a strike settlement by the

Mayor had failed.

On Monday, September 16, 1968, Circuit Court Commissioner Kuck rendered a judgment for possession in favor of the housing commission. Under the law, the Tenants' Organization had ten days to appeal or face mass eviction. The situation became ominous.

Prior to the regular weekly meeting of the tenants, the Tenants' Organization leadership made the decision to recommend to the membership that it vote not to appeal. In one of the most moving acts of courage of a long struggle, the group—at a dramatic meeting on September 12, 1968—in anticipation of Kuck's action, unanimously decided it would go to jail rather than return the monies held in escrow.

Here the M.C.R.C. made several moves during the Detroit Staff Meeting beginning on September 16, 1968. A member of the M.C.R.C. Housing Division secured the support of a newly formed state housing group, the Michigan Housing Federation, which issued a news release deploring the eviction process as a method for solving social problems. It also sent a telegram to the Mayor offering its services to help resolve the matter.

In discussion with a Field Representative of the M.C.R.C. Housing Division, it was decided to ask the Executive Director of the M.C.R.C. (who was to attend the Michigan Conference on Mayors that week) to contact the Mayor. The purpose of this contact would be to informally open the discussion with the Mayor and reinforce as much as possible the concept of tenant participation. It was felt that the Executive Director's status used this way might make the Mayor feel more comfortable about the idea of removal of Commissioners. Later in the week, the M.C.R.C. Executive Director, the late Burton I. Gordin, stated that the Mayor agreed to removal of the three Commissioners on a "phase out" basis—one every two months—and appointment of three new Commissioners from a list of fifteen persons drawn up by the tenants. He resisted the efforts of the Mayor to secure M.C.R.C.'s cooperation as arbitrator in the situation. The Mayor at this point was clearly feeling the pressure and wanted a "face saving" vehicle. He had hoped that the M.C.R.C. would serve as a fact-finding body for him and recommend to him the removal of the three Commissioners so he would not be centrally responsible. Gordin wisely side-stepped this invitation although he offered to come to Muskegon Heights at anytime to help in the crisis.

There was an overflow attendance at the Tenants' Organization meeting on September 19, 1968. In a stirring speech a popular local minister pledged his support. Another group, Blacks for Immediate Action (B.F.I.A.) offered to go to jail with the tenants. The courage of the tenants had fired the imagination and sympathy of many persons outside the project. A supportive telegram from the Michigan Housing Federation was read. These tenants were willing to risk possible family disorganization and legal as well as social hardship for a principle.

Four days later, the M.C.R.C. District Executive met privately with the Mayor. He stressed that tension was extremely high due to the eviction deadline. He suggested that community harmony was the Mayor's responsibility and asked him to seriously weigh whether retaining the three Commissioners was worth the tension. He pointed out the demands of a thousand whites at a nearby community who were demanding removal of school board members. This persuasive effort was necessary as the Mayor was waivering in his resolve to remove the Commissioners. At the end of a three-hour talk, the Mayor agreed to another meeting with the Tenants' leadership on September 26— the date of the evictions.

During the week the M.C.R.C. official met with the Tenants' leadership to invite them to the meeting and to persuade them that, in his judgment, the Mayor had made his final concession. On September 26, 1968, the community and the press were braced for a mass jailing. At the meeting with the Tenants' leadership, the Mayor agreed to the following terms:

(1) he would immediately stay the evictions;

(2) he would find a way to pay for the late fees which had been incurred by the tenants;

(3) he agreed to call the three Commissioners on the meeting date and request their resignations;

(4) he would issue a news release on the same day stating a resolution of the rent strike was imminent;

(5) he proposed that one of the three out-going Commissioners would be "phased out" every two months and that the new Commissioners would have to be approved by the Tenants' Organization;

(6) the first newly selected Commissioner would be selected by the Tenants' Organization and accepted unconditionally by the Mayor;

(7) the first Commissioner to be removed would be the one most objectionable to the tenants;

(8) he would work toward recommendations listed in the letter to him and the tenants.

In addition: (1) the Tenants' leadership agree to call a meeting on September 30, 1968, to vote on the agreement; (2) it was proposed by both the Mayor and the Tenants' Organization that the M.C.R.C. Executive Director participate in the Tenants' Organization's regular meeting on October 3, 1968, when the Mayor would publicly present his terms and (3) on the following day a joint press release approved by both parties would be released announcing the end of the strike and escrow monies would be reimbursed to F.H.A.

An important side light at this juncture was the curious role played by the Chicago Regional Office of HUD which up to this point seemed to view the tenants with antipathy. Upon learning of the agreement to place tenants on the Public Housing Commission, HUD representatives advised the Mayor that such a move would be illegal as a result of an Attorney General ruling that it would constitute a "conflict of interest." When challenged by attorney Kortering to produce the opinion or cite the source, the HUD representative could not do so. It appeared that HUD wanted to use its authority and status to frighten the Mayor from the agreement. However, since HUD could not verify its warning, he persevered. (Later, on December 12, 1968, Kortering received an unsigned letter from HUD citing an obscure ruling in California which did not apply at all.)

The District Executive invited the Tenants' Organization leadership, the Mayor, Mr. Gibson, and the Housing Division Director of M.C.R.C., James Rose, for a meeting at the district office prior to the public meeting. The format of the meeting and the roles each would play were frankly discussed. The thorny question of the penalty payments for non-payment of rent and court costs would be negotiated between the tenants' legal counsel and the Public Housing Commission. No one wanted this issue to become a last-minute bottleneck to the settlement. A news release was prepared incorporating the agreement terms and statements from each of the leading figures in the meeting—the Mayor, the Tenants' Organization President, and the M.C.R.C. District Executive.

The ending was uniquely simple; the public meeting was held and completed as planned. The rent strike was over. The East Park Manor Tenants' Organization celebrated their long-fought victory late into the night.

Aftermath

Within the next few months, the Mayor replaced three Public Housing Commissioners with three persons chosen from a list provided by the Tenants' Organization. The first new appointment to the Public Housing Commission was the President of the Tenants' Organization, Mary Daniels. As news of the historic strike settlement reached beyond the boundaries of the "Heights," recognition was deservedly received. At the University of Notre Dame, The Foundation for Freedom and Democracy in Community Life presented the East Park Manor Tenants' Organization a plaque citing its contribution toward bettering their community and furthering democracy. Members of the tenant organization, as well as attorney Kortering, were in demand as speakers as other groups wanted to organize. The Tenants' Organization sparked an effort to develop a strong Michigan Tenants' Union and, finally, delegates from the Tenants' Organization received a standing ovation from tenant union representatives throughout the country who assembled in St. Louis to adopt bylaws establishing a National Tenants' Organization. Tenant power had arrived in Muskegon Heights, Michigan.

CHAPTER 3

A Case Study of Tenant Union Legalism

Thomas Jennings*

The Ann Arbor rent strike was the largest and most ambitious attempt at fundamental alteration of the landlord-tenant relationship ever launched at an American college campus. Begun in early 1969, the strike at its height involved over 1200 active strikers. The strike lasted over a year, but ended with little permanent change. The purpose of this study is to analyze the growth of the Ann Arbor Tenants' Union and its attendant rent strike and to identify some of the legal and organizing factors causing its rise and subsequent fall. Lessons from the strike should be valuable to any group—whether student- or community-based—attempting to increase tenant involvement in housing.

The Initial Concept of a Tenant Union

For years, students at The University of Michigan have complained about the housing market in Ann Arbor. The 1960's had seen a great increase in the private sector housing of students. In that period (1960-67), spaces for 15,000 to 20,000 tenants were created in new apartments—called by some "housing for the affluent student." The remaining students usually lived in old, often delapidated houses or in University housing.

Except for a brief period between late 1966 and early 1968, the vacancy rate was much below the national average. The low vacancy rate, helped by an oligopolistic market in which three management companies controlled at least one-half of the central campus housing, created housing conditions termed by many students as oppressive. By the fall of 1968, students paid from $280 to $350 a month for a four-person, two-bedroom apartment. The leases were almost uniformly for 12 months, and students leaving for the

*Mr. Thomas Jennings, a graduate of The Univeristy of Michigan Law School, wrote much of this article while a member of the Michigan Law Review. He extends appreciation to the Law Review for the use of their facilities and resources.

summer were forced to lose considerable amounts of money subletting. Tenants usually had to put down three months rent in the spring for an occupancy beginning in the fall. Damage deposits were often not returned, even when no material damage had occurred. Finally, students constantly complained of shoddy maintenance.

In the fall of 1968, a number of radical students at the University developed the concepts of a tenant union and a rent strike. Believing that the housing conditions were in great need of improvement, they felt that enough tenant concern existed to facilitate concerted tenant action. Consultations with an attorney, Ron Riosti, who had served as counsel in a successful rent strike in Muskegon, Michigan, (described in the previous chapter) indicated that a rent strike would be feasible.

The goals of the initiating students were two-fold. First, they wanted to remedy the housing conditions which they found onerous. To achieve improvements, the students proposed that the Ann Arbor Tenants' Union (AATU) be created to negotiate and make agreements with the Ann Arbor landlords. They formulated three basic demands: "(1) that the AATU be recognized as bargaining agent for tenants; (2) that the landlords resolve the grievances of their tenants through collective bargaining; and (3) that landlords sign a contract with the AATU to ensure that the rights won by the tenants will be implemented." Thus, the students planned to establish the AATU as an established force to counter the bargaining power of the landlords.

Secondly, the students had more abstract goals. To an extent, achievement of these goals would further the progress of the Union by enhancing tenant commitment and participation, but the leaders also wanted to develop among the tenants and community at large a "radical consciousness" thought necessary for any program of lasting social change. The leaders sought to convince these two groups of their conception of political and economic realities by showing that the housing conditions in Ann Arbor had resulted from complicity among landlords, bankers, judges, and local politicians. They wanted to "demystify" the courts and the law—to illustrate their perception that the legal system had furthered the "interests of property rather than people." They also sought to show that participation in a broadbased, radical, and democratic collective activity could lead to real political power.

Any strategy developed by the leadership would be necessarily geared toward pressuring the landlords into acceding to demands of the Union. While some had argued that the development of a viable organization should precede any rent strike, the initial leaders decided to place primary emphasis on conducting the strike as soon as possible. They calculated that if a rent strike was publicized well enough it would generate the excitement necessary for tenant commitment.

Emphasis on the rent strike also led to subordination of other methods of pressuring the landlords. While activities such as picketing and sit-ins had been crucial for achievement of agreement in some tenant activities such as those in Chicago in 1966, the leadership decided that economic pressure would be more effective than attacks on the "prestige" of the landlord through publicity picketing.

The strategy of the rent strike called for the use of any tactic that would deprive the landlords of rents and necessitate expenditures, for it was felt that the resulting loss of profits and inability to meet financial commitments would force them to negotiate. Central to this strategy was the maximization of the numbers of strikers and the prolongation of the period during which they were able to withhold rent. Furthermore, all costs incurred by the landlords in seeking evictions would create an added strain on their funds. The Union proposed to prolong each eviction trial and jam the dockets. While they would try to win the trials, AATU leaders emphasized that winning was not central to their strategy. Finally, because of the cost and time involved, affirmative legal actions would be initiated only if they would have very significant benefits for the Union.

It cannot be overemphasized that certain peculiarities of Michigan landlord-tenant law were crucial to both their choice of the general strategy of a rent strike and the choice of specific strike tactics. In 1968, largely as a response to the Detroit riots, the state legislature had passed a set of five public acts known as the "Tenants Rights Package."

Three of these acts concerned public housing. The fourth act authorized a legal "rent strike" in some extreme cases. Under Michigan Comp. Laws Ann. §125.529. 30, tenants may pay their rent into an escrow account created by housing officers if their building has received neither a permanent nor temporary certificate of compliance with the state housing code. However, landlords can receive such certification despite code violations unless the conditions create a "hazard to the health and safety of the occupants."

Because code violations in Ann Arbor would generally not give rise to such a danger and use of the withholding statute would have required close involvement by housing enforcement officials, thus minimizing the power of the AATU to bargain with the landlords, the Union early decided to ignore the withholding provisions.

The final act in the Package appeared to modify basic rights and obligations in the landlord-tenant relationship.

As the strike developed, interpretation of the new statutes as creating a statutorily-required covenant by the landlord to obey the housing code, and authorizing reductions of back rent owed for breach of these covenants, allowed tenants to jam the courts with jury trials. They also were able to injure landlords economically by achieving sizeable reductions in rent.

However, at the outset of the strike the interpretation of the new legislation was in doubt. The organizers accordingly relied on an older section of the Michigan statute stipulating that a tenant losing an unlawful detainer action cannot be evicted if he pays the rent due and costs within ten days of the judgment. This redemption statute, existing in few other states, allowed the Union virtually to guarantee strikers that they would not be evicted if they chose to remain and promptly paid their back rent after judgment. In other jurisdictions, tenant unions have found either that they could not utilize rent strikes and had to rely on picketing and political pressure, or that if they *did* strike they had to rely on refusal of the authorities to enforce the eviction orders for fear of violent confrontation.

Organizing the Strike

The organizers who had developed the idea of a tenant union/rent strike held two meetings in the fall and early winter of 1968-69. At the second one, they created a fourteen-member steering committee and recruited about one hundred organizers.

While this committee was originally to be an *ad hoc* group formed to implement the basic policy decisions made by the organizers, it assumed the function of leadership because of the lack of structure among the organizers and the need for on-going decision-making. The members of the steering committee were given specialized positions—such as general coordinator, press, legal, etc.—and were also designated as group leaders for approximately ten organizers each.

The leaders had hoped to form a democratically-rooted structure as soon as the strike began. However, considerations of time and resources dictated that the creation of such a structure be postponed until the fall. A general meeting of organizers held in February, 1969, approved in principle a framework involving: (1) primary units of houses consisting of ten to twenty members; (2) a council of representatives, elected by the houses and possessing the general policy-making powers of the Union, and (3) a steering committee, elected by the council and mandated to carry out its policies. While two meetings of a provisional council were held in the spring of 1969, the council was not a viable force until the fall. In February, 1970, it approved a final constitution for the Union which basically incorporated the structural proposal approved the previous year. By spring, 1970 the council, made up of directly elected building representatives, was electing members of the steering committee and the two bodies were working together without serious disagreement.

Unfortunately, the steering committee—the core of the AATU—suffered from a large turnover in personnel. No members of the original group still served on it by spring, 1970, although some of them worked closely with new members.

When the Union was formed, the leaders decided to limit membership to those who were actually striking or fulfilling a work requirement. The purpose of this provision was to limit decision-making power to those who had real commitment to the strike. Later, membership was opened to any dues-paying non-strikers in order to broaden the base of AATU support.

Initial Organizing

The students who began the rent strike first conducted research on the apartment rental market in Ann Arbor. Their findings indicated that three management agencies controlled about 50 percent of the non-University housing in the central campus area and that several other large agencies controlled most of the rest. Because the students felt that these landlords set the rental pattern in the city and were particularly unconcerned with student complaints, they decided to place emphasis on striking against ten "target" landlords. Realizing that a sizeable number of strikers was necessary for success and that tenants would be more willing to strike if they knew they were part of a large movement, the AATU set a goal of 2,000 strikers out of the approximately 6,000 tenants renting from the target landlords. The students decided to collect pledges to strike from tenants and have the strike begin when they reached their goal.

There were several factors existent in Ann Arbor which suggested that large numbers of tenants would strike. First were the housing conditions themselves, about which students had complained for years. Second, many students perceived themselves as constituting a "class"—a unified group apart from the University administration and the landlords. This concept, coupled with the fact that most students lived in a relatively small area and in similar housing conditions, minimized the problems some tenant groups face in creating the consciousness of a common bond. Third, the campus was generally considered to be "radical." Many students, looking back at the disorders surrounding the Democratic Convention in Chicago in the summer of 1968 and faced with very few issues on the campus which could serve as the basis of a mass movement, seemed to be looking for a cause in which they could become involved. It also appeared that these students might be willing to adopt effective but "illegal" tactics which more moderate persons would eschew.

Despite these factors, the organizers found that there were several impediments to the tenants' willingness to strike. Many tenants did not recognize the value of collective action. Furthermore, they were afraid of the consequences of a rent strike—going to court, damaging their credit ratings, etc. Some felt that it was unfair to refuse to honor a contract signed with their landlord. It took many hours of work by well-trained organizers to dispel many of these fears; many of those approached still remained too apprehensive to strike.

Finding that the support of established groups, both on campus and in the community, could greatly legitimize the strike and help minimize the fears of many tenants, the Union also enlisted the support of the student government, the County Democratic Party, the UAW, and four members of the Ann Arbor City Council. Finally, effective use of the media as disseminators of information served to develop some tenant awareness of housing problems and of the AATU itself.

Results of Organizing

Within fifteen days of the commencement of organizing, the Union had obtained 500 strike pledges, and within the month they had acquired 1300. At that time, the Union decided to call an immediate vote of the pledged strikers on whether they should begin striking. The leaders felt that if the strike began immediately it would gain momentum and gain its original quota. Furthermore, as many students would be leaving the city at the end of the school term in April, it appeared that a delay could only hurt the strike. The vote was overwhelmingly in favor of immediate action, and on February 15, 1969, slightly more than 1200 rent strikers began withholding their rent.

Although tenant unions have utilized several different devices to handle the rent accumulated during rent withholding, the AATU collected full rent from its strikers and placed the bulk of it in an "escrow fund." The fund had four purposes: (1) located in a bank in Windsor, Canada, it protected the rents from landlords; (2) it impressed the public, the courts, and the landlords with the sincerity of the strike by creating assurances that the rent would be paid in full when the Union achieved agreement with the landlords; (3) it helped the tenants save their money so that they could pay their back rent upon settlement of the strike or a landlord's judgment for possession; (4) it helped finance the strike by accumulating interest.

The AATU received outright ten percent of the first month's rent deposited by all strikers. This fund, along with money raised from other sources such as donations, benefits, etc., was used to finance the strike. The remainder of the rents was placed in a savings or checking account. Tenants were allowed to remove their money from these accounts for any reason.

In the fall of 1969 the Union began to collect a fee based on five percent of each month's rent as dues. In February of 1970, the AATU decided instead to collect an initial dues fee of five dollars from all members and an additional two dollars per month from all strikers. While this policy lowered income by about $700 a month, the Union offset the loss by keeping 50 percent of all rent reductions received.

The Strike and the Courts

As mentioned before, the legal strategy of the rent strike centered upon the use of any tactic which would keep strikers in possession of their rental units while imposing economic hardship on the landlords.

A threshold legal problem faced by the Tenants Union was the possibility of "self-help" evictions, i.e., the landlord personally evicts his tenant. This remedy appeared to be extremely attractive for landlords. While re-entry alone would not provide the unpaid back rent, it would be a quick and relatively inexpensive means of regaining possession. Moreover, the remedy's greatest attraction was its psychological potential. A few quick and well-publicized self-help evictions could heighten the fear harbored by almost all strikers that they might actually be evicted. Such evictions could potentially break a strike at its inception.

Michigan law permits a landlord whose tenant has not paid his rent to re-enter the premises as long as he does not use force. The AATU's response to the possibility of self-help was largely "extra-legal" and largely successful. First, the union attempted to convince strikers that self-help was basically illegal. By doing this, it hoped to create an atmosphere in which attempts by landlords to regain possession without utilizing court procedures were politically damaging and added to the AATU contention that landlords were willing to exploit tenants in any way possible.

Secondly, when faced by actual threats of self-help by some of the smaller landlords, the Union established a "Tactical Mobile Defense Unit" which instructed tenants to prevent physically their landlords from entering their apartments. Because they were faced with the possibility that landlords would enter vacant apartments, remove the tenants' belongings, and change the lock, tenants were encouraged to act collectively by watching each others' apartments when they were vacant. The Defense Unit was on call to reinforce individual tenants when necessary. Due to these precautions, no self-help evictions were recorded.

Initial Eviction Proceedings

Because of the landlords' unwillingness to achieve self-help evictions, they turned to Michigan's summary eviction procedure. In the typical nonpayment of rent situation, the lessor must first make a written demand for possession—the "Notice to Quit." If the tenant does not either give up possession or pay the rent owing within seven days of the Notice, the landlord can file a complaint in District Court and a summons will be issued. The summons will be answerable in three to six days, and the matter will then be heard at a summary hearing. A crucial section of the Tenants Rights Package (Mich. Comp. Laws Ann. Sections 600.5637,.5646), defined the permissable issues to be litigated. The meaning of the statute was in doubt and it had not yet been interpreted by appellate court in the state. However, it seemed clear that the landlords would always be granted judgment for possession and at least most of the rent.

Before the strike had commenced, the AATU attorney and the law students began to develop a defense to evictions. In order to achieve their goal of postponing judgments and consuming the funds of the landlords, they decided to focus on methods to procure jury trials and avoid summary judgments. They established a set of affirmitive defenses which, they reasoned, would provide the foundation for factual disputes sufficient to avoid summary judgments. And while they realized that their chance of winning cases was slim, the effective assertion of tenant defenses would serve to add legitimacy to the strike for potential strikers who questioned the propriety of withholding rent.

At the heart of the defenses was the allegation that the lessor had failed to comply with the Ann Arbor and State housing codes. The tenant would argue that any violation of the housing codes constituted a "defense . . . upon the lease or contract" maintainable in an eviction action, or alternately a "counterclaim against the plaintiff by way of set-off or recoupment." A similar defense would be provided by breaches of specific written or oral covenants by the landlord.

Secondly, the legal staff planned to argue that various conditions in the apartments would constitute partial constructive eviction by the landlord. In asserting these defenses, the tenant would be using two of the rare instances in traditional landlord-tenant law in which the tenant was provided with a valid defense to a nonpayment-of-rent action.

Finally, it was decided that all tenants would assert two additional defenses of a highly unusual nature. They would first allege that the housing market in Ann Arbor created such an inequality of bargaining power that various clauses of the lease were unconscionable. Second, they would assert that the individual landlords had conspired to fix rental prices in violation of state and federal law and that the price was thus void. These defenses were given little chance of success but were seen by the AATU as important "political" assertions.

The mechanics of defending perhaps more than 1,200 strikers in court also posed serious problems. The legal coordinator planned to have law students conduct the initial investigations and draw up the pleadings. Each student was assigned to one or more strikers and given a comprehensive instruction sheet on defenses and possible code violations. They were instructed to encourage strikers to write the Ann Arbor Building and Safety Engineering Department with complaints of code violations to build an effective record. In anticipation of large numbers of summonses coming at once, the law students were encouraged to conduct as much investigation as possible in advance. The students were also given the responsibility of filling out form pleadings for the individual tenants.

The necessity of filing an answer in the required three-day period also posed serious problems. Union attorneys later informally worked out a procedure with the District Judge hearing the bulk of the cases by which they filed a standardized "shotgun" answer without interviewing the tenant. The answer could be amended up to 48 hours before the trial to state the specific code violations alleged. This procedure was crucial for conducting the defense of strikers, and the legal defense was dealt a serious blow when the judge began to refuse to allow the device in early 1970.

The AATU also moved to disqualify one of the District Court judges. In an affidavit they charged that the judge held a financial interest in an exterminating company with close ties to some landlords, managed and collected rents from an apartment house himself, and had sent letters threatening to revoke the probation of students convicted in a welfare sit-in if they continued in the rent strike. While concern that they would not receive fair trials from the judge was a major factor in the attempted disqualification, the AATU also reasoned that if the number of judges was reduced the trials would be effectively delayed. Further, they felt that exposure of a conflict of interest would help show the interrelationships of the various segments of the power structure of the city. After a series of manuevers, the parties worked out an informal agreement whereby the landlords would allow the disqualification of two judges and the tenants would not challenge a third. The fact that the arrangement was only informally arrived at was reinforced by the fact that the two "disqualified" judges began hearing cases again in early 1970.

If the AATU had been pleased by the course of events prior to the first trials, they were ecstatic when the first judgment was returned by a jury on March 20, 1969. A management company had sued a couple for possession and back rent totalling $300. In response to the tenants' argument that a faulty shower and inadequate garbage facilities constituted a breach of the landlord's statutory convenant, the jury granted possession to the landlord but held that the rent of only $280 was owing. By the end of March, only three cases had been concluded, all with rent reductions. One tenant had her back rent reduced from $250 to only $140. In each case the tenants paid their back rent and remained in possession.

Anti-trust and "Conspiracy" Suits

Two suits of a more comprehensive nature disrupted the pattern of individual eviction litigation. On March 13, 1969, eight tenants, assertedly representing the class of all tenants in the central campus area, filed a suit in Federal District Court against the Ann Arbor Property Managers Association and several of its members and associates. The suit was based on alleged violations of the Sherman Act and charged that the defendants had conspired to fix prices of apartments in the central campus area and control the supply of units. The tenants sought relief in the form of preliminary and permanent injunctions and treble damages for economic injury by all tenants in the preceding four years. While the suit was officially not filed by the AATU, it was closely coordinated with Union activities. As with other affirmitive legal actions, the Union felt the suit would publicize "landlord collusion" and would further harass the landlords. "Discovery" might provide valuable information of use not only in the suit but in other activities as well. But most importantly, the plaintiffs felt that they had a valid claim which, if successfully asserted, could reap millions of dollars for Ann Arbor tenants.

On July 25 of that year the suit was dismissed on the grounds that the "substantial adverse effect on interstate commerce" necessary for the jurisdiction of the court in a Sherman Act proceeding had not been shown (Marston v Ann Arbor Property Managers Ass'n, 302 F.Supp. 1276 E.D. Mich. 1969). When the dismissal was affirmed by the Sixth Circuit Court of Appeal and certiorari was denied by the U.S. Supreme Court, the AATU's most ambitious affirmitive action was effectively defeated.

The most concerted effort by the landlords was a suit filed in State Circuit Court on April 23, 1969 by five Ann Arbor realtors against 91 tenants. The complaint alleged that the defendants had engaged in a conspiracy to induce breach of contracts, obtain libelous articles about Plaintiffs in the news media, and harass Plaintiffs "so that all ownership and control of units of living accomodations will fall under public ownership and control." They sought injunctive relief to halt all AATU activities, an accounting of all money received and placement in a court escrow, individual damages of $10,000 and exemplary damages of $300,000.

A show cause hearing on a preliminary injunction—most feared by the AATU—was held in late April. However, by agreement of the parties it was postponed until June 6, 1969. At that time, the judge took under advisement a number of motions including mutual motions for summary judgment. One month later he denied all motions before him. This denial was apparently on the grounds that Defendant's answer had raised sufficient questions of fact on the issue of whether the inducement of breach of contract was reasonably justified by Plaintiff's failure to meet the housing code.

The status of the suit following the July decision became a matter of mystery even to the lawyer's involved. Although an August pretrial hearing date was set, the hearing was postponed—ostensibly because Plaintiffs were seeking to appeal the subpoena ruling. No appeal was ever filed, and at infrequent intervals the trial date was put forward, finally into 1971. By that time virtually all parties assumed that the case would not come to trial.

The unlawful detainer trials had recommenced on July 21, 1969. The trials continued throughout the fall, and in November the Union received its largest rent reduction of the strike: a jury cut the rent for a dilapidated house by 71 percent, from $1,088.60 to $323.30. Trials continued unabated.

Despite the fact that the Union had been able to achieve its original goal of forcing a multitude of trials and had received sizable rent reductions, the legal strategy began to falter in the summer and fall.

One of the greatest problems was legal help. While the Union had hoped to deplete landlords' funds through costly litigation, the AATU itself suffered from legal expenses and constant manpower needs. With the departure of the original attorney, the leaders had to produce more lawyers, yet they had limited funds at their disposal. They finally found two highly capable attorneys, but these men could not give the full-time services necessary for an effective legal struggle. Several other volunteer lawyers became involved at times, and a full-time attorney was hired in the spring of 1970.

Other factors led to legal difficulties. In the fall of 1969 landlords began to ask for court costs more effectively, cutting into the rent reductions. On October 31, a new District Court rule required that rents be deposited in a court-administered escrow fund before tenants could defend eviction notices. This led to a loss of leverage for the Union, for it no longer could promise immediate payment of rents upon recognition. The AATU also lost the accrued interest on such funds. Finally, a ruling was handed down forbidding the previously mentioned "shot-gun" amended answers. The tenants were now faced with administrative problems which would have taxed an efficiently-run law firm.

As a result of these factors, the AATU was forced to settle large numbers of cases out of court. These settlements generally involved rent reductions of between 10 and 20 percent. One of the major issues in these settlements was whether disposition involved a "dismissal" or "stipulated" judgment. While a dismissal had no effect on later withholding by the tenant, the stipulated judgments included a condition that future rents would be paid. If rent was not paid on time for the remainder of the lease, landlords were authorized to receive automatically a writ of possession after a five-day grace period. However, Union attorneys continued to litigate "attractive" cases which might yield large reductions.

In the fall, two landlord attorneys developed more sophisticated arguments to expedite evictions and eliminate the reductions. In a series of cases, they asked only for possession, choosing not to file a claim for back rent. The company argued that while the statute required the judge to determine the rent owing for purposes of the ten-day redemption period before execution, the new statute (Mich. Comp. Laws Ann. Section 600.5646), made no provision for the finding on rent. The tenant was therefore forced to pay *full* rent within ten days or face eviction. Only later could he litigate his counterclaim, and the landlord could make use of the dilatory tactics previously used by the tenants.

Although they succeeded in this argument in several cases, the court finally found it to be without merit. Clearly such an interpretation would have rendered both the protections accorded the tenant by the new legislation and the redemption clause as meaningless.

A more serious and fundamental attack on the interpretation of the Tenants' Rights Package was made by another landlord. Filing a motion for summary judgment on the issue of possession only, the landlord argued first that the legislation had not intended to make the new implied covenant "to fulfill the housing code dependent," i.e. had not meant that breach of the covenant to excuse payment of rent. Secondly, he argued that issues of landlord breach were not to be litigated in a motion for summary judgment brought under the new statute, Mich. Comp. Laws Ann. Section 600.5637(5). A decision was finally reached in the landlord's favor at the Circuit Court level. While the AATU appealed this ruling, the decision made the form of the rent strike originally envisioned by the Union no longer possible.

The rent strike helped create other legal issues as well. Some landlords sought to receive damages for supposed loss of credit and inability to make mortgage payments. Although such actions might endanger some rent strikes, no Ann Arbor landlord was able to win such damages. (In a related area, landlords in Berkeley, California dealt a rent strike there a severe blow by winning statutorily provided treble damages in cases of willful rent withholding. Such examples emphasize that particular state laws will always have a great effect on the viability of a rent strike.)

Secondly, several Ann Arbor landlords garnished the checking accounts of striking tenants. When the largest bank in the city repeatedly failed to inform its checking account holders of garnishments, the AATU launched an effective action in February of 1970 resulting in the withdrawal of over 600 accounts and $250,000 from the bank in one day. The previous spring, when landlords had garnished a few accounts, the AATU had retaliated by garnishing the landlords for the amount of their claim for last month's rent, damage deposit, and damages. The landlords promptly discontinued the garnishment procedure at that time also.

It is difficult to determine just how effective the Union was in jamming the Courts and delaying judgments. Clearly the fact that the spring, 1969 cases were still being heard in the fall indicates that the delay was considerable. Suits were brought against at least one half of the original strikers, and approximately four hundred suits were settled out of court. Certainly some of the tenants were able to escape without paying any rent. What is not known, however, is the extent of injury incurred by any of the landlords. They have never opened their books to the public.

The Second Organizing Drive

The AATU was hopeful as students returned to the University in the fall of 1969. The legal strategy of the strike, taken as a whole at that time, was probably going better than expected. The strike had received nationwide publicity. Leaders of the Union theorized that if they could get 1200 strikers in the spring, they should get between 2,000 and 4,000 in the fall . . . tenants would now be sure they wouldn't be evicted, and they would be anticipating victory.

A core of 100 organizers, trained in week-long workshops, fanned out over the city in mid-September, seeking pledges for the strike beginning with the October 1 rent payments. But tenants were more reticent to strike than expected. They had few complaints; they had promised their landlord they wouldn't strike; to some, he seemed like "too nice a guy to strike."

By early October, the Union had but a few hundred strikers. They were never to come close to the 1,200 they had so easily achieved last spring. By the spring of 1970, only about 600 tenants were withholding their rents.

A number of factors were responsible for the tenants' disinterest in the rent strike. Possibly most important was a fundamental miscalculation made by the Union. Leaders had assumed that tenants' grievances included not only poor maintenance and shoddy conditions, but high rents, the 12-month lease, and large damage deposits as well. However, organizers found that not all these factors were leading tenants to strike. Students were genuinely angry with shoddy maintenance, and were willing to strike to improve it. But because most University of Michigan students are members of the upper-middle class whose parents pay their rent, concern over high rents was not as great as had been expected. Furthermore, rents had not been increased over the previous year, and some landlords were now giving interest on the damage deposit.

This lack of concern with housing cost took on great importance in the face of the landlord response to the strike, for in the fall maintenance was greatly improved. The largest management company initiated a policy in which the company now made all necessary repairs. In previous years, it had made repairs only upon the authorization of the owners. Other management companies hired extra employees to supervise maintenance.

According to some maintenance firms in the area, management companies increased their maintenance six-fold. Further, landlords had tried to develop personal, individualized contact with their tenants. It was harder to strike someone who had actually vacuumed your rug.

In concert with the landlord "counter-offensive," the AATU's efforts at educating tenants on the basic goal of collective bargaining evidently failed to reach many of the tenants. The rent reductions in court had in a sense turned against the political aims of the organizing. Many tenants developed the impression from the trials that the purpose of the strike was to achieve rent reductions in the courts because of housing code violations. With increased maintenance, they could see no reason for striking. The tenants could envision no rent reductions in their cases, and they felt that it would be unfair to strike a "good" landlord. They did not recognize the need for pressure to assure an on-going relationship between Union and landlord, and they did not make the assumption made by the Union that as soon as the strike and the Union were removed, maintenance would return to its previously low standard.

More abstractly, the AATU was unable to maintain the psychological tempo of the strike present in the previous spring. According to one leader's analysis, both time and space had operated against the Union. Starting again in the fall, the strike lacked the charisma of six months previous. The strike had been *the* political activity in the spring—now it competed with other causes such as the struggle for a student-run bookstore. These activities also drained the AATU of some of its leaders and best organizers. Secondly, when students left Ann Arbor in the summer and returned in the fall, they lost the psychological involvement they had earlier felt. Finally, some noted that students were basically transients. Perhaps they considered their permanent, "real" homes as being with their parents and now just didn't care as much about their apartments as had been thought.

Negotiations and Agreements

When the strike began, the AATU placed its emphasis on organizing and the mechanics of the rent strike. Looking back, perhaps too little planning went into the mechanics of actual collective bargaining procedures. At the time, however, the Union demanded to be recognized as bargaining agent for a landlord's tenants. They also expected agreement on such factors as rents, handling of damage deposits, and grievance procedures. Only then, they planned, would the withheld rent be returned to the landlord.

Against this background, most landlords refused to negotiate at all. Much like employers in the 19th century, they argued that they could serve the interests of their tenants better than could the Union. To them, the AATU was little more than a group of outside radical troublemakers, bent on destroying their businesses.

One problem the Union never came to grips with was that besides back rent it had little to offer the landlords. While some inner-city tenant unions have been able to offer a lowered turnover and greater tenant responsibility, the AATU was unwilling and perhaps unable to make such promises. The notion of tenant discipline found little favor anywhere within the group.

In the spring of 1969, at least one management company entered into preliminary negotiations with the Union. These negotiations broke off when the company demanded payment of back rent before recognition, a condition the Union would not accept. Again in the fall a management company with 200 striking tenants entered negotiations, but the talks broke down when the company refused to negotiate specific agreements before officially recognizing the AATU as bargaining agent for the striking tenants. Finally, in the spring of 1970, a smaller landlord agreed to recognize the Union as the sole bargaining agent for any tenant choosing the AATU as his or her agent, but little substantive change occurred. Other preliminary negotiations with larger landlords also broke down over inability to define what "recognition" really meant to either party.

Reanalysis and Restructuring

By January of 1970, the AATU had recognized that it was in trouble. The strike had not generated enough participants and the legal strategy was floundering. The Union had fallen to relatively low visibility in the community, and almost all the original goals, other than temporarily-improved maintenance, were unachieved. The Union decided upon some very fundamental changes.

First, recognizing that the strike was not powerful enough to force recognition, the AATU deemphasized striking in favor of other tactics. For the first time nonstrikers were encouraged to join the Union. In order to increase the visibility of the landlords, several pickets were started. Perhaps most interesting of these was a series of actions against the landlord who had been the plaintiff in the suit which finally won summary judgment for the landlords; he was also the owner of the house which bore the largest rent reductions—71 per cent—of the strike. Furthermore, this landlord was then the Michigan State Crime Commissioner. For two months, about fifty demonstrators traveled weekly to the state capitol of Lansing and there factually documented how this appointed state official was one of the worst landlords in Ann Arbor, having received more than ten legal citations and "housing tickets" from the housing commission and the courts in the past two years. Under eventual pressure, the commissioner was soon forced to resign.

Secondly, the Union also determined that much of its emphasis was misplaced. An analysis of the housing market indicated that only massive new building could permanently alter the short supply and resulting high rents. Arguing that the University had created a situation which forced low-income tenants out of the city, the AATU moved to demand that the University engage in massive construction of low-income apartments on some of their available, tax-free land. A referendum to that effect was placed on the student government ballot that spring, and it passed by a five-to-one margin.

Plans for the fall of 1970 reflected the realization that tenant sentiment differed widely from that of the spring of 1969. Union leaders planned to develop more tenant consciousness by organizing massive participation at a relatively low level of involvement—peitions, letters, and small meetings with individual landlords. Only when more than 50 percent of a given management company's tenants were backing the Union, would they escalate tactics. Rent strikes would be used only as a last resort and only with the assurance of mass participation. The choice was also to focus pressure on only one or two management companies. The companies chosen for pressuring were those perceived to be most prone to injury from attacks on prestige and on loss of rental payments.

These theoretically sound plans never grew to fruition. By the end of 1970, the AATU seemed to many a thing of the past. A few persons remained dedicated and involved, but too often the Union operated merely as a service organization, handling individual tenant grievances but without the organizational emphasis of earlier times. Even then, however, the AATU was the only voice of outraged tenants. It continued to represent some tenants in court and it lobbied for change in the housing market. But the rent strike was over, and it appeared that the Ann Arbor Tenants' Union would never achieve the true "union" status it had so actively sought.

Conclusion

Ann Arbor tenants were fortunate in being able to utilize the best landlord-tenant law in the country. The combination of statutory covenants, dependence of promises, and the redemption statute all provided, for a while at least, a legal setting which made a massive rent strike feasible. Except for administrative difficulties, during the early stages of the strike the legal strategy worked extremely well. What was discovered, however, was the fact that the key to success is organization, long range planning, and massive tenant participation, not mere legal defense. As the strike progressed, these factors became sorely lacking, especially when the courts reversed themselves on a number of crucial judgments. Although the AATU was perhaps the most successful long-term student struggle at the University of Michigan, it ultimately failed.

In many ways this failure bodies ill to the future of tenant unions functioning under similar conditions found in a student community. While Ann Arbor seemed to provide an extremely good climate for organizing, and the student population appeared to be ripe for massive action, the Union eventually found that students may not be a good constituency for tenant activity. The fragmented academic schedule and the lack of commitment to permanent changes in local housing made permanent organization almost impossible. Those active in Ann Arbor found that higher commitment by other populations to better housing signalled greater likelihood for success.

One lesson from the experiences of the AATU is the recognition of the many alternatives for both goals and strategy. Different tenant populations and different legal structures may dictate fundamentally different approaches. Further, as Union activities evolve, new alternatives may open up and previously attractive alternatives may close. In short, a tenant union must be thoroughly planned while at the same time flexible enough to change as conditions require. Any fundamental alteration of the landlords-tenant relationship will be the product of only a hard and sustained effort.

Part II

CAUSES OF THE MOVEMENT: ECONOMIC AND LEGAL CONDITIONS BETWEEN TENANT AND LANDLORD

Causes of the Movement

Social movements often arise for unorthodox reasons. Some are begun by people of a particular philosophy or faith. For example, the Nineteenth Century Utopian communities were founded in the belief that man's innate goodness would lead him to live a correct and honest life if only given a setting in which to do so. Other movements are formed around one particular issue—such as the abolition of "Demon Rum." A few social movements grow so large in size and power that few remember that they were indeed once not institutions but movements. Such movements derive from social, economic, and political factors so complex that generations of writers spend lifetimes analyzing their origins. Naziism is a horrifying example of this latter movement type.

There is one distinctively American social movement as well—the "grass roots movement." It is the common title given to any widespread activity of poor, disenfranchised, or otherwise non-institutionalized groups which agitate for social change. These groups can be either progressive or reactionary. They are highly specific issue-oriented movements which often confront similar root problems. For example, two grass roots movements concerned with the same overlapping problems are the ecology movement and the tenants' rights movement. Both want an end to pollution and waste, both want the quality of life enhanced, both attack institutions unconcerned with the social costs of their own activity. It would appear that these movements would make natural allies.

However, political coalitions among social movements have been undercut by an American tradition that views political action solely in terms of "issues" or "causes." Over time, this traditional view has led new groups to organize first in terms of self interest and then in terms of political analysis. Such issue orientation makes understandable the substantive differences in style, depth of ideological analysis, and membership alienation from mainstream politics which are present among so many grass roots movements. For example, the ecology movement is today a predominantly white, middle class movement concerned with recycling processes and industrial waste; the tenants' rights movement is a predominantly black, poor movement concerned with rehabilitation of its members' housing and inequitable landlord-tenant relations.

This issue orientation can lead to other organizational problems. In Europe, where long-standing class traditions help subsume particularized movements into well-known political groups (as occurred with French students in May, 1968), individual issues soon become grist for ideological discussion and dissent. American grass roots movements, on the other hand, often have great difficulty in effectively moving beyond their agitational role. Sometimes a movement will simply disintegrate. This appears to be what has happened to the anti-war movement in the 1970's. Another alternative is co-optation of the issue by larger political groups. This second alternative has both positive and negative consequences. For example, the ecology problem is today discussed by every major political figure in the nation. Such widespread recognition of the problem is good. Yet with everyone being for ecology, it becomes more difficult for people to distinguish clearly who or what is at fault. In reverse of many European experiences, the issue has grown in importance at the expense of idelogical analysis.

A third, rarely realized alternative is the blending of different grass roots movements into one, larger political movement. Perhaps the best example of this alternative was the integration of different labor factions into a relatively cohesive force within the Democratic Party. Other more recent attempts at movement building are the anti-war movement and the civil rights movement (which proved ineffective) and the proposed linkage of the tenants' rights movement with the welfare rights movement. Until now, little has resulted from this latter coalition.

As long as these grass roots movements remain separate and distinct, the specific problematic causes for each one's development must also be analyzed separately—not only to understand how they differ from those of other movements, but in what ways they are alike. This section sets out to explore the particular economic, social, and legal problems underlying the tenants' rights movement. Other topics (such as land development costs), while important to a thorough discussion of the entire housing problem, are not considered here. The following articles address the unique economic conditions within the housing community which directly relate to tenants and landlords, the actual effects of such economic factors on tenants themselves, and the legal situation which helps reinforce those economic and social conditions.

The first article, prepared by Michael Beckman, describes the economic realities underlying ownership of urban apartments in both slum and non-slum areas. The types of landlord behavior created by these economic conditions are carefully analyzed to help explain why some of our urban problems are so difficult for tenants alone to combat.

In case study form, Ted Vaughan analyzes the actual effects which the above-mentioned economic factors have upon poor urban tenants. While written separately, the first two articles together help explain the economic and social realities of many tenants now living in poor areas of our cities.

On another front, Thomas Quinn and Earl Phillips have written a legal history of landlord-tenant relations. Using a developmental approach, the authors carefully and fully document how little landlord-tenant relations have changed since feudal times. They go on to discuss the effects that such a static response has had upon urban housing conditions.

Finally, the legal picture confronting tenant unionism is described by Richard Cotton. In an enlightening comparison with previous labor and civil rights experiences, the author explains what tenant groups can expect to achieve in organizational and membership self-defense as they work for greater tenant equity within the housing community. This comparison, coupled with an analysis of the distinct legal problems faced by tenant unions, makes the article a valuable piece for lawyers, tenants, and planners.

CHAPTER 4

The Realities of Being an Urban Landlord

Michael Beckman*

A tenant union, if it is to work effectively towards the improvement of its members' housing, must understand the economic realities under which they live. The success or failure of the tenant union depends primarily on its understanding of these economic realities, and secondarily on its abilities to shape its tactics and programs so that they deal adequately with such realities. In this brief paper, we will examine some of the important economic features of the housing market which affect tenants and their organizations. Concentration will be on the creation and maintenance of the slum housing market. This discussion will not be all-inclusive; rather it is hoped that it will provide a guide for the investigation by tenant unions of their specific housing markets. Slum housing markets differ greatly from city to city; any treatment of the important features must be of a general nature.

There are two actors of importance in the housing market. While the landlord is the more important actor in terms of economic position and power, tenant unions must not overlook the economic position and motivation of the second actor—the tenant.

The Tenant

People with low incomes have relatively little flexibility regarding the amount of money they can spend on housing.[1] They will tend to seek inexpensive housing, and the cost of that housing will be a more important consideration to them than the condition of the housing. Hence, a demand is created which is satisfied by slum housing—low-cost deteriorated or dilapidated dwellings. However, because of the limited amount of housing available at relatively low prices, and because of the large numbers of people who

---

*Michael Beckman, a graduate of Harvard University, has been an organizer in the tenant movement in Boston, Ann Arbor, and Cincinnati. Presently he is housing chairman of a local community action center in Cincinnatti.

must because of their income inflexibility, bid for that low-cost housing, the price of the housing tends to be pushed upwards to the highest feasible level.[2] A tenant living in slum housing is paying not only as much as he is willing to pay, but he is probably paying as much as he can pay.

Thus, it is important to understand that improved housing cannot be financed by higher rentals. Concomitantly, low income tenants are unlikely to choose vastly improved housing at even only slightly higher rentals.

The Landlord

The prime motivation for the property owner or investor in the housing market is his desire to earn a profit. The operation of the housing market in general, as well as the slum housing market in particular, reflects this motivation. Since housing is rarely constructed as slum housing, it is necessary to examine first the non-slum housing market, and trace within it the creation of slum housing. Then we will examine some of the mechanics of the slum housing market.

A clarifiction is perhaps in order here. This discussion deals with generalized behavior, assuming that a landlord will be whom the economists call a "rational economic man," that is, that the property owner will operate in a way that will bring him the largest possible profit under existing economic conditions. This assumption may not be true when dealing with specific landlords who may have economically irrational motivations, i.e. refusing to sell a building at a good price because it "belongs in the family." Such landlords are discovered by investigation by the tenant union and may have to be dealt with on non-economic grounds.

There are two sources of profit in the non-slum housing market, and those are the resale potential of the building and the tax advantages of ownership.

Resale Potential

An important factor in the profit picture of the owner of non-slum housing is the ability to resell his property at a price higher than that at which he bought it. Essentially, he is speculating in real estate, gambling that his property will increase in value during the time which he holds it. The difference between the cost of the property—his buying price plus improvements and other expenses—and his selling price will be his gross profit. If he makes no further investments or improvements, the entire difference will be gross profit. The primary factors which cause increase in value over time are a continued demand for rental housing and an inflationary economy. Secondary factors, such as the location of the building, the general condition of the neighborhood surrounding the building, the nearby presence of a captive tenant market such as students, the probability of governmental purchase in the future also exert influence.

The creation of the profit that arises from the resale of the building is often independent of the actual physical presence of the building itself. When this is so, there is no economic incentive for the owner to make repairs in the buildings he owns. While the owner must make minimal repairs that will keep the building habitable, he realizes that significant investment in maintenance and rehabilitation will not result in a corresponding increase in the value of the building in the resale market, and thus such money is seen as unrecoverable. The same considerations hold true for each successive owner of the non-slum property. The building may stand for years without significant improvement.

Tax Advantages[3]

Though the possibility of profitable resale provides a long-range incentive to investment in non-slum housing, it is the tax advantages inherent in real estate ownership that provide the initial and short-term attraction to property investment. Indeed, these tax advantages are so important to the investor that they may increase the price of a building.[4]

The tax advantages in apartment house investment are three-fold. First, income tax laws permit accelerated depreciation during the earlier years of ownership, which allows the owner a greater write-off than would be available under straightline depreciation.[5] Such depreciation is treated as a deduction from ordinary income. Second, tax laws also provide for the deduction of the interest on a loan secured by a mortgage on a building. So the purchaser of rental buildings usually tries to obtain as much borrowed money as possible to finance the acquisition of the building, putting up as little money of his own as he must. (This is known as a "highly leveraged" purchase.[6]) The larger the ratio of interest to principal in the loan payments, the greater the tax deductions. And, although the purchaser may, in reality, have very little money of his own invested in the property, he is still entitled to claim the entire value of the property in calculating his accelerated depreciation deductions.

There is a time element involved in these two tax advantages, and the longer the building is held, the less important the tax advantage. The accelerated depreciation tends to flatten out after a certain period of time, and the longer that loan payments are made the greater the portion of the payment the principal becomes. The investment becomes less attractive, and the owner looks for other properties offering maximum potential of a new cycle of these tax advantages.

A third tax advantage derives from the tax treatment of the profit made from the resale of the property.[7] Provided that the building is held a maximum of ten years, the profit from resale is treated as a capital gain, and is taxed at a lower rate than is ordinary income.

Certain conclusions appear from these observations concerning resale and tax advantages. First, profit in non-slum housing often does not depend primarily on rental income. Rather, in many cases tax advantages and resale are the primary sources of profit. This is not to say that rental income is not important to the property owner. The building may be highly leveraged, and the owner may depend on rental income to make the mortgage payments. But his profit comes from other sources.

Second, there is little economic advantage in long-term ownership of rental property. Given the way tax laws are written, profits realized under the tax advantages discussed above reach a point of diminishing returns around the tenth year of ownership. When this stage is reached, the owner of the property takes advantage of the strong resale market in non-slum housing, sells at a profit, and reinvests a portion of the gain in new property. Some of the data collected by Chester Rapkin in New York's West Side, and presented in Sternlieb's *The Tenement Landlord*, seem to confirm this trend of ownership turnover every tenth year. In a total of 1,108 properties examined, there were —during a seventeen-year period from 1938 until 1955—a total of 1,619 conveyences, or an average of 1.46 conveyences per property during that time period.[8]

Third, there is little reason for a property owner to invest in the maintenance or rehabilitation of his property. The sources of his profit are not dependent on, or affected by, the physical condition of the building. There is small incentive, financial or otherwise, to induce the property owner to make repairs. The building gradually deteriorates as a succession of owners realize their profits with no measurable re-investment of those profits in maintenance of the building. Finally, the building becomes slum property. Rothenberg, in the *Economic Evaluation of Urban Renewal*, succinctly sums up this process:

> "When the property has been completely depreciated for tax purposes, it is still habitable, despite a lack of physical maintenance of the property with little impairment of its competitive market position relative to the rest of the neighborhood, due to the neighborhood effects and the bargaining disabilities characteristic of the tenants. The property can then profitably be sold, because the new purchaser can subsequently take the depreciation on the property anew, while failing to maintain it, and can in turn resell it profitably. The same property, many times delapidated, is passed into lower and lower occupancy use while continuing to be depreciated for tax purposes."[9]

Slum Housing

The slum housing market differs in several fundamental ways from the non-slum housing market. Basically, in the slum housing market, rent is the primary source of profit.[10] There are two reasons for this dependence on rent to provide an adequate return on the investment. First, the resale market for slum housing is weak. Secondly, since the resale market is weak, the owner will probably remain in possession of the building past the ten-year limit for realizing profits from tax advantages.

The resale market is weak for several reasons. There may be a scarcity of prospective buyers of the property because the process of deterioration has reached such proportions that the prospective buyer realizes that he will never be able to resell the building. This lack of bidding for the building tends to bring down the selling price of the building; this downward trend may reach a point where the owner cannot sell because he will be unable to recoup his original investment.

There is also the problem of refinancing the sale of the building. Although the owner may find a prospective buyer at an advantageous price, the prospective buyer may not be able to secure financing on terms that would make the purchase a profitable one. Institutions which normally loan money for real estate purchases may require relatively unfavorable terms for buildings located in slum areas, e.g. high interest rates. Another possibility is that financial institutions may have a perhaps informal but nevertheless real policy of refusing loans secured by properties within certain geographical areas of the city. This may occur regardless of the actual condition of the building or neighborhood where it is located (this practice is known as "black-listing.") The seller may find it necessary to take back a large junior mortgage in order to finance the purchase. Such a condition may make the transaction less profitable and therefore less attractive.

Contributing to the weakness of the resale market in slum housing are such factors as vandalism, high vacancy rates, possible city citations for code violations, and increasing property taxes—all of which make investment in slum housing less attractive and which therefore tend to depress prices. Selling becomes that much more difficult. Money which might have been invested in slum neighborhoods is drawn to safer investments in more "respectable" neighborhoods with more "respectable" tenants.

The structural weaknesses of the resale market means that many owners of the slum properties hold their properties beyond the ten years during which tax advantages are prominent in the profit picture. This seems to lead to wide fluctuations in respect to the return on investment, with some owners reportedly returning up to two-thirds of their equity in the first year, while others simply abandon their properties as unprofitable.

However, each owner will attempt to maximize the return on his investment. This has several important consequences for the tenants and the building. It means that the landlord will try to charge the highest possible rent per unit. He will try to create the maximum number of dwelling units in his building by dividing up existing units. He will try to minimize the amount of money that he needs to reinvest through maintenance in his property. In addition, he will try to minimize the costs of operating the building. It is obvious that this set of policies, designed to maximize profit, also are designed to accelerate the deterioration of the building. Furthermore, these policies contribute to the cost-increasing problems of non-payment of rent, vacancies, and vandalism, which in turn force the landlord into more ruinous rental and maintenance policies.

The only really effective response the unorganized, low-income tenant can make against the inadequate services and facilities provided by the landlord is non-payment of rent. Such action may be accompanied by moving out, or the tenant may simply choose to wait until the landlord, either legally or illegally, evicts him. In either case, the landlord's costs of operation are increased and his income is decreased. The increased costs may either be direct, in the form of fees to lawyers and/or sheriffs to obtain and enforce the eviction, or indirect, as in the costs resulting while an apartment unit stands vacant. Though long-term vacancy does not seem to be a serious problem for the slum landlord, the fact of frequent moves by his tenants causes a cumulative vacancy rate that can seriously increase his costs. This increase in costs is compounded by the fact that vacancies are usually accompanied by non-payment of rent.

Another cost of renting slum property is that of vandalism. A great deal of vandalism is probably outside the control of either the tenant or the landlord. Nevertheless, the rental and maintenance policies of the landlord are a contributing factor. The tenant may feel that what happens in the empty unit downstairs is of no concern to him, for the landlord is already taking what he, the tenant, feels is an exorbitant amount of money from him and doing nothing in return—why should he care what happens in the rest of the building? If the tenant leaves, he may feel justified in taking some of the furnishings or fixtures, or his anger at being forced to move may express itself in destructive actions against the landlord's property, since actions against the landlord's person are more vigorously prosecuted.

The property owner in the slum housing market may thus find himself in an inexorable cost squeeze. On the one hand, the rent he charges and the number of units he has created have already reached their maximum limits. Yet, on the other hand, the costs of operating that building continue to rise. There are the costs of non-payment, vacancy, and vandalism, as noted above. Those minimal maintenance costs necessary to keep the building habitable, such as the costs of maintenance of the heating and plumbing systems, inevitably rise as the building gets older. The only flexible cost that the landlord can reduce is maintenance beyond that necessary minimum. Hence, the landlord is likely to avoid doing any repairs and rehabilitation. Furthermore, he is kept from doing those repairs by the realization that any investment in significant repairs done to the building is likely to be money that cannot be recovered. Such investment would not improve the value of the building in the resale market, and could not be recovered through increases in the already-maximized rent levels.

Some Implications

The above is a brief and intentionally over-simplified description of the economics lying behind the slum housing market. The popular stereotype of the rapacious landlord, growing immensely wealthy off the outrageous rents paid by slum tenants, exists but he is not universal. Some landlords—those with large holdings in slum areas—do fall into that category. However, others are struggling to survive economically. These people are every bit as trapped by the system as are their tenants; they are caught by the pressure of rising costs and stable or declining incomes and are unable to get rid of their buildings except at a loss too great to sustain. And surely there is a sizable population between these two extremes.

Certain implications for the activities of a tenant union arise out of the foregoing discussion. Briefly mentioned, here are a few of the more important ones:

1. Rent strikes can be effective in slum housing because they apply an immediate economic pressure, but the union should be aware of possible outcomes of this action. The owner may decide to meet the demands of the union, but he may also decide to abandon the property. Either outcome has great potential, but only if the tenant union is equipped to handle it.

2. A rent strike in non-slum housing may not be an effective means of economic pressure on the landlord, especially if the landlord owns many properties or is a corporate property owner. Other tactics, perhaps directed at the reputation of some of the owners, might prove to be more effective.

3. A tenants' union should not assume that every building is capable of being rehabilitated if the rental income was to be reinvested in it. Some buildings are just beyond repair. Rents may cover only mortgage payments and daily maintenance, with nothing left over for improvement.

4. The landlord's costs would not necessarily be the costs of operating the building if the tenant union were to take it over. Tenant participation could very well reduce the costs of vacancy, frequent moves, and vandalism. In addition, repairs might cost the tenants' union less if there existed some form of tenants' participation in the repairs.

---

1. The President's Committee on Urban Housing, *A Decent Home,* U.S. Government Printing Office, Washington, D.C., 1969, p. 121.

2. Charles Abrams, *The City is the Frontier,* Harper and Row, New York, 1965, pp. 22-25.

3. This discussion on tax advantages closely parallels Myron Moskovitz's work for the Urban Housing and Development Project, *Handbook on Housing,* Prentice-Hall, Englewood-Cliffs, New Jersey, 1970, pp. 86-87 of "The Tenant Union Guide."

4. Patricia Leavey Hodge and Philip M. Hauser, *The Federal Income Tax Relation to Housing,* prepared for the National Commission on Urban Problems, Washington, D.C. 1968, p. 16.

5. *Ibid.,* p. 14.

6. *Ibid.,* pp. 119-121.

7. *Ibid.*

8. Cited in G. M. Sternlieb's *The Tenement Landlord,* Rutger's University Press, New Brunswick, 1966, p. 99.

9. Jerome Rothenberg, *Economic Evaluation of Urban Renewal,* Brookings Institute, 1967, pp. 48-49.

10. Sternlieb, *op. cit.,* p. 119.

CHAPTER 5

The Landlord-Tenant Relation
in a Low-Income Area

Ted R. Vaughan*

Given the fundamental importance of housing, a fairly extensive literature has accumulated on the causes, consequences, and correctives of poor quality housing.[1] Yet, despite the range of the literature on the subject, a crucial social consideration—the relationship between landlord and tenant—has been largely ignored.[2] This state of affairs has existed despite the fact that the rental of housing accommodations is still the predominant tenure pattern among low-income people today.[3]

This paper addresses itself to this anomaly. Our specific problem was to investigate the nature and effects of the landlord-tenant relationship in one area in Columbus, Ohio. The absence of previous sociological studies of this relationship necessitated an exploratory approach. Thus, we have not presented herein a set of specific propositions but a theoretical framework which we have illustrated by our case study findings.

The concentration of rental tenure in low-income areas introduces an inherent conflict of interest between landlords and tenants and raises the possibility that the relationship itself may contribute to the inadequate and deteriorated housing conditions of the poor. Current area rehabilitative plans ignore this theoretical possibility in favor of an essentially historical position on the problematic condition. This reasoning focuses upon deteriorating physical structures principally occasioned by changing land use patterns and age. As a neighborhood begins to deteriorate, the area is invaded by lower-income people who, this view argues, encourage further deterioration. Successive invasions of even lower-income tenants eventuate in an area of dilapidated

*A version of this paper was read at the meetings of the Ohio Valley Sociological Society, April, 1966. Ted Vaughan expresses indebtedness to College of Commerce Research Committee, The Ohio State University, for a grant that made the research possible, appreciation to Roger G. Krohn for his theoretical stimulation, to Elias M. Poston for his field work, and to Gideon Sjoberg for his helpful comments on the earlier draft of the paper. This paper first appeared in *Social Problems*, Vol. 16, No. 2 (Fall, 1968) pp. 208-218. *Social Problems* is published by The Society for the Study of Social Problems.

structures populated by people who cannot afford to live any place else. Against this image of slum formation, area reconstruction is a plausible program.

The invasion-succession sequence obviously occurs, but the thesis of this paper argues that this is the surface manifestation of a more basic social process. If we conceive of suburban migration at least in part as an effort to avert the landlord-tenant relationship and if we regard those who remain as powerless to escape the relationship, then we can direct attention to the structure of this basic relationship as a contributor to the origin and maintenance of the problematic situation. Under these circumstances, poor housing is not necessarily an abnormality that can be corrected by altering those features that present themselves as problems. Poor housing may, rather, be the normal, inevitable product of the social organization of the housing market as it is presently constituted.

Theoretical Framework

That housing in American society is a commodity item is an elementary fact. Housing accommodations are not afforded one simply because of human necessity or because one is a member of the society. In order to obtain housing facilities, one must contract with another person who controls such facilities. If the commodity is purchased outright, the buyer-seller contract is terminated with the close of the transaction. If, on the other hand, housing accommodations are rented, a contractual exchange relationship is established. The tenant exchanges rent for the use of the landlord's facilities.

The contractual exchange is not simply an economic one; rather it entails complex social elements that profoundly affect the terms of trade as well as the actions of the participants involved. A contractual relation is characterized by its specificity (the participants are oriented to the acquisition of a single end), its short-term duration (the length of the notice is the length of the contract), and its substitutability (one person with the requisite qualifications is as good as any other). Given these characteristics, the participants use the relationship as a means to achieve their respective goals which often reflect a conflict of interest.

Thus, the nature of the broader societal arrangements in American society establish the conditions under which the landlord-tenant relationship is carried out. The landlord who, for example, conceives of housing exclusively in terms of service does not participate in the housing market as such and cannot utilize this means to acquire the resources necessary to enter other contractual relationships in the broader society. As the rental relation normally operates, each participant is oriented toward a different goal and the other party is a means to that end. Although the simultaneous accomplishment of differential ends is not impossible, when this situation is paired with exchange between unequals the divergent ends are unlikely to be simultaneously attainable.

In the ideal sense, contractual exchange exists between relative equals. Despite the norm of equality associated with market exchange, the party controlling the commodity has a superior position in the interchange that is not easily offset. Even the classic advocate of such exchange—Adam Smith— noted in another context that mutual interdependence has its limitations: "In the long run the workman may be as necessary to his master as his master is to him, but the necessity is not so immediate."[4] Given the nature of the commodity, the rental relation nearly always involves a degree of inequality; the tenant, having an immediate and constant need for housing, is more dependent on the landlord for housing than the landlord is dependent upon him for rent.

This immediate independence in each rental relationship is made even greater because the landlord ordinarily participates in many rental contracts. Whereas each tenant is dependent upon one landlord, the landlord typically diffuses his dependency among many tenants. As a result, the owner can rather easily retain an independent position in each relationship. And collective tenant action is made difficult by, among other things, the spatial dispersion of the units controlled by one owner.

But differential dependence involves much more than the accrual of power that can be used in the event the owner has occasion; it involves the exercise of privilege in the most elemental routines of the relationship. Given his position of power, the landlord—within certain limits at least—sets down the terms of the contract. It is he who decides to whom the unit will be rented, and the conditions the tenant must meet. And he is generally the judge of the extent of compliance. Only rarely does a landlord specifically agree to maintain the unit, and even then the tenant is in no position to enforce compliance. Even if the landlord forgoes enforcement of certain agreements or does improve the premises, it is typically his unilateral decision to do so.

The landlord's power over the tenant is further enhanced by more extensive knowledge of the situation. He can easily determine the tenant's occupation and approximate income, for example. The tenant has more difficulty in determining in advance of his occupancy undesirable or hidden defects in the premises.

Rental housing as a commodity item embodies, by its very nature, differential power and interests. Whenever two positions are so related, there is a structurally induced conflict potential. But just as sustained conflict in the broader society is suppressed, expressions of overt conflict in contractual exchange are minimal. In a situation in which conflict is endemic but its expression is infrequent, we can surmise that conflict is taking some sublimated, covert form of expression. That is, in a conflict setting, patterns of adjustment and strategies are worked out to minimize the conflict. Such efforts are of substantial benefit to the person in a less dependent position in the relationship, and this line of reasoning would argue that strategies minimizing conflict most often emanate from the more powerful participant.

Against the theoretical perspective adumbrated here, we investigated the structure and content of the landlord-tenant relationship.

Procedure

Since we were concerned with observing the landlord-tenant relationship in a variety of situations, we selected a sector of Columbus, Ohio that increased this possibility through the following characteristics: a high percentage of rental units, low median family income, multi-family dwelling units, and a bi-racial population. Although the census tract selected was not the most extreme case in the city on each of these criteria, its combined characteristics madé it fairly representative of the surrounding slum area.

For our purposes and resources, the entire census tract was too large to work with; so we delineated a smaller core area of approximately four by six irregular blocks.

The chosen area had some features of a "neighborhood" in that a small commercial center served as a common meeting place for many area residents.

We chose to study in depth a limited number of rental relationships. A graduate research assistant moved into the area as a participant observer and resided there for one year. While he concentrated his attention upon tenants living in the area and observed their interaction with landlords, he also contacted landlords independently. He also participated in a neighborhood community center, talked with managers, agents, real-estate personnel, and the representative of an owners' association, and obtained supplementary information from official records and other published sources. Legal authorities were also contacted with respect to the legal aspects of housing.

The renters involved in the study are fairly representative of the general characteristics of the census tract with respect to the data from the 1960 census. Inasmuch as the census data combine information on renters and owners, it is understandable that tenants would differ in some respects from the overall census tract figures. Table 1 provides comparative data on the characteristics of the study area, the census tract, and the city.

TABLE 1

CHARACTERISTICS OF TENANTS IN THE STUDY AREA
COMPARED WITH CHARACTERISTICS OF THE
CENSUS TRACT AND CITY (1960)

	Tenants in Study Area	Census Tract	City
Median family income	$3,200	$3,953	$5,982
Percentage of non-white population	49%	46%	16%
Percentage living in rental units	100%	73%	45%
Percentage living in multi-family dwelling units	95%	67%	32%
Percentage unemployed	13%	10%	5%

The conditions found in the study area generally reflect the conditions of low-income people as they exist in other American cities. It should be noted, however, that the area is probably atypical as a slum with respect to the very largest cities in that large tenements do not exist and the concentration of ownership and management is rather limited.

Findings

That rental housing is a beleagured enterprise is attested by the fact that it has experienced a steady decline during the past three decades, although some counter trends are underway. But rental housing continues to exist in the poorest sector of the economy. Although rental tenure is heavily concentrated in the lowest one-third of all American families, owners find rental property in low-income areas a profitable enterprise.

Persons with restricted incomes contribute most to the success of owners, because the landlords can use their power position in the relationship to tie rent levels to income rather than quality of accommodations. The landlord has control over the commodity that the low-income person needs—low cost housing. Housing that he can afford is that purchased cheaply by owners. In other words the rental rate, though less than is elsewhere available, bears little relation to the investment. Several owners stated they had amortized their debts in five to seven years; amortization in as little as three years was also reported. While providing the poor a place to live within their incomes, the owners in this study exacted a comparatively large rental share from the tenants' small incomes. Every tenant in the study paid in excess of 25 percent of their monthly income for rent; most paid between 30 and 33 percent but went as high as 38 percent in one case.

More directly supportive of the argument that rental levels are related to income rather than to the size and quality of housing is the fact that the percentage of income paid for rent remains relatively constant despite variations in the quality of housing accomodations. That is, for comparable housing facilities, tenants with incomes above the median consistently paid higher rental rates than those whose income was below the median. And conversely, tenants with approximately the same incomes paid similar rates despite considerable differences in the number of rooms per unit. In the case of rent, as in many other spheres, "the poor pay more"—considerably more—in comparison with rental rates paid for demonstrably better housing.[5]

The implications of this power imbalance are portentous. Inasmuch as his clientele is restricted in its choice of accommodations, the owner has no economic motive to improve or actively maintain the property, but there are important reasons for not doing so. If he keeps the building in a good state of repair or if he makes improvements, he cannot reasonably expect to charge the present tenants higher rents—they are already paying out one-third of their income for rent—and he is unlikely to attract a higher income clientele. But he will have to pay for upkeep and repairs or alterations.[7] In not doing any of these things, he still retains his low-income clientele. The strategy that enables him to make a profit from low-income people commits the landlord to a policy and practice of further property decline and deterioration. Quite obviously, the owners don't want their property to deteriorate and a recurring sentiment expressed by these landlords was that low-income renters do not know how to take care of property. They do not see that their own actions and inactions contribute directly to these conditions.

The same factors that permit the landlord to affix rent to income levels rather than to housing itself underlie a second feature in the rental relation that has adverse implications for the housing conditions of the poor—a pervasive aura of suspicion and tension. Although each made reference to unpleasant aspects of rental tenure and frequently expressed the desire to disassociate themselves from it, both landlords and tenants routinely disavowed any animosity toward the other party. And to an important extent this seems to be the case, for neither attributes the malaise directly to the self-interest of the other. They do not articulate the problem clearly, but they show an awareness that the issue is not purely personalistic. Uncertain of the nature of the issue, they react ambivalently to it.

As an example of this, take a generalized case that forms part of the experience of the low-income rental relationship. The landlord routinely requires an advance property deposit. Since the prospective lessee frequently has an immediate need for housing and is unable to secure it without a deposit, the deposit is extracted, in a sense, under duress. In addition to the deposit, the tenant typically agrees to forfeit the deposit if the unit is not returned in substantially the same condition as at initial rental, excepting, of course, normal wear. Against this background, and even if the owner is defined as a "good landlord," the tenant suspects that the deposit will not be returned. The outcome of this suspicion is that it frequently becomes a basis for behavior, not in the sense of keeping up the property (Why should he make repairs, he asks, that will accrue to the owner or the next tenant?) but in the sense of avoiding projected exploitation. In consequence, owners can recall tenants who have literally taken the kitchen sink. Anticipating such behavior, owners feel justified not only in demanding but in retaining the deposit. Thus, a circle of suspicion is joined, the projected action of the other guiding the conduct of each.

These owners have few reasons to maintain or improve their property and powerful pressures work against their doing so. Additionally, tenants have limited interests in such repair, and even if they desired to, most could not because of their poor financial condition. The result is that property decline is systematically abetted and this becomes legally institutionalized.[8]

Against this backdrop of his own need for housing, the owner's virtual monopoly of power in the relationship and the legal institutionalization of his own dependency, the tenant has one power leverage—the threat to move. While they carry the threat out with considerable frequency, this maneuver is relatively weak and both they and the owners know it. With their limited resources, they cannot hope to do appreciably better. The mobility is largely restricted to the immediate area. Even were it a renter's market, the tenant would still operate at a structurally induced disadvantage. As it is, the very tool that is supposed to improve the living conditions of the poor—urban renewal—has served, at least in the area of our investigation, to diminish the bargaining power of the poor.

The above findings and discussion suggest some of the principal features of the landlord-tenant relationship as it exists in a low income area, but these findings do not reveal how such matters exist without engendering overt conflict between the particpants. Confronted with the nature of the relationship, we may now pose another basic question: What are the strategies that minimize overt conflict, and what are the implications of these strategies?

Inasmuch as tenants are in the weaker position in the relationship, we might expect strategies that minimize conflict to emanate from owners. However, their strategies as well as the reactions of the tenants vary. The key structural element producing this variation is that of social power. Some owners are not as independent of their tenants as are others.

For purposes of analysis we dichotomized the owners in terms of their place in the rental market. Those owners controlling in excess of 12 rental units were regarded as having a strong position. Owners controlling eight or fewer units were regarded as relatively weak. Although there were many differences among the tenants observed in this study, they had one commonality; they were all relatively powerless. Even those who had incomes matching or exceeding the city median were limited in other respects such as education. We have, then, two general types of landlord-tenant relations: (1) a relationship in which the owner has a powerful market position and can clearly dominate the tenant; and (2) a relationship in which the owner has greater power than the tenant but not to the extent that exploitation or dominance can be freely exercised.

The Landlord Dominated Relationship

When the owner's position in the rental housing market was strong, the nature and content of the relationship was noticeably different from those involving a weak owner. The most noticeable thing is the marked impersonal nature of the relationship. Frequently, there is little if any personal interaction between the contracting parties. Rent is often paid by mail or is paid to a collection agent or manager. Twelve of the seventeen tenants had no regular contact with the landlord. When interaction does occur, it is likely to have a specific purpose. Contact may occur when the owner makes occasional inspections or, as in a few cases, when he personally collects the rent. Amenities are almost always exchanged, but they do not take the form of personal relations. The terms of the relationship are stipulated by the owner, but only occasionally in the form of a lease; only five of the 17 tenants in this type relation had signed legally binding lease arrangements.

Owners usually consider it to their business advantage to maintain the characteristics of the contractual relation in which the relation is a means to the end of business success—profit. As long as the property is rented, the occupant and his personal life are of little relevance or concern to the owner. His is a captive clientele and the emotional costs of personal involvement— and the potential economic costs—are not necessary inducements.

Behind the impersonal appearance of the relation, there is not an accompanying personal indifference. Although tenants constantly aver that they feel no hostility toward the landlord and would do nothing purposefully damaging against the property, they just as consistently complain about the housing situation. They are most likely to complain that the rent is too high for the quality of housing; less frequently they complain that requested repairs aren't made, or mention the slowness with which such repairs are attended. With some consistency, tenants imply a lack of trust in and some fear of exploitation by landlords. These feelings are hardly ever explicitly verbalized, but are suggested by a variety of cautious statements by the tenants. When they are asked directly if they would join other interested people in an organization attempting to get rent lowered or the units improved, they almost uniformly state that they would. Yet, several volunteer workers in the area stated that organizing the people in the area in an action front had proved to be very difficult.

While tenants are suspicious and complaining of the owners, landlords are convinced that tenants don't take care of property. They explain this not so much in terms of malicious destruction or hostility directed toward them, but as the result of the way of life of lower-class people. As an indication of their feelings, landlords in this relationship often express a desire to get out of the low-income rental business: "too many problems," they say. And there seems to be a good deal of property exchange, although it appears to occur mainly as business expansion or contraction rather than withdrawal.

In behavioral terms, this type of relationship is characterized by a considerable degree of mobility. Over one-half of these tenants had moved to the present location within the past two years and over one-third had resided in the present unit for less than one year. Most of the movement had occurred within the same general area of the city.

Other than moving, there seems to be a lack of concern with the housing condition—not necessarily in the neatness or cleanliness sense, but as a matter about which something can be done. This is more than just an attitude of indifference; it is a practice. Except in the case of emergency conditions, these tenants live with a variety of irritating problems. When the light fixture in the bathroom doesn't operate and the toilet doesn't flush properly, these are conditions that call for adjustment, not comment or action.

How are we to account for this resignation on the part of tenants' despite the fact that they feel they are being exploited to some extent? This seeming paradox is partly explained in terms of the tenants' image of the landlord, which is a highly ambivalent one. This ambivalence effectively immobilizes the tenants in that while feeling dissatisfaction with the accommodations they usually bear no antagonism toward the owner and feel that he is likely to be the one to suffer from their efforts at improvement. This may account, in part, for the discrepancy between those who talk an action line yet do not become involved in action organizations. When the discrepancy is pointed out, they respond by suggesting that such an organization probably wouldn't be effective anyway.

Strategies of some owners are not consistent, however, with their positions of power. For example, one owner who has built up his holdings to the point that he now owns over one hundred units continues to relate to a few tenants in a very personal way. He regularly takes one of his elderly renters to her doctor and has done so over a period of years. Thus, a practice developed in one period may very well be carried over to another time. This strategy utilized by some whose market positions are strong constitutes the major pattern for a sizeable proportion of the less independent owners.

The "Pseudo"-Reciprocal Relation

When the power of the owner in the market is more nearly the equivalent of the tenant, the ability to unequivocally dominate the relationship is substantially reduced. Although the owner retains the power advantage through his control of the commodity, inasmuch as he derives his immediate income from the rent of a few tenants, he is more nearly in the position of the tenant with the immediate need for housing. Responding to the smaller differential in power, his strategy differs considerably from the more powerful owner. The distinctive difference that sets this pattern off from the owner dominated relation is the owner's willingness to personalize the relation. In a number of cases these landlords have aided their tenants not only in times of crises but also in terms of acts of friendship. Several cases exist in which the landlords have made interest-free loans to their tenants. Some of the loans are for as much as fifty dollars, although they are typically for much less. In other cases, owners have purchased groceries, paid utilities, permitted late payment of rent, and engaged in an assortment of helpful and friendly acts. Examples of this type are represented in their most completely developed form in cases where health problems exist. In the area under study, there were several cases in which the landlord performed an important health service function.

While these patterns have a personal quality, their effect is to bind the tenant to the landlord in terms of non-economic ties of personal dependence. To be sure, not all landlords adhere to this strategy, nor do all those who effect reciprocity do so with identical intent. Yet, such relations do occur almost exclusively among those whose market position is poor and who consequently have a higher dependence level. Tenants in this relationship fairly uniformly paid as much as 30 percent of their income in rent and the percentage went as high as 38 percent in one case. This compares with approximately 25 percent among those in the conventional contract relation. Furthermore, repairs and upkeep tend to be at the discretion of the owners with the initiative of the tenant counting for little.

Once the reciprocity is initiated, the ties of personal dependence are likely to be increased. The intial favor is acknowledged and conventionally returned. Once inaugurated for whatever reason, a ring of reciprocity is likely to be developed. When health problems are involved, the ring of reciprocity sometimes extends to relatives of the tenant. The total impact is to constantly increase the personal dependence of the tenant upon the landlord and emotionally bind the tenant to the rental relationship.

The personal knowledge of the tenant's affairs also aids the owner in maximizing his advantage. In one case, for example, when the owner learned that a tenant had received an increase in income, he raised the rent. To be sure, owners who utilize this personalization of service strategy do not look on their activities as insincere or exploitative. They are more likely to think of their activities as being motivated by norms of friendliness and neighborly assistance.

This is not to suggest that the element of hostility is removed or even more subtle. Some of the most direct charges of exploitation came from tenants in this type of relationship. Landlords, too, complain that their tenants are not sufficiently appreciative of the services they have performed.

While there are exceptions to the pattern of personalization, they are less numerous than one might expect. In over 60 percent of the cases in which the owner was in a poor market position this pattern was clearly discernible.

Summary and Implications

The commodity nature of rental housing produces a relationship characterized by differential power and interest of the participants in it. When two positions are differentially related, there is a potential for conflict. But overt conflict of a widespread nature has not developed. We find, rather, that various strategies are developed to minimize such conflict. These strategies largely emanate from owners and differ according to the owners' dependency level. If the landlord is not immediately dependent on a given tenant, the relationship tends to be marked by impersonality and consequent disinterest in the housing situation. When owners are less independent of their tenants, personalization of the relationship occasions non-economic reliance by the tenant upon the landlord.

In channeling the effort to prevent or minimize conflict, the conditions that underlie potential conflict are not relieved. The consequence is that the conflict is channeled into more subtle expressions. In some important respects the very efforts to minimize conflict contribute to deterioration since these produce disinterest and sublimation. Instead of the participants acting out their conflicts, they convert them into practices that lead to unpleasant conditions for all concerned.

If additional evidence should support the findings suggested in this exploratory research, questions would have to be raised about current efforts to deal with problems of low-income housing. Programs that are concerned only with the elimination of sub-standard housing will be unsuccessful over the long run. Only the elimination of the sources in the structure of the broader society that produce such conditions can effectively deal with the issue.

---

1. See, as a convenient guide, *Housing and Planning References,* Washington, D.C.: U.S. Department of Housing and Urban Development, issued bi-monthly.

2. Even in works dealing explicitly with the social aspects of housing, the landlord-tenant relation is typically omitted; it is not, for example, treated at all in G. H. Beyer, *Housing and Society,* New York: Macmillan, 1965; nor in such a social survey of housing as that by Beverly Duncan and P. M. Hauser, *Housing a Metropolis—Chicago,* New York: Free Press, 1960. A comprehensive housing reader by W. L. C. Wheaton, Grace Milgram, and M. E. Meyerson, editors, *Urban Housing,* New York: Free Press, 1966, not only does not include articles addressed to the landlord-tenant relationship, but it omits reference to the topic in a discussion of important topics previously omitted in housing studies.

3. For a summary of the income characteristics of owners and renters, see Beyer, *op. cit.,* p. 275. In conjunction with low-income, rental tenure is heavily concentrated among non-whites. Whereas 64.4 percent of all white families owned homes in 1960, 61.1 percent of the non-white families rented. *Statistical Abstract of the United States,* 1964, Washington, D.C.: U.S. Government Printing Office, 1964, p. 759.

4. Adam Smith, *The Wealth of Nations,* New York: Modern Library, 1937, p. 66.

5. For a discussion of the consumer practices of low-income families, see David Caplowitz, *The Poor Pay More,* New York: Free Press, 1963.

6. Other factors in the property situation reinforce this structurally induced trend. Foremost among these is the tax structure in most American communities that systematically penalizes property upkeep while rewarding—through writeoffs—deterioration. Local property taxes, capital gains taxes, and federal income tax depreciation allowances collectively contribute to this state of affairs. For a brief discussion of these features, see Alvin Schorr, *Slums and Social Insecurity,* Washington, D.C.: U.S. Department of Health, Education and Welfare, n. d., pp. 90-93.

7. See Richard Robbins, "Landlord-Tenant Relations and the Impoverished Tenant," in *Course on Law and Poverty,* Columbus, Ohio: Ohio State Legal Services Association, 1966.

CHAPTER 6

The Legal History of
Landlord-Tenant Relations

Thomas M. Quinn
Earl Phillips*

The purpose of this article is to explain the law of Landlord and Tenant emphasizing its application to the leasing of residential space within a multi-
family dwelling: what it is, how it developed and what can be done about it. It
is not a very happy subject, for the law in this area is a scandal. More often
than not unjust in its preference for the cause of the landlord, it can only be
described as outrageous when applied to the poor urban tenant in the multi-
family dwelling. There it views with complacency the most wretched living
conditions, littered and unlit hallways, stairways with steps and banisters
missing, walls and ceilings with holes, exposed wiring, broken windows, leaking pipes, stoves and refrigerators that do not work or work only now and
then. And always the cockroaches, the rats, and the dread of the winter cold
and uncertain heat.

Surely the law in a civilized urban society cannot tolerate such conditions.
But it does! Let that be said frankly and without hedging. Admittedly, there
are building and health codes and there is a law that governs the landlord's
obligations to the tenant; but the bitter fact is that they do not adequately
protect the tenant. Indeed, there is a savage mockery in the little tenant-
oriented law that exists. Pronouncements in the building and health codes
and even the sometimes harsh threat of criminal sanctons contrast painfully
with the hard realities of living conditions. The deteriorating conditions per-

*Reprinted by permission of copyright holder from Fordham Law Review, Volume 38, pp.
225-258. Business Office: Fordham Law Review, Lincoln Center, 140 W. 162nd. St., New York,
N.Y. 10023. ©1969 by Fordham University Press. Abridged by permission of the authors.

The authors, associate professors of Law at Fordham, wish to thank Nancy LeBlanc, Esq.,
Mobilization for Youth, and Mort Cohen, South Brooklyn Legal Services for their valuable
suggestions.

sist, and grow worse. Still the landlord collects rents. That unfortunately is the system. The trouble is not that we fail to apply properly and effectively the law that is in force, but that the present law is grossly inadequate. It is just bad law. One can understand how it developed, but it is incomprehensible that responsible men and women who are normally alert to intolerable social conditions in other societies can be so blind and complacent with respect to their own shameful system. Perhaps they do not really know.

Understanding of landlord-tenant law is best obtained by reflecting on what it is not. It is *not* similar to the law with which most people are familiar. This is contract or sales law. Although it is not difficult to find instances of serious injustice in these fields, by and large, their rules seem reasonably fair. The rights and duties of one party are related to and dependent upon those of the other. The house painter who fails to paint does not get paid, and if he performs poorly he will ultimately get less than the contract price, or perhaps nothing at all. Indeed, the result may be that he pays out considerable sums to remedy the situation he set wrong in the first place. The homeowner, in turn, must also perform, not only by paying but also by cooperating as required, e.g. by selecting the paint, making the premises available, etc. There is an interrelationship and dependence here not only between the rights and duties of the parties, but also in the remedies available to them.

Although the lease can be viewed as a type of service contract with the rights, obligations and remedies of the landlord and tenant related to one another in a manner similar to the contract between the house painter and the householder, such a view is misleading. Indeed, if one assumes as a first principle of basic fairness that whenever two people enter into an agreement one's performance is always interrelated and dependent upon the other's, he will never understand landlord-tenant law. The simple reason is that it is built on a different first premise.

The relationship between the landlord and the tenant can also possibly be viewed as similar to that which exists between a seller and a buyer. This would furnish a familiar analogy, i.e. the marketplace. Thus, it is possible to think of the landlord as leasing an apartment the way one thinks of Hertz or Avis renting a car.

However sensible this approach, it is also incorrect. In the vendor-vendee situation not only are the rights and obligations of the parties related and mutually dependent, but there is also a long tradition of imposing definite quality standards on those who market goods. This tradition, however, is foreign to the marketing of apartments.

If the more familiar legal analogies fail, where are we to go? The only course left is to approach the subject as one approaches a foreign country. One must leave behind one's preconceived notions as to how the law operates, suspend one's sense of basic fairness since this can distort the picture as well, and be prepared to accept this area for what it is, i.e. foreign country, different and sufficient unto itself. Thus, what the stranger to landlord-tenant law finds novel and singularly bewildering, the seasoned practitioner in landlord-tenant law accepts as commonplace.

In order to understand landlord-tenant law one must forget the modern urban complex with its towering office buildings, its sprawl of huge apartments, and its teeming slums. The place to start is with the countryside, i.e. the grass, trees, and grazing sheep. We are back to the land now, and land is really what *land*lord-tenant law is still all about. That may seem curious to the man who gets off the elevator fifteen stories up in the air to go to an apartment where even a dandelion could not grow, but such is the fact. The land is the thing. It is the fields, orchards, pastures, and streams and their possession and use that are important. To comprehend the law it is helpful to envision the tenant leaning on a fence at twilight, watching his fields and awaiting the call to dinner. It is against this simple background that landlord and tenant law took the shape it has essentially retained to this day.

With this background as a starting point, the crudities and eccentricities of landlord-tenant law become at least understandable. Still more important, it focuses our attention on not only where things started to go wrong in this body of law but also on the reason why.

Landlord-Tenant Obligations: Part I

The landlord's primary obligation was to turn over possession [1] of the land to the tenant and to agree to leave him in peaceful possession. [2] The tenant, in turn, was expected to pay the "rent." [3] In technical terms, the tenant "covenanted" to pay the rent while the landlord "covenanted" to keep him in quiet possession.

Significantly, the landlord was not being paid to do anything. He was turning over the land to the tenant with the rent serving as continuous compensation for the transfer. The landlord was *not* expected to assist in the operation of the land. Quite the reverse, he was expected to stay as far away as possible. In other words, for the term of the lease, the lands were subject to the tenant's, not the landlord's care and concern. Should the landlord interfere, he risked violating real property law.

A landlord's or tenant's failure to perform his basic obligation led to the problem of remedies in landlord-tenant law. Once again even a rudimentary knowledge of remedies as they are found in other areas of the law, for example, in the law of sales, can cause great confusion and consternation here. One expects to find in any advanced legal system a certain sophistication where remedies will be measured at least roughly to meet the needs that gave rise to their use. However legitimate the expectation, it does not come to fruition in landlord-tenant law. Remedies, like everything else in this field, are based upon a single notion, i.e. the possession-rent relationship.

Rent was the quid pro quo for possession. If the tenant failed to pay the rent, he would be deprived of possession. The landlord, once he had conveyed the leasehold, was obliged to leave the tenant in quiet possession of the premises. Where the landlord failed in this basic possessory obligation by actually interfering with the tenant's possession, the tenant's one effective remedy was to "interfere" with the rent which stood as the surrogate for possession. [4]

The crudest form of violation of the tenant's right to possession occurred when the landlord entered the land prior to the expiration of the lease and forcefully removed the tenant. As a result of this intrusion, the law abated the rent completely, and even permitted the tenant to sue for his injuries.[5] The point, of course, was that rent stood for possession, and since possession was gone, so was the obligation to pay the rent. Further, if the tenant wanted to recover the actual possession of the premises, that too was possible by an action in ejectment.[6] Once possession was recovered the rent obligation was reinstated. The law's chief concern, therefore, was with correcting in one way or another any imbalances in this basic possession-rent relationship.

This preoccupation with the possession-rent relationship, however, was carried to extremes. Concededly, no theoretical problem arose where the landlord physically evicted the tenant. In this case the abused tenant certainly had no actual possession of the premises. The disequilibrium in the relationship was clear. However, suppose the tenant had not been physically evicted, but rather was subjected to such harassment and vexation that life on the premises became a misery. This situation presented a serious problem with regard to the tenant's remedy. The landlord was certainly not performing. Indeed, let us assume that he was flagrantly interfering with his tenant's "quiet enjoyment" of the premises. Was the tenant free to stop paying the rent since his use and enjoyment had been clearly diminished? The answer was no.

There were two reasons for this strange but entirely consistent result. First, the landlord had not physically interfered with the tenant's actual hold on the premises. He had stopped short of physical eviction. Second, and infinitely more important, was the evident fact that the tenant still retained possession. As a result, although under stress, the fundamental possession-rent relationship remained in balance. The tenant was still holding onto the full leasehold, and thus, the landlord retained his right to the full rent. The rent was the surrogate for possession.

Suppose the tenant abandoned the premises? The possession-rent relationship certainly appeared to be in disequilibrium. Did the landlord still retain his right to the rent? The ancient answer is yes.

The point that emerges and which bears emphasis is that the basic remedies peculiar to landlord-tenant law are possession oriented. The tenant who failed to pay the rent was evicted from possession. In turn, the landlord violated the law when he deprived the tenant of possession.

These measures are still the law. However, it is the contemporary man who experiences the sense of shock and not the ancient farmer. Historically, the land was the thing and its possession the whole story, more than the fabled nine-tenths of the law. It yielded grain from the fields, fruit from the orchard, water from the stream, and heat from the woods. So long as the tenant remained in possession equilibrium was maintained. He had his part of the agreement, and so long as he clung to possession, and quite literally reaped the fruits of possession, he was obliged to render to the landlord the law's substitute for possession, i.e. the rent.

Landlord-Tenant Obligations: Part II

It all made sense back in those days with the landlord off on the hunt or drinking port in the quiet of the evening, and the tenant asking only to be left alone to tend his fences and to shear his sheep. The heart of the system was land and its possession. The model landlord was the one who did the least. The tenant, in turn, was expected to run the farm, to be the omnicompetent man fully prepared to see to his own shelter, heat, and light.

Get away from the simplicities of the rural scene, however, and the old ideas get strangely and radically out of joint. What once made sense now looks more like nonsense.

The scene shifts from the countryside to the city, and the subject is not land but space in a building. In place of the farmer leaning on his fence at twilight there is now a clerk, newspaper under his arm, climbing the stairs to reach his flat on the second floor. The farm acreage gives way to square feet of board floor enclosed by walls and ceiling. Of course, this is to be the pattern of the future which will culminate in buildings so high that an internal transportation system will be necessary.

How did the landlord-tenant law, developed for the farm, function when applied to the apartment in the multi-family dwelling? Well enough, at least on the surface. The basics were still there, important and workable. The landlord's job was still to turn over possession and then to assure the tenant that he would not be disturbed in his tenure. The tenant, in turn, was bound to make his rental payments.

The trouble, of course, was that once you scratched below the surface even the basics began to fall apart. The tenant in the multi-family dwelling was not an independent farmer. He did not share the farmer's interest in being left alone to work the fields. Indeed, there were no fields. The object of the lease was now a building, or more accurately, a part of a building, i.e. the flat. The new type of tenant was anything but self-sufficient and the last thing he wanted was to be left alone. Since he occupied only a part of a building, he was dependent on the rest of it. He relied upon the building's water system, lighting system, and heating system; he was sharing walls, doors, corridors and stairways. Agrarian self-reliance in this context is simply not possible. Indeed, if the hypothetical farmer were somehow transposed to the flat and there attempted to be self-sufficient, he would be physically thwarted at every turn. The law itself would impede and threaten him with the risk of serious liability were he to make the effort.

Just as the real property law served the agrarian tenant, it worked against the tenant in the multi-family unit. True, he had possession of part of the building and the older law assured him of his quiet possession in his assigned area, but the rest of the building was not only owned by someone else, but also was possessed by others whose quiet possession was also protected by the law. Consequently, he could no longer assure warmth in his dwelling, for doing so involved entering areas outside the leasehold and tampering with another man's boiler. His own "quiet possession" in this context assured him the undisputed possession of a cold apartment that he could not heat even if he were prepared to spend the time, the effort, and the money.

Clearly, the ancient landlord-tenant idea of the lease is woefully out of line with the changed physical circumstances. Possession, even possession of apartment space, is no longer the whole story. Possession is only part of the agreement. Indeed, it may not even be the prime component. Just a very short stay in an apartment without heat or light, with broken plumbing and rodent infestation is all that is needed to make this point painfully clear. A roof and a floor are admittedly important, but hardly the only aspect to the renting of an apartment.

Surely the landlord assumed added obligations more consonant with the changed situation. Who else could supply the needed services? He did, of course.

Or did he? On the surface he certainly did. This type of obligation is commonplace even in the form lease; at least some of the standard clauses, e.g. heat and water[7] have been included for a long time. But even these, unfortunately, come accompanied by a variety of waivers and disclaimers. The crucial question, however, is not whether the landlord has a stated obligation to render services, but rather what can be done about his failure to do so. It is here that one of the more bizarre features of landlord-tenant law surfaces.

One would have anticipated a give and take between landlord and tenant in this area. The landlord's failure to supply heat would justify the tenant in withholding rent or reducing it somewhat to cover the costs of his own attempts at interim heating. The prospect of a tenant's being forced to continue paying rent under pain of summary eviction when heat is not supplied seems preposterous to one who expects basic fairness from the law. However, this is exactly how the law of landlord-tenant operates.[8] The reason for this legal monstrosity lies in the inability of the courts to adjust the old law satisfactorily to the new circumstances. There had to be adjustments where the landlord had assumed new obligations beyond the mere assurance of quiet possession. The only question was what adjustments.

What the law did was to preserve the old landlord-tenant law with its fixation on possession as the crux of the lease, and with rent as the quid pro quo for possession. Onto this was engrafted a new set of rights and duties (concerning heat, hot water, and repairs) which were independent of the possession-rent relationship and considered incidental and unimportant relative to possession[9] The result was a double set of relationships between the landlord and the tenant, i.e. a two level relationship.

On level one, the basic level, whether the tenant happened to be a farmer or a dweller in a multi-family unit was quite immaterial. He was first and foremost a tenant, and that meant he was entitled to possession, whether it happened to be land or space in a building. He was assured of quiet possession, and in return was bound to pay the full rent under pain of eviction.

On level two, the newer and less important level legally, he had a right to heat, light and other services from the landlord. Level two constituted a separate agreement. The landlord was expected to perform and if he did not the tenant was free to sue him for redress.

Significantly, the two levels were separate and distinct. A failure to perform on one level generated a remedy on that level, but in no way affected the other level. In technical terms, the covenants on one level were not reciprocal with the covenants on the other.[10] What it actually meant was that the tenant had to pay the full rent so long as he had possession of the premises (level one), even though the landlord failed miserably in the delivery of services (level two).[11] The sophisticated legal structure was a velvet glove which concealed an iron fist.

Theoretically, the tenant was free to go into court to seek redress for the breached service contract,[12] but the route was so cumbersome, time consuming, and costly that it was neither practical nor realistic. Moreover, it meant that even when the tenant went into court, he did so in a cold apartment with small pressure on the dilatory landlord. Stopping the rent was language the landlord was likely to understand, but this was not available.[13] The tenant, who assumed that basic fairness permitted him to operate on a "no heat, no rent" basis, was in trouble. The tenant was here confusing the two levels, attempting to apply level one remedies to level two problems. On level one the tenant was bound to pay the rent so long as he was assured possession. In addition, the landlord was fulfilling his obligation by assuring the tenant quiet possession. By withholding the rent, however, the tenant was violating his part of the level one relationship. He had possession and full rent was due. His refusal to pay the rent, therefore, was without legal justification. He was the wrongdoer.[14] In addition, the landlord had every right to apply his basic level one remedy, i.e. eviction of the tenant from the premises. The result was a legal proceeding where only two questions were asked: (1) Are you in the apartment? (2) Did you pay the rent? Everything else, the heat, the garbage, the plumbing, was technically quite irrelevant. It is unfortunate that this sort of vicious legal in-fighting should be sanctioned by the law.

More startling still was the plight of the tenant who simply abandoned the apartment. The service in the apartment had been defective and he had a right to complain. Indeed, he had a legal right to redress of his grievances. But that right existed on level two. Abandoning the apartment was level one action. He had contracted for possession, possession had been given, it had not been interfered with and thus, he had a rental obligation. If he chose to leave that was his business, but his duty to pay the rent continued for the term of the lease.[15] The fact that there was no heat in the apartment had nothing to do with the possession-rent relationship of level one. After all, covenants were not reciprocal.[16]

Only when living conditions became unbearable did the law intercede. It did so by stretching the old idea of the landlord's physical eviction of the tenant to fit the new situation. This was the doctrine of the "constructive" eviction. Here, the landlord had not actually removed the tenant from the premises, but he had certainly harassed the tenant to such an extent that leaving the premises became the only feasible alternative. The legal question was whether this type of situation should be equated with a physical eviction and treated the same way? The answer was yes.[17]

The revealing point is that the law was unwilling to classify the harassment alone as an act equivalent to an eviction. It was insistent that the tenant actually abandon the premises before the doctrine could be invoked. The doctrine was not so much one of "constructive" eviction as it was one of "constructive" eviction *with abandonment*. The abandonment was the critical element that placed the case into the category of an "eviction." The reason was that the abandonment affected the possession component of the possession-rent relationship, placing it in disequilibrium. Granted, it had been caused by the voluntary act of the tenant, but the landlord was ultimately responsible for the decision to leave. Given this actual abandonment, an analogy exists between the true eviction and "constructive" eviction. In both the result was the same. Possession had been taken from the tenant, in one case by crude force, i.e. the true eviction, in the other by indirect measures, i.e. the "constructive" eviction. Where the harassment was not accompanied by an abandonment of the premises, it was not treated as an eviction. The tenant could not abate the rent, but rather had to pay in full while he remained in possession of the uninhabitable premises.

This appeared very traditional. The law was not talking about the landlord's failure to supply services, but rather of his obligation to assure quiet possession. That was the old idea, and that was what triggered the old remedy, i.e. the tenant's power to abate the rent by leaving the premises. Beneath the traditional exterior, however, a radically new idea was really at work. What the law was doing was taking an obligation that clearly situated itself on level two, i.e. the landlord's service obligation, and shifting it down to level one. On this level, there was a relationship of dependence between it and the rent. Here a failure to supply service, at least a gross failure to supply service, did affect the rental obligation. What the law was accomplishing, therefore, was the fusion of the two levels in the limited situation where the failure to provide services was so severe that it shocked the court's conscience.

Although the effort was praiseworthy, it contained a radical defect. It was a possession-oriented remedy. Harassment of the tenant worked a rental abatement only when the tenant actually abandoned the premises. But if he chose to remain and use the land, the full rent was due. For the tenant in the multi-family dwelling, this meant that the tenant was free to abandon the premises where the failure of service was extreme, but had to pay the full rent so long as he stayed.[18]

The remedy's value became even more ephemeral in the modern context of a housing shortage. Assuming gross abuse of the service obligation by the landlord, abandonment by the tenant may not be a very real option. All too familiar in the urban ghetto is the family in an apartment with peeling plaster, broken windows, random heat, faulty plumbing and appliances, and rats. The family can leave and be rid of the rent obligation, but where are conditions any better, and if the same situation develops there, as it normally does, what are they to do? So they usually stay and the full rent remains due.

If it is not paid they are subject to eviction, defective services and poor living conditions notwithstanding.

This final horror led to still another quite recent attempt to find a remedy within the creaky system. This was the development of the theory of "constructive eviction *without abandonment.*"[19] Here lawyers were attempting not merely to stretch the old law, but to develop a radically new idea under the guise of a recognized and accepted legal doctrine. The starting point was the "constructive eviction *with abandonment.*" Why not continue classifying the gross failure of services as a constructive eviction and permit the tenant to abate the rent without abandoning the premises?[20] As a matter of simple justice, to do so makes eminently good sense. What blocked this most sensible development was the old landlord-tenant law's inability to relinquish the hoary possession-rent correlation. What had made the "constructive" eviction an "eviction" was the fact that the premises were actually abandoned by the tenant. The crux was not so much the failure of services as it was the actual abandonment. The law equated the situation with a crude physical eviction. Moreover, the crucial rental abatement did not depend on the harassment by the landlord, but on the fact that the harassment resulted in the actual abandonment of the premises. Possession had been surrendered and this affected the rent. The old possession-rent relationship, therefore, was in disequilibrium because of the landlord's misconduct. This justified the abatement of the rent.

Where there was no abandonment by the tenant it was hard to see how there could be talk of an "eviction" constructive or otherwise. After all, the tenant was still in possession.[21]

As previously noted, what the "constructive eviction *without abandonment*" doctrine was attempting to do was to permit an abatement of the rent even though the tenant remained fully in possession.[22] This was a radically new idea and had it succeeded it would have linked the rental obligation not just to possession, as was traditional, but to a failure to provide service. In effect, the landlord's covenant to render service would now be reciprocal with the tenant's rental obligation, at least where the failure of service was so gross as to be classifiable as a "constructive" eviction. Beneath the jargon was a direct attack against the two level system.

A number of courts have approved the doctrine,[23] but unfortunately it has not yet been widely accepted.[24] Perhaps it is simply too sophisticated a fiction, however sensible its intentions, to bridge the gap between the two levels upon which landlord-tenant law operates. If it had been fully accepted, landlord-tenant law would have been developed to the point where the tenant's rental obligation was dependent upon the landlord's performance of his service function as well as upon the fulfillment of the covenant of quiet enjoyment.[25]

However, the old law was maintained. The landlord's routine failure to perform his service obligation is, therefore, as a practical matter, without remedy. Gross failures may be remedied in some extreme cases by abandonment of the premises. Short of this the tenant must continue to pay the rent whether he stays or leaves.

With the law of landlord-tenant so radically out of balance in favor of the landlord, the consequence was predictable. In ghetto areas, deteriorating structures, rat infestation, and health and fire hazards are widespread. Surely this could not be tolerated by civilized men and women. It was not, of course. A variety of legislative efforts designed to correct the situation were made. The private law had failed to develop a clear set of really enforceable service obligations between the landlord and his tenant. Legislatures, therefore, imposed on the landlord civic obligations which the landlord would now owe to the community at large. These obligations were imposed on the landlord in the form of building and health codes. [26]

Landlord-Tenant Obligations: Part III

Criminal Sanctions. The usual way to force a citizen to observe higher standards of conduct is by the use of criminal sanctions. [27] With the sanction threatening, presumably the one threatened will do his civic duty. Should he fail, the pain of fines and prison walls stand ready to instruct him in the error of his ways.

Criminal law designed to coerce landlords into the maintenance of decent building and health standards have an ancient tradition. [28] Their value in the context of the modern urban setting, however, is questionable at best. Although there are laws designed to eliminate substandard living conditions, these conditions still prevail. There exists a frightful gap between the high promises of the building and health codes on the one hand, and the hard reality of dreadful living conditions on the other.

Enacting laws is one thing; translating them into action is another and quite different thing. The criminal law on its most superficial level is merely words on paper. The reality of enforcement is that the interdicted activity must be identified, and a case must be assembled, prepared, and presented to the trier of fact. Manageable things, such as physical conditions and actions, along with not so manageable things like subjective intentions and a criminal state of mind must be proven. It takes time and effort; a lot of people and money are needed. There are only so many policemen, public prosecutors, and judges. Consequently, there has to be a screening process. It is only the extreme violation that has any chance of being remedied in the major city setting, where large numbers of old buildings are deteriorating rapidly. The present costs of municipal government are extremely high, taxable revenues always insufficient, and the demands on the criminal enforcement system intense. Even when the case does move through the system to court action, there is still the human element, a variable that is difficult to define, but no less real. For example, there is the problem of the imposition of a penalty at the conclusion of a successful trial. Shall the court impose a fine or send the landlord to prison, and how much of a fine, or how many days in jail are there to be? These are hard questions to answer, but ones that will have a profound affect on whether tenants sue landlords. Sending landlords to prison is not very popular. Even in New York, a major housing area with countless structures in fearsome disrepair and more than its share of professional slumlords, a prison sentence in a housing case is rare indeed.[29] The fine is the usual remedy, and if the experience in New York is any indication of its effectiveness, it is simply not significant. The average fine per case in New York City has been variously estimated as $14[30] and $16.[31] What does it all amount to when the law has run its course and the fine imposed? Very little indeed, and honesty compels a frank admission of that fact.

For the knowledgeable landlord, the whole process is simply a matter of risks and basic economics. How likely is it that the law will penalize him and how long will it take the law to get around to doing so, if it does so at all? If the landlord is threatened with suit what are the options available to him to smooth things out along the way, e.g. a start at some repairs? If the matter actually terminates in conviction and a fine, how does the cost of the fine compare with the cost of maintaining the building properly or even rectifying the complained of conditions?[32] At the base of the process lie these economic questions. Actually, it is far cheaper to pay the fine than to make the repairs, much less maintain the building in a habitable condition. What about the opprobrium of a conviction? That carries about the same sting as a traffic ticket.

Although this recital is discouraging, it is not the entire story, since all that has been considered is the handling of the housing offense after it has come to the attention of the criminal enforcement system. That is the tail end of a process, not the beginning. Before the case gets there it must work its way through several different bureaucracies. With the housing and health codes come departments of buildings, health, gas, water and electricity, sanitation and fire, etc. This generates yet another and a different set of problems. The first is the problem of jurisdiction. What department is charged with remedying the particular complaint? Since serious complaints come in clusters, what departments are to be contacted, and how do they relate to one another? In the modern city the answer to a jurisdictional question requires a knowledgeable housing expert. The inexperienced may wander for days, weeks or months just looking for the right place to go.[33]

After finding the right department, the second problem is the awesome one of getting the department's machinery into operation to serve the complaining tenant. Here again the tenant is faced with a self-contained bureaucratic system. It is burdened with waiting lists, heavy daily work loads, too few inspectors, too few substitutes, intense paperwork levels, and on top of all that, other equally important work to do, e.g. fighting fire, repairing water mains, etc. Once again complaints must be screened in order to handle the graver violation. Policies of adjustment are adopted in the hope of reducing costs and caseloads. Moreover, before the case is even suggested for prosecution, decisions on higher levels must be made. This leads to further delays.

The process is slow, to say the least. When and if all the wheels get moving up and down the bureaucratic line and into the court process, a small fine is the result. Obviously, something more effective is needed.

What is needed is a remedy that is closer at hand and more immediately available to the tenant. Since abating the rent seemed to be the most effective sanction, laws were passed which sought to control the landlord's abuse of his service obligation by altering in some way the tenant's rental obligation. Here was a weapon available to the tenant himself designed to force the landlord to maintain decent housing conditions.

Rent Impairing Remedies[34]. The idea behind this new direction was familiar enough. Simply stated, it was that the tenant's rental obligation was to be reciprocal with the landlord's service obligation. This same idea, it will be recalled, was latent in the "constructive eviction *with abandonment*" doctrine and emerged full blown in the constructive eviction *without abandonment*" doctrine. [35]

With new laws enacted, the tenant was now free to stay in possession of the premises. He gained the power, if not to abate fully the rent, at least to prevent or delay its payment to the landlord. [36] It was anticipated that this economic pressure would cause the landlord to perform his service obligation.

These laws took a variety of forms. Some permitted the tenant to channel the rent to those institutions, e.g. the courts. [37] Others provided the tenant with a defense should he stop paying rent and then find himself faced with summary eviction proceedings.[38] Despite their good intentions these laws were all subject to the same critical weakness. This was the simple fact that a tenancy only lasts a limited period of time. When the tenancy expires, the tenant must leave or the law will eject him. Should the landlord permit him to remain beyond the lease, his tenancy continues, but for brief periods, e.g. month to month. He is now a tenant at the pleasure of the landlord and can be evicted without reason after notice of termination of the periodic tenancy. The court called to evict the tenant is concerned with only one question: did the lease expire? [39] If it did, the tenant is removed.

Consequently, the tenant's bargaining power vis-a-vis the landlord wanes as the termination of the lease approaches. At this point, even the legitimate complaint of the luxury apartment tenant is made obliquely and courteously. Once the lease has ended the tenant is subject to the landlord's plenary and arbitrary power for the landlord alone decides whether the tenant may renew the lease. Obviously, the holdover tenant is in the poorest possible position to complain or threaten to withhold the rent.

Unfortunately, the urban ghetto tenant is usually a tenant by sufferance. As a result, the landlord has the power to evict him. The tenant is well advised, therefore, not to complain. Nagging complaints about the service, a call to the department of buildings, a discussion of common complaints with other tenants, invite the landlord's wrath. This is the retaliatory eviction. Quite simply, it turns out the "troublemaker," however legitimate his grievance and desperate his state. Further, the landlord does not have to give a reason for the eviction. The risk of retaliatory eviction must be reduced before a tenant can consider altering his rent payments to force the landlord to improve basic services. Direct attacks on the retaliatory eviction have been made in an effort to erase this inequity in the law. However, this effort has not been notably successful.[40]

The problem, of course, is that the tenant needs a measure of permanence if he is to carry the fight to the landlord, and that is precisely what the hold-over tenant does not have. One exception to this exists in the rent control situation. One of the hidden and seldom acknowledged advantages of rent control is its permanency of tenure feature. Once in possession, the tenant stayed there. The landlord's power to evict on the ground that the lease had run out is sharply circumscribed; indeed it is virtually nonexistent.[41] In this context a retaliatory eviction is no longer possible. Free of this threat, the tenant's position vis-a-vis the landlord is strengthened. It now becomes possible to talk intelligently of rent impairing remedies available to the tenant himself.

Section 755 of New York's Real Property Actions and Proceedings, for example,[42] is designed to give the individual tenant the power to withhold rent when the landlord fails to perform his service obligation. The law requires, however, that a serious violation against the landlord be recorded by a government bureau before the process commences. When this occurs, the tenant may stop paying the rent. Should the landlord later seek to evict the tenant for nonpayment, the tenant can deposit the rent in court and continue to deposit it until the repairs are made. At that time, the accumulated rent is turned over to the landlord.

The most striking feature of this new law is its similarity to the basic ideas present in the older landlord-tenant law. First, the statute is not designed to compel the landlord to maintain his full service obligation, nor even to comply totally with the housing and health code. Quite the contrary. Only the gross failure to maintain minimum standards is singled out for treatment. This, it will be recalled, is the type of failure that was characterized as "constructive" eviction, and described as a situation where conditions were so unbearable that the tenant was justified in abandoning the premises.[43]

The second significant point is that it is not merely a gross failure to provide service which triggers the statute, but one that has been recorded as such by the municipal authorities. This brings into play the whole bureaucratic process outlined above in connection with the use of criminal sanctions. The tenant must initially enlist the aid of the municipal department concerned, and then support the complaint until a recorded violation characterized as serious, i.e. sufficient to warrant a recommendation of prosecution, is made.

A further cruel twist peculiar to the New York law is that the serious recorded violation must also be serious enough *in the estimation of the court* to constitute a constructive eviction and to warrant section 755 treatment. Judges vary, and the tenant's lawyer in New York is never quite certain how things will go in court, recorded serious violation notwithstanding.[44] All too frequently the court sweeps it aside, finds for the landlord, and grants a warrant of eviction.[45] When this occurs, the now evicted tenant has only the consolation of knowing that the landlord is seriously at fault, but not seriously enough. The tenant will not even learn what constitutes an actual violation because normally the court gives no reason for its decision. Unfortunately, second guessing the judge is simply part of the process.

Should the tenant's lawyer be successful and convince the court that the recorded violation is indeed serious enough to warrant section 755 treatment, then the rent is paid into the court and stays there until repairs are made. As noted previously, when repairs are made, the accumulated rents are returned to the landlord, less such amounts as the court may direct to be used to pay for repairs, fuel, electricity and the like. This, too, is a very old idea which fails to shock only because it is so familiar. What the law is stressing is the ancient idea that the landlord has a right to the full rent so long as the tenant is actually in possession. The full rent is the quid pro quo for possession, and so long as possession is retained by the tenant, the full rent is due and payable.

What startles the reasonably neutral observer is the treatment of the tenant. The landlord has seriously failed to fulfill his obligation. This has resulted in premises so seriously below standards as to warrant intervention by municipal authorities and perhaps, criminal prosecution. The conditions have persisted for a long time, certainly through the long delays incident to departmental inspection, formal recordation, eviction proceedings, and final court action. In the meantime, the tenant remains in the miserable apartment, which admittedly is a hazard to life and health. Yet, when the landlord finally decides to repair, he regains a right to all the accumulated rent. What of the real losses the tenant has suffered in the interim? Human misery aside, the apartment itself failed to be minimally tenantable for significant periods of time. However, the full rent, even for those periods, still accrued to the landlord. This result can only be characterizied as preposterous.

It is as if a leased car turned out to be defective in its heating, lighting, gas and electrical systems. It is a misery to the driver, a hazard to the rest of us, and cause for the criminal prosecution of the lessor. Yet, the entire rental payment would remain due. At best, rental payments could be paid over into court and returned in full to the leasing company if and when repairs were ultimately made. A statute built on these lines is simply shocking in its callous disregard for basic justice. The reason is historic. The rent is the ancient price for possession and the tenant had possession. Thus, the newer law repeats the inherited formula of the older landlord-tenant law. However that formula is incorrect. When the rent is paid a good deal more is expected than mere possession. Everyone knows that. That courts should repeat and laws incorporate the old bromide is a monument to either ignorance, complacency or callousness.

Rental abatement for the landlord's failure to supply services, as distinguished from merely withholding and subsequently depositing the rent into court, is also available in New York, through section 302A of the Multiple Dwelling Law.[46] A study of this law is instructive. Again, a serious recorded violation is required to get the law into operation. Six months after the landlord has been notified of the recordation, the section 302A abatement takes effect.[47] What this means is that six months after notification the tenant can stop paying rent and, when a nonpayment proceeding is commenced, deposit the accumulated rent into court,[48] and seek a section 302A abatement. If he succeeds in obtaining the abatement he can retain the rent and need pay no further rent until repairs are made.[49]

The startling thing is that we have reached such a point in the radical inequality between landlord and tenant that this example of New York law presents itself as remedial legislation. Observe that we are talking about a gross abuse of service by the landlord which constitutes a serious violation of the housing or health code. The tenant must suffer this violation for a full six months before the law accords him the abatement remedy. He is held to the full rent during that period. In addition, the landlord can defeat section 302A by singling out the critical violation, repairing it, and leaving everything else in the same condition. If the tenant loses in his action, he loses not only the case but also can be ordered to pay $100 in court costs.[50] plus the rent! This results notwithstanding the fact that the apartment is definitely substandard and the landlord is in default on many points.

The remedies geared to governmental intervention to reduce the rent have been more successful. Thus, under New York's Spiegel Law,[51] the Department of Welfare can cut off rental payments where the tenant is on welfare and there are serious recorded violations, i.e. the apartment is "dangerous, hazardous or detrimental to life or health."[52] Infinitely more sophisticated, although rarely recognized for its radical theoretical importance, is the power of the New York Rent and Rehabilitation Administration to decrease the permissible rent in a rent controlled dwelling by way of adjustment for the decline in services.[53] This remedy, although dependent on rent control, is extremely enlightened.

First, the rent control law is not only geared to remedying the landlord's flagrant failure to supply services. In theory, at least, it provides a possible remedy for any substantial failure of services. Second, it takes as a first principal that the rent is made up of something more than merely the transfer of possession. Rent is conceived rather as a package sum which contains compensation for both possession and the basic services that give possession its real value. Third, the law operates on the premise that the covenant to pay the rent is indeed reciprocal with the landlord's obligation to render service. Theoretically, as one varies so should the other.

All of these ideas are as novel as they are fair. The unfortunate fact is that the ideas required the context of rent control to attain articulation in the law. This confines them to a single city in the nation. The wonder is that such insights have not found more universal application in one form or another elsewhere.

A different approach to the problem is found in Article 7-A of the Real Property Actions and Proceedings Law.[54] This is New York's Rent Strike Law and is similar to a number of other state's in its provision for rent withholding. It is an affirmative remedy accorded to one third of the residents of multi-family dwellings.[55] The statute permits them to go to court, deposit the rent, and get an administrator appointed to run the building and to make the repairs.[56]

This brief summary of Article 7-A underplays the awesome complexity involved in organizing the tenants, presenting the case, and administering the building.   The process discourages all but the hardiest ghetto lawyer, and more often than not, even he will refuse to go the 7-A route.

Yet, in New York, the 7-A proceeding is among the first things the ghetto lawyer considers after he has noted the obvious ones of simply relocating the family, getting a rent reduction from the rent control board or stopping the rent via the Spiegel Law for the welfare client.

The tragedy is that these are all the remedies available to the tenant. Landlord-tenant law, not only in New York but also across the nation, as it regulates the private obligations between the landlord and the tenant comes to very little. At best, the law justifies the tenant in moving out in horrendous situations without fear of being later charged with a demand for further rent. However, it offers very few practical ways for the tenant to hold the landlord to minimum standards of housing decency. Yet, all admit that the tenant is utterly dependent on the landlord's affirmative activity in the multi-family dwelling unit. The housing and health codes provide high hopes and promises, but little else. It is comforting to know that the landlord can be threatened by the law, but the law is exceedingly cumbersome and carries in this area a painless sting. Rent impairing remedies are noted, but even in a jurisdiction like New York where rent control blocks the retaliatory eviction and assures the tenant a measure of permanence, they are insignificant.

The urban ghetto tenant is the leper in our midst. Even the law purporting to remedy his more desperate needs, only mocks him with a promise that it consistently fails to deliver. There he sits, and even the sophisticated urban lawyer is largely powerless to help him. Small wonder that rumblings of violence are heard in the ghettos of the nation and that our best young minds raise angry questions we are hard put to answer honestly.

---

1. In technical terms the landlord conveys a leasehold estate which gives the tenant the legal right to possession. This has had interesting consequences in some jurisdictions where it has been held that the landlord has fully performed his obligation if the lease gives the tenant the legal right to possession at the beginning of the term. No obligation, however, is imposed on the landlord to see that the tenant actually gets into possession, e.g. by evicting a holdover tenant. Gardner v. Keteltas, 3 Hill 330 (N.Y. Sup. Ct. 1842); Hannan v. Dusch, 154 Va. 356, 153 S.E. 824 (1930). In other jurisdictions there is an implied convenant by the landlord that the premises shall be open when the time for possession arrives. Canaday v. Krueger, 156 Neb. 287, 56 N.W.2d 123 (1952) (Tenant prevented from taking possession by landlord's failure to complete construction of building on premises); Adrian v. Rabinowitz, 116 N.J.L. 586, 186 A. 29 (Sup. Ct. 1936); Barfield v. Damon, 56 N.M. 515, 245 P.2d 1032 (1952) (Tenant prevented from taking possession by a holdover). The cases are collected in Annot., 70 A.L.R. 151 (1931). . . .

2. This does not mean that the landlord has an affirmative duty to maintain and protect the tenant's use and possession. Quite the contrary. His duty is negative, i.e. to refrain from disturbing the tenant's possession and use. Therefore, a landlord cannot be held responsible for an unauthorized interference with the tenant's use by a third person who does not have a title paramount to that of the landlord. Katz v. Duffy, 261 Mass. 149, 158 N.E. 264 (1927).

3. Technically, rent was the consideration furnished by the tenant for the leasehold estate, i.e. for the tenant's legal right to possession and use undisturbed by the landlord. Automobile Supply Co. v. Scene-In-Action Corp., 340 Ill. 196, 172 N.E. 35 (1930). See Coogan v. Parker, 2 S.C. 255 (1870).

4. Inherent in the conveyance of a possessory estate for a term was the duty of the landlord to leave the tenant in possession for the term of the lease without interference. It was in return for this estate and the continuing right to quietly possess the land that the tenant covenanted to pay the rent. This inherent duty of the landlord was imposed by the law through the device of an implied covenant. Thus, every lease contained by implication, if not expressly, the landlord's covenant not to oust the tenant from possession of the demised premises or any part thereof during the term of the lease. Thurman v. Trim, 199 Kan. 679, 433 P.2d 367 (1967); L-M-S Inc. v. Blackwell, 149 Tex. 348, 233 S.W.2d 286 (1950). The cases are collected in Annots., 62 A.L.R. 1257, 1258-66 (1929), and 41 A.L.R.2d 1414, 1420-23 (1955).

5. Although covenants in a lease were viewed as independent, the obligation to pay rent was in fact dependent upon the landlord's observance of his duty not to interfere with the tenant's possession. True, the breach of the landlord's covenant of quiet enjoyment did not, as such, release the tenant from his covenant to pay rent because property law held that covenants in a lease were independent. However, when the tenant was deprived of possession, there was truly a failure of consideration for the rent. Royce v. Guggenheim, 106 Mass. 201 (1870); Fifth Ave. Bldg. Co. v. Kernochan, 221 N.Y. 370, 117 N.E. 579 (1917).

6. By the year 1500, the English courts recognized that a lessee could recover not only damages but also the land itself in an action in ejectment. 3 W. Holdsworth, History of English Law 216 (3d ed. 1927).

7. For example, The Real Estate Board of New York, Inc., Standard Form of Apartment Lease, clause 13 provides: "As long as Tenant is not in default under any of the provisions of this lease Landlord covenants to furnish, insofar as the existing facilities provide, the following services: (a) Elevator service; (b) Hot and cold water in reasonable quantities at all times; (c) Heat at reasonable hours during the cold seasons of the year."

8. Automobile Supply Co. v. Scene-In-Action Corp., 340 Ill. 196, 172 N.E. 35 (1930); Barone Bldg., Inc. v. Mahoney, 16 La. App. 84, 132 So. 795 (1931). Also, the landlord's breach of his statutory obligation to make repairs, etc., does not permit the tenant to withhold rent.

9. Frazier v. Riley, 215 Ala. 517, 111 So. 10 (1926).

10. Stewart v. Childs Co., 86 N.J.L. 648, 92 A. 392 (Ct. Err. & App. 1914).

11. See Reaume v. Wayne Circuit Judge, 299 Mich. 305, 300 N.W. 97 (1941); Peters v. Kelly, 98 N.J. Super. 441, 237 A.2d 635 (App. Div. 1968) (per curiam); Edgerton v. Page, 20 N.Y. 281 (1859); Waldorf Sys., Inc. v. Dawson, 49 R.I. 57, 139 A. 789 (1928).

12. Thomson-Houston Elec. Co. v. Durant Land Improvement Co., 144 N.Y. 34, 39 N.E. 7 (1894).

13. Wurz v. Watts, 73 Misc. 262, 132 N.Y.S. 685 (Oneida County Ct. 1911). See cases cited note 13 supra.

14. See Reaume v. Wayne Circuit Judge, 299 Mich. 305, 300 N.W. 97 (1941).

15. Stewart v. Childs Co., 86 N.J.L. 648, 92 A. 392 (Ct. Err. & App. 1914).

16. Stone v. Sullivan, 300 Mass. 450, 15 N.E.2d 476 (1938). As previously noted, the lease was considered as fundamentally a conveyance to the tenant of a right to possession for a term. Once the conveyance was made, and the tenant had acquired a legal right to possession for an agreed period, the main thing had been accomplished. Except for the covenant of quiet enjoyment, therefore, the covenants in a lease were viewed as incidental and relatively unimportant when compared with the conveyance to the tenant of his estate, i.e., his right to possession. 1 American Law of Property § 3.11 (A. J. Casner ed. 1952). Consequently, a subsequent breach by either party of the promises incidentally inserted in the lease was considered immaterial and, therefore,

gave the aggrieved party no right to rescind the conveyance or terminate the estate conveyed. Moreover, it did not excuse the injured party from the performance of his covenants. E.g., Ravkind v. Jones Apothecary, Inc., 439 S.W.2d 470 (Tex. Civ. App. 1969).

17. Dyett v. Pendleton, 8 Cow. 727 (N.Y. Ct. Err. 1926). The text refers, of course, to the now traditional "constructive eviction with abandonment" doctrine in its modern urban context. For a discussion of this doctrine see 1 American Law of Property § 3.51 (A.J. Casner ed. 1952).

18. Herstein Co. v. Columbia Picture Corp., 4 N.Y.2d 117, 149 N.E.2d 328, 172 N.Y.S.2d 808 (1958).

19. See generally Schoshinski, Remedies of the Indigent Tenant: Proposal for Change, 54 Geo. L.J. 519, 529-31 (1966).

20. It is also possible to view a failure of services as a constructive partial eviction. Therefore, although the tenant remains in possession of the "incomplete" premises, he may refuse to pay rent without fear of eviction until the landlord's wrong is corrected. Boreel v. Lawton, 90 N.Y. 293 (1882); Barash v. Pennsylvania Terminal Real Estate Corp., 31 App. Div. 2d 342, 298 N.Y.S.2d 153 (1st Dep't 1969).

21. Edgerton v. Page, 20 N.Y. 281 (1859).

22. The suspension of the tenant's obligation to pay rent even while he is in possession would not be unjust were the landlord permitted to recover the reasonable value of the use of the premises in their defective condition. This was done in Pines v. Perssion, 14 Wis. 2d 590, 111 N.W.2d 409 (1961), a case of breach of warranty of habitability.

23. See Barash v. Pennsylvania Terminal Real Estate Corp., 31 App. Div. 2d 342, 298 N.Y.S.2d 153 (1st Dep't 1969); Robb v. Cinema Francais, Inc., 194 Misc. 987, 88 N.Y.S.2d 380 (Sup. Ct. 1949).

24. See Gombo v. Martise, 44 Misc. 2d 239, 253 N.Y.S.2d 459 (App. T.) (per curiam), rev'g 41 Misc. 2d 475, 246 N.Y.S.2d 750 (Civ. Ct. 1964).

25. As with other fictions which permit the development of the law without a radical dislocation of traditional modes of thought, the cumbersome "constructive eviction without abandonment" device could have been later dropped and, in the interest of clarity and realism, its underlying purpose frankly acknowledged, i.e. that covenants in a lease are actually reciprocal. Indeed, the way would have been open to carry the realism a step further by expressly noting that the two level relationship that previously structured landlord-tenant relationships in the law wa no longer so evident a fact.

26. Housing codes designed to protect tenants, as opposed to regulations intended to protect the public from fire and building collapse, were first enacted at the beginning of this century. Gribetz & Grad, Housing Code Enforcement: Sanctions and Remedies, 66 Colum. L. Rev. 1254, 1259 (1966).

27. See generally Comment, Rent Withholding and the Improvement of Substandard Housing, 53 Calif. L. Rev. 304, 314-23 (1965).

28. Gribetz & Grad, supra note 26, at 1262-63.

29. In New York City in 1963 only 36 out of 14,786 landlords convicted of housing code violations were imprisoned. Id. at 1277 n.102. The District of Columbia's record is even better. Through 1965 no landlord had ever been sent to jail for a housing code violation. P. Wald, Law and Poverty 1965 15 (1965).

30. Gribetz and Grad, supra note 26, at 1276.

31. P. Wald, supra note 29, at 15.

32. In once case a fine of $50 was imposed for violations of the Multiple Dwelling Law and New York City's Administrative Code. The correction of the violation would have cost $42,500. Even so, the court of appeals might have reversed the conviction because the landlord did not have the money to correct the violations and could not procure a loan. People v. Rowen, 9 N.Y.2d

732, 174 N.E.2d 331, 214 N.Y.S.2d 347 (1961), rev'g 11 App. Div. 2d 670, 204 N.Y.S.2d 74 (1st Dep't 1960).

33. A housing complaint's guide for New York City clearly demonstrates the maze through which a citizen must wander when looking for help. In 1964, no water in an entire building was a matter for the New York City Department of Health; no cold water in one apartment, no hot water in one apartment and insufficient water were matters for the Department of Buildings. Leaking pipes, sinks, and radiators were also for the Department of Buildings. If the leak was a large one, however, wasting a lot of water, the Department of Water Supply, Gas and Electricity had jurisdiction. Leaking toilets were under the jurisdiction of both the Buildings Department and the Health Department. An overflow of water from the apartment above was a Police Department matter. WMCA: Call For Action, Housing Complaints Guide: The Book you SHOULDN'T Need 3 (1964).

34. See generally Comment, supra note 27, at 323-31.

35. "Constructive eviction with abandonment" is much closer to actual eviction since both are characterized by the tenant's absence from the premises. The difference lies in what leads to the absence. In the case of actual eviction the landlord physically dispossesses the tenant. The "constructive" eviction involves something short of this, e.g. harassment, and now the landlord's gross failure to service the apartment which renders the apartment untenantable. E.g., Rome v. Johnson, 274 Mass. 444, 174 N.E. 716 (1931) (failure to supply heat in breach of covenant to do so).

36. Malek v. Perdina, 58 Misc. 2d 960, 297 N.Y.S.2d 14 (Civ. Ct. 1969).

37. Such as, N.Y. Real Prop. Actions Law § 755(2) (1963).

38. Such as, N.Y. Mult. Dwell. Law § 302-a(3)(c) (Supp. 1969).

39. The landlord's reasons for wanting the holdover tenant removed are immaterial. DeWolfe v. Roberts, 229 Mass. 410, 118 N.E. 885 (1918); Wormood v. Alton Bay Camp Meeting Ass'n, 87 N.H. 136, 175 A. 233 (1934).

40. There are a few statutes expressly prohibiting retaliatory evictions. E.g., Ill. Rev. Stat. ch. 80, § 71 (Smith-Hurd 1967); Mich. Comp. Laws § 600.5646(4) (Supp. 1969). A regulation of the Department of Housing and Urban Development dated February 7, 1967, requires that a tenant in a federally assisted, public housing project who is given notice to vacate must be told the reasons for the eviction. Thorpe v. Housing Authority, 393 U.S. 268 (1969). The regulation goes a long way toward prohibiting retaliatory eviction, especially when a housing authority concedes, as it did in the Thorpe case, id. at 282-83, that it may not evict a tenant for engaging in constitutionally protected activity.

Moreover, the courts seem to be tending toward the prohibition of retaliatory eviction. See Edwards v. Habib, 397 F.2d 687 (D.C. Cir. 1968), cert. denied, 393 U.S. 1016 (1969).

41. N.Y. Unconsol. Laws § 8585(1) (1961); New York City, N.Y., Admin. Code § Y51-6.0 (1963).

42. N.Y. Real Prop. Actions Law § 755 (Supp. 1969). Similar statutes are Mass. Ann. Laws ch. 239, § 8A (1968); Pa. Stat. Ann. tit. 35, § 1700-01 (Supp. 1969).

43. In New York, effective September 1, 1969, the violation need not amount to a constructive eviction. It will be sufficient if the condition "is, or is likely to become, dangerous to life, health or safety." L. 1969, ch. 820 § 1. What that adds to the law is not clear.

44. N. LeBlanc, A Handbook of Landlord-Tenant Procedures and Law, With Forms 13 (2d ed. 1969).

45. Comment, supra note 27, at 324 H.96. But see Malek v. Perdina, 58 Misc. 2d 960, 297 N.Y.S.2d 14 (Civ. Ct. 1969).

46. N.Y. Mult. Dwell. Law § 302-a (Supp. 1969).

47. Id. at § 302-a(3)(a). See Ten West 28th St. Realty Corp. v. Moerdler, 52 Misc. 2d 109, 275 N.Y.S.2d 144 (Sup. Ct. 1966).

48. N.Y. Mult. Dwell. Law § 302-a(3)(c) (Supp. 1969).

49. Id.

50. The tenant can be required to pay costs of up to $100 only when he raises the defense frivolously, i.e., when he claims a rent impairing violation of at least six months duration when there is not one; when the tenant caused the violation and when he refused the landlord entry to his premises to repair the violation. If the tenant loses because, though there is a rent impairing violation on record, the landlord has repaired it, the tenant cannot be made to pay costs of $100. N.Y. Mult. Dwell. Law § 302-a(3)(e) (Supp. 1969).

51. N.Y. Soc. Services Law § 143-b (1966). A similar statute is Ill. Ann. Stat. ch. 23, § 11-23 (Smith-Hurd Supp. 1969).

52. N.Y. Soc. Services Law § 143-b(2) (1966).

53. New York City, N.Y., Admin. Code Y51-5.0(h) (Supp. 1969); 1 City of New York, Rules and Regulations of New York City Agencies § 34.2 (1967). As the rent control law in New York is now greatly weakened, these positive effects may be further weakened—eds. note.

54. N.Y. Real Prop. Actions Law §§ 769-782 (Supp. 1969). Massachusetts has a similar law, Mass. Ann. Laws ch. 111, § 127F (1967). Other statutes permit tenants to cause repairs to be made and to deduct the cost from the rent: Cal. Civ. Code §§ 1941-42 (West 1954); La. Civ. Code Ann. arts. 2692-94 (West 1952); Mont. Rev. Codes Ann. §§ 42-201 to 02 (1947); N.D. Cent. Code Ann. §§ 47-16-12 to 13 (1960); Okla. Stat. Ann. tit. 41, §§ 31-32 (1954); S.D. Comp. Laws Ann. § 43-32-9 (1967).

55. N.Y. Real Prop. Actions Law § 770 (Supp. 1969).

56. Id. at §§ 776(b), 778(1).

CHAPTER 7

Tenant Unions and Their Legal Status

Richard Cotton*

More than 15 million people throughout the country live in substandard or
deteriorating rental housing units.[1] Many municipal housing codes or state
tenement-house laws declare such housing conditions unlawful.[2] But if the
landlord chooses to ignore complaints, the tenant usually has no quick, effective remedy to compel even emergency repairs.[3] He can protest to the building department or initiate a costly, drawn-out court proceeding.[4] Or the tenant can move—provided, of course, he can find another flat to rent.

In several Chicago apartment buildings, however, tenants now have an alternative: grievance machinery under a collective bargaining agreement between landlord and tenant union.[5] Recently, for example, a Chicago slum
tenant discovered that several floorboards on his back porch had rotted
through.[6] The tenant reported the condition to the union grievance committee. Upon investigation the committee decided that the whole porch was
about ready to go, and at its weekly meeting with the landlord asked him to
replace the entire structure. The landlord denied that the porch was dangerous but suggested that he would fix it the following year. The committee was
unimpressed; it demanded that the issue go to the arbitration board created
by the collective bargaining agreement. The three-member board, composed
of landlord and union representatives and a third person selected jointly by
landlord and union, found the porch unsafe; but upon verifying the landlord's limited financial resources, it directed him to replace only floorboards
actually rotting away. Had the landlord still refused to repair, the tenant-
union members could have withheld their rent and paid their money instead
into an escrow account, until either the landlord made the required repairs or
the union could finance the work itself through the accumulating funds.

The alluring tenant union model has spurred the negotiation of collective
bargaining agreements between tenants and landlords not only in Chicago

---

*Reprinted by permission of the Yale Law Journal Company and Fred B. Rothman and Com-
pany from the *Yale Law Journal,* Vol. 77, pp. 1368-1400. Edited for inclusion in this volume.

but also in other cities across the country.[7] As early associations have gained experience, the sophistication of their contracts and of their negotiations with landlords has increased. In some cases landlord as well as tenant has come to appreciate the advantages of a stable tenant organization. Even the federal government has recognized the institution.[8] Although few unions have been in existence long enough to justify any firm conclusions about their ultimate usefulness, their initial successes and failures suggest that they can play a significant role in some housing situations where other techniques are unavailing.

The Origins of Tenant Unionism

Tenant organizations are not exclusively the product of present conditions. As long ago as the 1890's, severe economic depressions and housing shortages triggered the formation of tenant groups.[9] In New York City, for example, the acute post-World War I housing shortage and the depression of the 1930's both produced large scale tenant organizations.[10] Such groups, arising in response to extraordinary conditions, sought and received temporary legislative palliatives such as moratoria on evictions as well as rent reductions. Predictably, the organizations were short-lived; once the pinch had eased, they melted away. More recently, the grievances animating tenant organizations have shifted to the chronic ills of city slums: deteriorated housing, high rents, and absentee landlords. The most recent and well-publicized wave of tenant protests swept New York in 1964, when the massive rent strikes (see Chapter 1 herein) led by Jesse Gray gained wide publicity. Even there, however, the tenant groups demanded only one-shot repairs from the landlord. Some tenants won, but even they must start the whole struggle afresh as soon as another defect appears.

The goals and tactics of tenant unions differ sharply from those of earlier groups. Their emphasis is on a stable organization dealing directly with the landlord on a continuing basis. Like a labor union, the tenant union begins by joining individual tenants into a cohesive association, and then negotiates an agreement with the landlord defining the obligations of both parties and providing specific procedures for the resolution of disputes. Although the similarities between tenant and labor unions are evident enough, tenant unions neither derive exclusively from the labor model nor represent so sharp a break with past landlord-tenant law as might appear at first glance. Tenant unions reflect the convergence of two developments: a trend in recent landlord-tenant statutes toward increased tenant participation in efforts to improve housing conditions, and the civil rights movement with its offspring, the war on poverty.

Remedial Statutes

The common law of landlord-tenant relations has long been incapable of dealing satisfactorily with the problems of private housing in an urban industrial society. Traditional notions of property rights have sharply restricted the (tort) liability of apartment house owners for even dangerously dilapidated structures so long as the tenants were in possession of the premises.[11] In order to collect his rent the landlord had no obligation even to maintain the apartment in a habitable condition.[12] By a relentless adherence to the doctrine that covenants in a lease are independent, the courts preserved the landlord's right to collect the rent even when he breached a written promise to repair.[13] The courts conceded only the principle of constructive eviction to the tenant, but that relief was scant comfort except in the most outrageous circumstances.[14] The common law, in short, gave the landlord the right to keep his property in whatever condition he desired. Its sole solution for tenant complaints was the right to terminate the lease and quit the premises.

Legislatures, however, have not regarded property rights with such awe. Slums are ancient phenomena, and statutes have long recognized that the public interest in adequate, safe, and sanitary housing conditions may override private property claims. In the late nineteenth and early twentieth centuries state legislatures responded to the inadequacies of the common law by enacting tenement-house statutes in an effort to set minimum housing standards. Over the next fifty years the early regulations evolved into the elaborate housing codes of today. But administrative enforcement of housing codes did not eliminate substandard housing; where the landlord's operation was profitable, fines for housing-code violations effectively amounted only to a tax on his business. Consequently, some states established receivership,[15] permitted welfare departments to withhold rents,[16] or authorized public agencies to make emergency repairs with bills over to the landlord for costs.[17] The courts have consistently upheld such measures as valid exercises of the state police power.[18]

Until recently, most statutes could be enforced only at the initiative of an official arm of the government, either judicial or administrative. Now, however, tenant-initiated remedies are receiving increased attention because they are thought more effective.[19] Also implicit in tenant-initiated remedies is a growing awareness that the tenant has a special interest in adequate housing in preserving the public health and welfare generally.

In the past few years, Massachusetts and New York, among other states, have passed provisions authorizing the tenant to rely on the legal process as sword rather than shield; he may initiate a lawsuit against the landlord to compel correction of dangerous housing conditions.[20] The New York statute is the first explicitly to legalize *collective* tenant action and establish its ground rules. Article 7A of the New York Real Property Actions and Proceedings Law[21] allows one-third of the tenants in a slum dwelling to petition for an order directing the landlord to repair conditions "dangerous to life, health, or safety" without a prior inspection by the building department; if necessary, the court may place the building in receivership.[22] Article 7A allows organized tenants an effective initiative to seek and obtain receiverships; the state, however, still insists on injecting itself into every landlord-tenant dispute by requiring a cumbersome, time-consuming, and expensive court proceeding.

Civil Rights and the War on Poverty

The emergence of tenant-initiated statutory remedies gave some impetus to the formation of tenant unions; another catalyst was the sudden popularity of community organization in the civil rights movement and the war on poverty. The herculean task of organizing apathetic slum residents has required organizers to focus on an issue that can catch and hold the interest of the poor. Housing is an obvious choice. Many of the original organizers of tenant unions hoped that the organizations would expand into broadly based community and political groups. While those hopes have yet to materialize, the effort to mobilize the poor for better housing has created, at least in some cases, a spirit of self-sufficiency and self-help.

The Economics of Slum Housing

The success of the tenant union will ultimately depend upon judicial tolerance of its activities, and upon its bargaining power with the landlord. But its potential for achievement must be gauged by the economics of slum housing. Improvement in the condition of slum housing requires either capital investment for rehabilitation or increased expenditures for maintenance and repairs. Without government assistance or higher rents, such funds can come from only three sources: economies that lower other operating costs, tenant labor, and the landlord's profits.

Poor Tenants, Old Housing

Most proposals for improving slum housing focus single-mindedly on the landlord,[23] but funds for maintenance may also be released by lowering operating costs. For while the landlord will resist vigorously if his profits are threatened, he should have no objection if better housing can be provided for his tenants without changing total expenditures. Because of the nature of slum housing, there is reason to hope that this can be done.

In the American city, housing for the poor is old housing. As a building ages, the pattern of income and expenses that it generates changes significantly. Operating expenses for heat, repairs, and janitorial services rise and rents fall.[24] As the building moves toward its fortieth or fiftieth birthday, operating expenses often climb from 40 percent of income to almost 60 percent.[25] In addition, keeping the building in adequate condition requires at least occasional capital improvements. In this respect a building is like a car: the older it becomes and the more intensely it is used, the more expensive it is to maintain.

Moreover, the slum tenant's rent covers more than "normal" operating expenses. The lessee who plunks down $35 for the week's rent pays for the right—and the right of his neighbors—to vandalize the apartment, to have large numbers of children jumping on the furniture, to live in illegally small apartments, to skip out without paying the preceding month's rent, to move frequently, and to pay in weekly installments. Vandalism, children's wear and tear, harassment by housing code agencies, rent skips, high turnover, frequent collections—all are costs that the landlord must cover by charging higher rent for less housing.[26] Since poor people by definition cannot afford to pay high cash rents, the landlord increases his price by offering fewer square feet of space and fewer services.[27]

The tenants themselves, acting in concert through a tenant union, can help reduce the operating costs of housing. Tenants driven by personal frustration or anger at the landlord to vandalize or dump garbage in the hallway can be counseled and cajoled most effectively by other tenants. Organization itself can be a major solvent; many tenants do not bother to keep their building clean because they feel other tenants will tear it up anyway. The existence of grievance machinery may break the vicious circle in which the tenant vandalizes his apartment in retaliation against the landlord's refusal to make repairs, and the landlord makes no repairs because the tenant vandalizes his apartment. In short, the union may be able to provide the supervision and incentive that presently characterize owner-occupied slum tenements—usually the best maintained buildings in the slum.

The tenant union may also be in a position to reduce the high rate of turnover and rent skips. One study has suggested that lack of sufficient space and complaints about present housing conditions motivate families to move.[28] Tenant union organizers believe that exasperation with specific defects causes many slum tenants to move, despite the knowledge that new housing is likely to be as bad as what the tenant left behind. Without hope of improvement in the present dwelling, however, a poor family will pick up and move anyway. Since a new landlord ordinarily requires a security deposit, a tenant often omits the last month's rent at the old apartment. By creating a sense of group participation among tenants in the management of the building, the tenant union might halt the constant movement from one substandard apartment to another. Of course, to the extent that rent skips are the last resort of impoverished people spending money they do not have, not even the union can accomplish anything useful.

Tenant Labor

Besides cutting costs to the landlord, tenants can contribute their own labor to improve their living conditions. Informal, in-kind rent payments already occur in large areas of the slum housing market. Many landlords, for example, offer the new tenant a month's free rent if he cleans his own apartment when he moves in. Mutual distrust between landlord and tenant sharply limits the value of such agreements. The mere existence of the arrangements, however, suggests that they could become an additional "rent" payment plowed directly back into the building where lessor and lessee are both assured of adequate supervision. A tenant union can devise varieties of "sweat rent",[29] a landlord, for example, might reduce the rent where the tenant repairs the apartment with landlord-supplied materials. Obviously such arrangements will depend on the desires of the tenants. But if they want better housing and are willing to invest additional effort to get it, they should be allowed—if not urged—to proceed. The tenant union remains the only feasible device to ensure the workability of tenant-labor plans.

Picking the Deep Pocket

The tenant union, of course, need not limit its goals to the housing improvements which can be financed through lowered operating costs or tenant labor. The landlord as investor and profit-maker represents the most obvious potential source of increased maintenance funds. The extent to which a landlord has profits to yield to a tenant union, however, will depend on several variables: the rate of return demanded by the landlord; the condition of the housing market; and the stage of deterioration of the building.

The ultimate constraint on the rewards the union can hope to win from the landlord is the rate of return the landlord requires to stay in the housing business. This required rate of return takes account of (1) the return presently available on safe investments, e.g. government bonds; (2) the probability that the property will continue to generate income; and (3) the property's liquidity (how easily it can be sold and the collateral value of the property)[30]. Uncertainty about a steady flow of income, about the eventual ease of selling the property, and about the effort required to run the building will cause an investor to demand a high rate of return. Investors regard all rental housing as a risky investment, and slum housing is not only the most uncertain market, but the social disapproval attendant upon the epithet of "slumlord" tends to push the necessary rate of return even higher.[31] The tenant union, if it can reduce some of these risks and uncertainties by stabilizing landlord-tenant relations, may be the only institution capable of exerting a downward pressure on the rate of return necessary to keep landlords in business.

In many instances, however, the landlord's profits exceed the return necessary to keep him from abandoning his buildings. Housing markets vary widely in different parts of the country.[32] In some cities housing for the poor may be a dying industry,[33] but in a substantial proportion of slum markets demand outruns supply.[34] Even though the central cities have been losing their white population to the suburbs for nearly 20 years, in-migration of the poor—and chiefly the Negro poor—has replaced most of the fleeing middle class. Racial and social discrimination, as well as the more conventional disabilities of impoverished consumers, such as lack of knowledge, have kept the recent arrivals crowded into much smaller geographical areas than those deserted by middle-class emigrants.[35]

Not only is the demand for low-cost housing high, but the supply of low-cost housing is limited. Given the rents low-income people can pay, it is not economically feasible to build new units. Additional housing for low-income tenants becomes available as higher-income households vacate older for newer housing units. The older units then "filter down" to low-income tenants. Even the limited housing made available by the filtering process is further restricted by "block patterning" which allows only buildings on the fringes of already-existing slums to filter down. [36] In such a tight housing market, landlords often can increase rents without fear of losing tenants. Under these circumstances, the tenant union should be able to attack the "spread" between the required rate of return and the rent charges based simply on what the market will bear.

If the structure of the slum market creates one opportunity for landlord profiteering, the rhythm of housing deterioration creates another. When a building first enters the slum market, it is a prime candidate for "milking"; that is, while in later years the building will require significant repair expenditures to stave off actual collapse, during the period of descent the landlord need perform no maintenance work at all. The landlord may find it more profitable to collect the rents and milk the building as it deteriorates than to attempt to maintain his investment through repairs. In order to serve a low-income market, the landlord must be permitted to reduce services somewhat; however, when a landlord attempts to extract huge profits in a short period of time by a cataclysmic change in maintenance policy, permitting the building to deteriorate rapidly and totally, the tenant union can attempt to reverse the policy without driving the landlord out of business. . .

However, even if the union's bargaining power brings the landlord to the conference table, the checkered history of legal efforts to improve slum housing may still cast doubt on the tenant union's ability to obtain significant improvement of slum housing. But arguments based on the inadequacy of traditional legal remedies fail to note both the inherent limitations of earlier legal devices and the correspondingly greater potential of the tenant union.

The irreversible nature of housing deterioration makes the tenant union an especially promising tactic against the landlord intent upon milking a presently adequate building. The process of deterioration is asymmetrical: it is easy to let a building go, but virtually impossible to reverse the process. [37] Once the building has deteriorated substantially because maintenance requirements have been ignored, the building may cost more to rehabilitate than it is worth. Traditional legal remedies for inadequate housing have not been able to prevent the landlord from carrying out the decision to allow his structure to deteriorate into a slum tenement. The landlord will make token efforts to mask the deterioration taking place. Particularly because of the haphazard enforcement of such laws, by the time the building has clearly fallen below the minimal standards set by the housing code it will be too late. [38] The landlord has milked the building of the profits in it; only the badly deteriorated husk is left; the damage has been done with crushing finality. Legal action after the fact cannot force restoration of the building.

The tenant union, in contrast, can act early enough to prevent the landlord from profiting by his own inaction; before the structure is fatally blighted, the union can negotiate for an acceptable standard of maintenance based on rent paid and earnings withdrawn. [39] Moreover, the tenant union builds on its own success. It creates machinery to bring continuing pressure to bear on the landlord, unlike traditional legal remedies where enforcement is intermittent at best and the time and effort involved in bringing a second code prosecution or rent-withholding action are the same as in the first. [40]

Even where the building has deteriorated to the point that it cannot generate enough income to bring it up to code requirements, the tenant union enjoys an advantage over traditional legal remedies. Code prosecutions and welfare receiverships set unrealistic goals for many buildings. [41] Invoking administrative remedies precludes a strategy of flexibility and gradualism; to avoid the threatened sanction, the landlord must bring his building up to code requirements. Yet demanding all or nothing too often gets nothing. When the structure has already been milked, capital investment to meet requirements is simply uneconomical: the landlord will abandon the building rather than waste money upon it. Serious penalties, such as jail terms or high fines, have never materialized to deter this type of behavior. The tenant union, on the other hand, can tailor its demands to the possible. Many tenant complaints fall far short of an insistence upon major repairs; they look only for a few trash containers, janitorial service, locks on doors, mailboxes, or patching for the walls. Rehabilitation may be the ideal, but where it is unattainable a formalized procedure for handling complaints which the landlord can afford to remedy represents considerable progress.

The Law of Tenant Unions

Most landlords have stoutly resisted tenant-union organization from the time the first leaflet was slipped into the tenant's mailbox until just before they signed on the dotted line; several have turned to the courts for help in resisting tenant organizing. Generally, the cases have been settled before a decision came down. Consequently, few opinions have indicated the tenor of judicial reaction to tenant unionism. But several lines of precedent exist to which courts are likely to turn for guidance in adjudicating the conflicts that arise between union and landlord at the various stages of union organization.

Organizing: the Foot in the Door

At the outset union organizers canvass door-to-door and distribute leaflets to inform tenants of the union's activities and to recruit tenants for union meetings. The tenant's right to possession should protect such organizing activities from the landlord's attack on grounds of trespass or invasion of privacy. Unlike the laborer who has no right to possession in the company-owned factory, the tenant in an apartment building has the right to receive anyone he desires in his leased premises. [42] In addition, he holds an easement or right-of-way over the common hallways even though the landlord retains possession there.[43] Either an implied license arising from the existence of a bell in the front hallway or the "habits of the country,"[44] or an actual invitation to enter extended by the tenant will defeat the landlord's charge of trespass.[45]

Recognition: Purposes, Picketing, and Strikes

Once organized, the union typically has demanded that the landlord recognize it as the sole bargaining agent for the tenants and negotiate an agreement. With equal consistency, the landlord has refused, thereby precipitating a union campaign of picketing and rent withholding. Judicial scrutiny of such tactics is likely to be extensive, and courts will undoubtedly turn to the labor precedents for guidance.

The broad first amendment right to picket sprang from the utility and effectiveness of picketing as a means of conveying and publicizing information.[46] In later cases, however, the Supreme Court realized that picketing involved more than just communication; the physical presence of patrolling pickets produced not only traffic problems such as the blocking of sidewalks or entrances to buildings, but also coercion. . . .[47]

Even where picketing generates coercion—as it almost always does when the union pickets a business establishment—the Supreme Court has carved only a specific exception to the scope of first amendment protection. The state may enjoin the picketing only where the object sought by the picketers violates a legitimate, clearly defined state law or policy. Provided the state law is valid, a state court may enjoin the picketers either from breaking the law themselves or from coercing a third party to break it. In upholding injunctions against labor picketing, the Supreme Court has consistently based its decisions on a finding that either the union was violating a law or that it was attempting to force an employer to violate it.[48]

Recognition picketing[49] of a landlord's building and offices by a tenant union does involve economic coercion. Its purpose is to force the landlord to the bargaining table. The courts will consequently face the question whether the purposes of the picketing are lawful. They may retrogress to the "unlawful object" and "prima facie tort" doctrines formerly invoked in criminal conspiracy and business interference cases against the labor unions.[50] But unlike the older courts, which had few legislative pronouncements to guide them in their handling of early labor disputes, the judges today can look to the Housing Act of 1949, state housing statutes, and municipal housing ordinances for relevant policies to define their treatment of tenant unions. By picketing, the tenant union seeks to force the landlord to bring his building up to the legal minimum prescribed by the housing code, to create orderly machinery for the resolution of tenant grievances, and to improve substantially the quality of his tenement housing. Such objectives, far from being unlawful or against public policy, parallel the statutory purposes enunciated by Congress and state legislatures. Even if the tenants' demands exceed the minimum requirements of the local housing code, the more general legislative policy should lead the courts to conclude that the picketing is lawful in its purpose. Congress has committed the nation to "the goal of a decent home and a suitable living environment for every American family," and to "the policy of . . . opening to everyone . . . the opportunity to live in decency and dignity."[51] State and municipal housing laws imposing minimum standards on multi-family dwellings coincide even more exactly with the tenant union's aim of improving existing housing stock.

Consequently, the courts should not enjoin tenant union picketing on the ground of unlawful purposes. They may instead question whether the tenant union represents an appropriate means of accomplishing the end sought. Here the union's greatest burden will be its novelty. But tenant unions are no more novel than congressional desire for the participation of the poor in many recent government programs. In states where the legislature has authorized the welfare department to withhold rent or where statutory remedies have otherwise come to recognize the value of tenant-initiated remedies, courts should find no justification for enjoining tenant union activity per se.

In addition, code enforcement is irrelevant to the tenant union's basic demand of union recognition and negotiation of a collective agreement. Such demands violate no law or policy of any state but instead further the policy of self-reliance enunciated in the Economic Opportunity Act. In labor disputes the early common-law courts, recognizing the possible improvement in wages and working conditions to be as valid an economic concern as the avoidance of possible harm to employers, never laid down a per se law outlawing labor unions.[52] Tenant unions offer the state the potential of a self-regulating system to ameliorate housing conditions in the cities. Such considerations should prevent the courts from subordinating the tenant union's potential for improving housing to the protection of a landlord's pocketbook.

Many tenant unions, however, have found that picketing alone does not bring the landlord to the bargaining table, and have also resorted to rent withholding. Landlords have a medley of theories on which they can seek to enjoin such union conduct. . . Such doctrines underlay the notorious labor injunctions of the first third of the century, and they share a tortured common-law history. In all of them, the landlord's claim for relief will rest, as did that of his employer counterpart, on the injury intentionally inflicted by the union.[53] And in both situations, "the damage inflicted by combative measures of a union—the strike, the boycott, the picket—must win immunity by its purpose."[54] In defending rent withholding, the tenant union will find itself back in the means-ends analysis prevailing in the picketing cases, but with no first amendment considerations to weigh in the balance.

Still, the tenant union does stand in a better position than the early labor union, insofar as the economics of rent withholding differ from those of the labor strike. In the withholding action the union collects the rent from tenants and places it in an escrow account. Unlike the irretrievable loss caused an employer by a labor strike, the economic "harm" inflicted on the landlord by rent withholding is temporary and conditional solely upon his continued recalcitrance. To the extent that the tenants stay on in the building, the land-lord suffers no business loss analogous to that incurred by the struck em-ployer. The landlord has a right of action against the tenants (and probably against the union as well) for rent accruing from use and enjoyment of the premises.[55] It should be emphasized that the union's promise to repay the funds at the end of the dispute is no fiction: in many instances the union has furnished the landlord with an accounting of its rent collections and has not intervened to prevent the eviction of tenants who paid their rent to neither landlord nor union. The tenants are not after free apartments; they want their money's worth in better housing.

Courts, therefore, should find no justification for injecting their power of injunction into such a situation. The landlord cannot satisfy equity's require-ment of irreparable harm as a prerequisite to the issuance of an injunction.[56] With no immediate, irreparable harm in prospect, the landlord should be re-mitted to his existing, adequate legal remedies. Meanwhile, as the lease actions or summary eviction proceedings drag on, both tenants and landlord come under strong pressure to reach an agreement. Neither can find the un-certainties and disadvantages of the strike situation attractive. Self-interest should move each side to negotiate, compromise, and settle on the basis of a realistic appraisal of the other party's economic strength.

The Collective Bargaining Agreement

The final negotiation of a collective agreement with the landlord represents the fruition of the tenant union's efforts. The contracts vary widely in sophis-tication, specific terms, and the number of buildings covered. The typical agreement contains the following provisions:

Substantive promises:
- a union commitment to encourage and oversee tenant efforts in respon-sible apartment maintenance;
- a landlord commitment to make certain initial repairs and to meet basic maintenance standards thereafter;
- a maximum rent scale for the life of the contract;
- a union commitment not to strike;

Enforcement provisions:
- machinery for the regular transmission of tenant complaints and de-mands to the landlord;
- an arbitration board to resolve disputes over grievances with power to compel repairs;
- a procedure for rent withholding if the landlord fails to comply with the agreement;

Landlord-union relations:
- landlord recognition of the union as exclusive bargaining agent;

- a landlord commitment not to discriminate against union members;
- a requirement that the landlord inform the tenant union of the addresses of all buildings owned and managed by him, and of the names of all new tenants as they move in.

Increasingly, collective bargaining agreements provide for a dues checkoff by the landlord.

Most important to the union is the landlord's acceptance of binding arbitration and the private enforcement mechanism of the rent withholding provision; their combined effect produces considerable economic pressure on the landlord to make necessary repairs rather than delay or take the matter into court. A Chicago tenant union that failed to include the enforcement provisions in its contract found itself little better off than if it had no contract at all. Under present common law the tenant can sue for damages for breach of a covenant to repair, [57] but the expense and delay of legal action often deter litigation. A collective agreement with no private enforcement provisions simply trades one lawsuit for another. The landlord is under no incentive to act and may simply await litigation, knowing that it is unlikely to come.

In exchange for his promises the landlord receives a union commitment to encourage responsible tenant maintenance of apartments. The union's promise is not empty, and in fact landlords have placed great reliance upon it. The potential for reducing vandalism and turnover played a large part in convincing several landlords to sign their first collective bargaining agreement with a tenant union. One landlord estimated that he could increase maintenance expenditures by 20 per cent if vandalism and turnover were reduced. It is still too soon to evaluate the union's effectiveness in promoting tenant responsibility, but after extended dealings with the unions, several landlords have come to look favorably on the prospect of their continued existence. As the union increases its control over the buildings, the tenants, adopting a more proprietary attitude toward their apartments, may take better care of them.

Courts are likely to approach the collective agreement as warily as the once-burned child the kitchen stove, but painfully acquired familiarity with the labor agreement should encourage acceptance of the landlord-tenant arrangement. [58] The judicial eye should experience little trouble in discerning sufficient consideration to validate the agreement in the exchange of promises between landlord and tenant. Consideration has moved to the landlord in the union's promise to attempt better tenant maintenance. True, tenants are already under a legal duty to maintain their apartments imposed by most housing codes and the terms of their leases. [59] Still, the union's promise should not come within the pre-existing legal obligation rule. [60] In the expectations of the parties tenant vandalism, no matter how illegal, is a fact of life in the slum housing market. Landlords budget for it, municipal code enforcement agencies despair over it, and no one can cope with it. As an empirical matter the landlord attaches value to the commitment of the union *qua* organization to encourage tenant responsibility. The union's promise gives rise to a new obligation along with a cause of action that the landlord did not have before the contract. The promise bears no relation to the situation that the pre-existing legal obligation rule is designed to meet. The union is not engaging in a hold-up, unless every pressure for contractural advantage is defined as such. Furthermore, the union has committed itself to encourage more than the minimal maintenance duties the tenant is already obligated to perform. The union's promises not to withhold rent and to abide by decisions of the arbitration board also constitute consideration moving to the landlord. In the labor context the courts have long recognized that the promise not to strike was good consideration for company undertakings. To the extent that the bargaining agreement also induces present tenants to remain in the building and new tenants to move in, the collective contract should further bind the landlord by virtue of third-party detrimental reliance.[61]

To inspire judicial confidence in the value of its commitments, the tenant union will do well to grant specific enforcement of a collective bargaining agreement to a plaintiff union noted that the organization had backed up its promises by the apparent ability to make good on them:

> Two organizations, one composed of employers and the other of employees, have entered into an agreement. Each had power through the consent of its members to enter into a binding obligation in their behalf. By the constitution or by-laws of each, power is given to the organization to enforce, through disciplinary proceedings which have been demonstrated to be effective, compliance with the terms and conditions to which it has subscribed. This contract has mutual obligations binding on the parties thereto. Each party knows the obligation that it has assumed . . . . Through its control of its members it can compel performance.[62]

The courts have traditionally had far less difficulty in detecting the movement of valuable consideration from employer to labor union, and it is unlikely that anyone will challenge the validity of the landlord's consideration. His promises to repair and to submit to binding arbitration constitutes sufficient consideration in exchange for the undertakings of the tenant union.

A second difficulty in contract analysis arises if the landlord claims that he signed the agreement under duress. In one case,[63] the landlord pointed to the union-organized rent withholding and picketing. Since every bargaining situation entails some degree of compulsion, the landlord asserting duress must demonstrate that he really had no choice, and that he was compelled to manifest his assent "without his volition." If the tenant union's conduct is lawful, the labor cases holding that a lawful strike cannot constitute legal duress should control.[64] If the tenant union's conduct is unlawful, though, the landlord may still not prevail. Some labor cases have held that under such circumstances the employer should seek legal relief in the courts. Moreover, even if the landlord establishes that he signed under duress, he still must show that he repudiated the agreement at the earliest opportunity after removal of the duress. If the landlord accepts any of the benefits arising from the agreement, remains silent for a considerable time after he has had the chance to repudiate, or acts on the provisions of the agreement, he ratifies the contract.[65]

* * *

Tenant unions do not represent a panacea for the country's low-income housing problem. No solution can be advanced without provision for large-scale infusion of money—either public or private—for rehabilitation and new construction. But even the most ambitious government proposals do not envision the construction of an adequate housing supply within a decade; realism suggests a considerably longer period before the country approaches its housing ideal. Interim steps are required, and the tenant union represents an alternative which may be beneficial in a variety of situations. There are, of course, circumstances where tenant unions will be of little use, as, for example, where the landlord is as destitute as his tenants. But even where unions fail to attain their housing objectives, they have an equally important potential for creating better community organization in the slums.

While the tenant unions may be able to emerge intact from judicial scrutiny, legislation probably represents the best method of structuring the growth and formation of tenant unions. The real growth of labor unions did not take place until the Wagner Act had given labor organization the stamp of legislative approval.[66] Undoubtedly legislative endorsement of tenant unions and settlement of housing disputes through collective bargaining would provide a substantial stimulus to the organization of tenants. Passage of landlord-tenant relations laws might go far to minimize the strife and friction so characteristic of present relations between the low-income tenant and his landlord.

---

1. This figure somewhat understates the situation. There are 5.3 million deteriorating or dilapidated occupied rental housing units in the United States. G. Beyer, Housing and Society 144 (1965). The average household in the United States has 3.8 people. Bureau of the Census, U.S. Dep't of Commerce, Statistical Abstract of the United States 35 (1966). These figures yield an estimate of approximately 18 million people living in substandard rental housing units. Most substandard housing is rented. *Cf.* B. Duncan & P. Hauser, Housing a Metropolis—Chicago 84 (1960).

2. See Gribetz & Grad, *Housing Code Enforcement: Sanctions and Remedies,* 66 Colum. L. Rev. 1254, 1254-55 (1966).

3. See, for example, Department of Housing and Urban Development, Department of Justice & Office of Economic Opportunity, Tenants' Rights 5-6 (1967) [hereinafter cited as Tenants' Rights]; Illinois Legislative Commission on Low Income Housing, For Better Housing in Illinois 21-22 (1967) [hereinafter cited as Illinois Commission]; Massachusetts Special Commission on Low-Income Housing, Final Report 64 (1965) [hereinafter cited as Massachusetts Commission].

4. See p. 111, *infra.*

5. "Tenant union," as it is used in this chapter, refers only to a tenant organization which seeks a collective agreement with the landlord defining the obligations of both the tenants and the landlord. See Tenants' Rights 16-17.

6. The example in the text is an amalgam of several incidents. Interviews with Charles Love, Richard Rothstein, and Tony Henry, tenant union organizers, in Chicago, May 2 and 3, 1967.

7. For example, Chicago Sun-Times, Nov. 18, 1967, at 16, col. 1; Chicago Sun-Times, Nov. 17, 1967, at 12, col. 1; Wall Street Journal, Nov. 16, 1966, at 1, col. 1; Tenants' Rights 16-17; Glotta, *The Radical Lawyer and the Dynamics of a Rent Strike,* 26 Guild Practitioner 132 (1967).

8. The Federal Savings and Loan Insurance Corporation in its capacity as lessor of 84 foreclosed properties in Illinois signed a three-year contract with a newly organized tenant union. Chicago Sun-Times, Nov. 18, 1967, at 16, col. 1; the Department of Housing and Urban Development also approved a lease for a Muskegon, Mich., public housing project which recognizes a tenant union and establishes formal grievance machinery. Letter from Ronald Glotta, attorney for the East Park Manor Tenants' Organization, to the *Yale Law Journal,* Feb. 24, 1968.

9. Piven & Cloward, *Rent Strike,* The New Republic, Dec. 2, 1967, at 11.

10. W. Rudell, Concerted Rent-Withholding on the New York City Housing Front: Who Gets What, Why, and How?, May, 1965, at 20-28, 39-45, 61-63 (unpublished divisional paper in Yale Law School Library).

11. Chambers v. Lowe, 117 Conn. 624, 169 A. 912 (1933); [Restatement (Second) of Torts §§ 355-56 (1965); 2 F. Harper & F. James, Torts § 27.16, at 1506 (1956); 1 H. Tiffany, Real Property § 99 (3d ed. 1939).].

12. Widmar v. Healy, 247 N.Y. 94, 159 N.E. 874 (1928). Nor is there any duty on the landlord to keep leased premises in good repair, Withy v. Matthews, 52 N.Y. 512 (1873); 1 H. Tiffany, Real Property § 103 (3d ed. 1939).

13. Johnson v. Haynes, 330 S.W.2d 109 (Ky. 1959); Stone v. Sullivan, 300 Mass. 450, 455, 15 N.E.2d 476, 479 (1938); see Annot., 28 A.L.R.2d 446 (1953). In some jurisdictions, a landlord may be liable for injuries which would have been avoided if he had honored his agreement to repair. 2 F. Harper & F. James, Torts § 27.16 at 1514 (1956); 1 H. Tiffany, Real Property § 106 (3d ed. 1939).

14. Dyett v. Pendleton, 8 Cow. 727 (N.Y. 1826); 1 American Law of Property § 3.51 (A. J. Casner ed. 1952).

15. Conn. Gen. Stat. Rev. § 19-347b (Supp. 1965); Ill. Ann. Stat. ch. 24, § 11-31-2 (Smith-Hurd Supp. 1967); Mass. Gen. Laws Ann. ch. 111, §127H-J (1965).

16. Ill. Ann. Stat. ch. 23, Public Aid Code, § 11-23 (Smith-Hurd Supp. 1967); N.Y. Soc. Welf. Law § 143(b) (McKinney Supp. 1966).

17. Note, *Enforcement of Municipal Housing Codes,* 78 Harv. L. Rev. 801, 834-36 (1965).

18. E.g., *In re* Department of Bldgs. of the City of New York, 14 N.Y.2d 291, 200 N.E.2d 432, 251 N.Y.S.2d 441 (1964) (receivership).

19. Tenants' Rights 1, 7; Illinois Commission 23-25; Sax & Hiestand, *Slumlordism as a Tort,* 65 Mich. L. Rev. 869, 871-75 (1967).

20. N.Y. Real Prop. Actions Law §§ 769-82 (McKinney Supp. 1967); Mass. Gen. Laws Ann. ch. 111, §§ 127C-H (1967).

21. N.Y. Real Prop. Actions Law, §§ 769-82 (McKinney Supp. 1967). See Note, *Tenant Rent Strikes,* Colum. J. L. & Social Prob., April 17, 1967, at 2.

22. N.Y. Real Prop. Actions Law § 778 (McKinney Supp. 1967).

23. Most reforms are designed to wring money from the landlord. Schoshinski, *Remedies of the Indigent Tenant: Proposal for Change,* 54 Geo. L. J. 519, 520-21 (1966); Gribetz & Grad, footnote 2, at 1281; see Sax & Hiestand, footnote 19, at 874-75.

24. Institute of Real Estate Management, 1967 Apartment Building Income Expense Analysis 4, 11 (1967); Arnheim, *Evaluating Expense Statistics in Property Management,* 31 J. Prop.

Management 66, 70-73 (1966). In middle-class buildings the profit squeeze produced by rising expenses and falling rents is offset by two factors: the percentage of collections rises and the vacancy rate falls. *id.* 73.

25. Institute of Real Estate Management. The selling price of a building usually does not fall to allow for increased maintenance costs. W. Grigsby, Housing Markets and Public Policy 234, 238 (1963).

26. See G. Sternlieb, The Tenement Landlord 73-75 (1966) [hereinafter cited as Sternlieb]. A New Haven, Conn. landlord estimated that he could reduce rents by 20 percent if vandalism and turnover were substantially reduced. Speech by Herbert Cohen to Yale Law School seminar, Nov. 17, 1967. Public housing for low-income tenants also faces these added costs. National Association of Housing and Redevelopment Officials.

27. A. Schorr, Slums and Social Insecurity 99-100 (1963).

28. P. Rossi, Why Families Move 97 (1955).

29. Self-help and sweat equity plans have traditionally been associated with home building by future owners. See Nesbitt, *"Self-Help" Homebuilding,* 24 J. Housing 275 (1967); Wall St. Journal, Nov. 13, 1967, at 1, col. 1. In addition, sweat equity plans have been advocated for building low-income cooperatives or condominiums. See Davis, *Cooperative Self-Help Housing.* 32 Law & Contemp. Prob. 409 (1967). Tenant unions may, of course, prepare the way for cooperative or condominium ownership of buildings. Letter from Victor de Grazia, executive vice-president, Kate Maremont Foundation, to the *Yale Law Journal,* July 11, 1967; *cf.* Quirk, Wein & Gomberg, *A Draft Program of Housing Reform—The Tenant Condominium,* 53 Cornell L. Rev. 361, 390-93 (1968).

30. See Hollebaugh, *Income Approach to Value* in Encyclopedia of Real Estate Appraising 54, 60-63 (E. Friedman ed. 1959); L. Winnick, Rental Housing: Opportunities for Private Investment 103-09 (1958).

31. Sternlieb 95-96.

32. Vacancy rates, rent levels, and expenses vary wildly from region to region, and city to city. See Institute of Real Estate Management, 1967 Apartment Building Income Expense Analysis 3, 6-9 (1967).

33. For example, Sternlieb 88-93, 103-06. Newark may be a special case, however, since it has one of the highest ratios of public housing units to population of any city in the country.

34. The housing market is very fragmented; for example, large apartments able to house adequately the many large, low-income families of the slums are in terribly short supply in most slum housing markets. Interview with Tony Henry, tenant union organizer, in Chicago, May 2, 1967.

35. J. Rothenberg, Economic Evaluation of Urban Renewal 44, 45-46 (1967) [hereinafter cited as Rothenberg].

36. See B. Duncan & P. Hauser, Housing a Metropolis—Chicago 219 (1960).

37. Rothenberg 47-48; *cf.* Note, *Tenant Initiated Repairs: New York's Article 7-A,* 2 Harv. Civ. Rights-Civ. Lib. L. Rev. 201, 207 n.48 (1967).

38. Both administrative and equal protection probelms have prevented housing code enforcement agencies from achieving completely effective code compliance. Note, *Enforcement of Municipal Housing Codes,* 78 Harv. L. Rev. 801, 810-11 (1965).

39. The analogy to the labor union here is striking; if an employer claims economic inability to meet the union's demands, the Court has held that the employer must substantiate his economic hardship. See NLRB v. Truitt Mfg. Co., 351 U.S. 149, 153 (1956); Yakima Frozen Foods, 130 N.L.R.B. 1269 (1961).

40. In old buildings, there must be constant supervision and maintenance. Even if court action produces repairs, the building may rapidly deteriorate to its pre-repair condition unless

maintenance is continuous. If the tenants have to go to court following each deterioration, the expense and trouble may not prove worth the result. See Note, *Tenant Initiated Repairs: New York's Article 7-A,* 2 Harv. Civ. Rights-Civ. Lib. L. Rev. 201, 207 n.48 (1967).

41. See Note, *Enforcement of Municipal Housing Codes,* 78 Harv. L. Rev. 801, 811-12 (1965); Sternlieb, *Slum Housing: A Functional Analysis,* 32 Law & Contemp. Prob. 349, 354-55 (1967).

42. The tenant has the right to possession of the leased premises. 1 American Law of Property § 3.38 (A. Casner ed. 1952).

43. Commonwealth v. Richardson, 313 Mass. 632, 639, 48 N.E.2d 678, 682 (1943); Totten v. Phipps, 52 N.Y. 354, 357 (1873). See Annot., 24 A.L.R.2d 123 (1952).

44. Commonwealth v. Richardson, 313 Mass. 632, 640, 48 N.E.2d 678, 683 (1943).

45. Nor can the landlord rely on any blanket anti-solicitation statute to keep organizers away. The organizers can claim a strong first amendment right to be heard—a proposition dating back to the leaflet and doorbell cases of the 1940's. Martin v. Struthers, 319 U.S. 141 (1943); Cantwell v. Connecticut, 310 U.S. 296 (1940). There the Supreme Court upheld the speaker's right to intrude on the privacy of an *unwilling* listener, at least for non-commercial purposes; *cf.* Breard v. Alexandria, 341 U.S. 622, 642-43 (1951).

46. 310 U.S. 88 (1940), at 104.

47. Teamsters Local 695 v. Vogt, Inc., 354 U.S. 284, 293 (1957); Giboney v. Empire Storage & Ice Co., 336 U.S. 490, 501, 503 (1949); Cox v. Louisiana, 379 U.S. 536, 554-55 (1965) (dictum). See Jones, *Picketing and Coercion: A Jurisprudence of Epithets,* 39 Va. L. Rev. 1023 (1953).

48. See, for example, Teamsters Local 695 v. Vogt, Inc., 354 U.S. 284 (1957); Teamsters Local 309 v. Hanke, 339 U.S. 470, 477 (1950); Building Service Local 262 v. Gazzam, 339 U.S. 532, 539-41 (1950); Giboney v. Empire Storage & Ice Co., 336 U.S. 490, 498 (1949).

49. Hughes v. Superior Court, 32 Cal. 2d 850, 855, 198 P.2d 885, 888 (1948), *aff'd,* 339 U.S. 460, 466 (1950).

50. See F. Frankfurter & N. Greene, The Labor Injunction 24-46 (1930).

51. 42 U.S.C. § 2701 (1964).

52. Commonwealth v. Hunt, 4 Met. 111 (Mass. 1842); see F. Frankfurter & N. Greene, footnote 50, at 2-5.

53. See Holmes, *Privilege, Malice, and Intent,* 8 Harv. L. Rev. 1 (1894).

54. F. Frankfurter & N. Greene, supra note 50, at 25.

55. 1 American Law of Property § 3.64 (A. J. Casner ed. 1952).

56. See 1 J. Pomeroy, Equity Jurisprudence § 221 (5th ed. 1941). For a discussion of general factors militating against injunctive relief, see *Developments in the Law—Injunctions,* 78 Harv. L. Rev. 994, 1004-13 (1965).

57. See 1 American Law of Property § 3.79, at 351-52 (A J. Casner ed. 1952).

58. Collective agreements have long been confusing phenomena to fit into the law's tidy pigeonholes. Lenhoff, *The Present Status of Collective Contracts in the American Legal System,* 39 Mich. L. Rev. 1109 (1941); Witmer, *Collective Labor Agreements in the Courts,* 48 Yale L. J. 195, 196 (1938); Note, *The Present Status of Collective Labor Agreements,* 51 Harv. L. Rev. 520, (1938).

59. See Note, *Enforcement of Municipal Housing Codes,* 78 Harv. L. Rev. 801, 810-11 (1965); 1 American Law of Property § 3.39 (A. J. Casner ed. 1952).

60. For a discussion of the pre-existing legal obligation rule, see 1A A. Corbin, Contracts § 171 (1962).

61. See Mabley & Carew Co. v. Borden, 129 Ohio St. 375, 195 N.E. 697 (1935); *cf.* Lawrence v. Oglesby, 178 Ill. 122, 52 N.E. 945 (1899); Note, 7 U. Chi. L. Rev. 124, 133 (1939).

62. Schlesinger v. Quinto, 201 App. Div. 487, 498-99, 194 N.Y.S. 401, 410 (1922).

63. 66 CH 4827 (Cook Cty., Ill. Cir. Ct. 1966).

64. E.g., Lewis v. Quality Coal Corp., 270 F.2d 140, 143 (7th Cir. 1959), *cert. denied*, 361 U.S. 929 (1960).

65. See, for example, Gallon v. Lloyd-Thomas Co., 264 F.2d 821 (8th Cir. 1959); Annot., 77 A.L.R.2d 426 (1961).

66. Congressional endorsement was, of course, not the only reason for the rapid rise of labor unions since 1935. See H. Faulkner & M. Starr, Labor in America 209-12 (1957).

Part III

TENANT ORGANIZATIONS AND THE ORGANIZING PROCESS

Introduction

Tenant organizers face a series of extraordinary problems. They range from the immediately obvious one of decreased tenant mobility in a tight housing market to those concerning the amorphous yet threatening presence of the landlord. But even more importantly, organizers will soon realize that tenants live in a world that purposefully obstructs collective effort. Labor organizers have found that the physical setting of the work place is common ground on which workers can be united. Tenant organizers will find that the "living place"—the apartment building—functions not to unite people, but to reinforce the uncommon, diverse elements of its occupants' lives. Unlike the work place, the building is designed to separate people from each other.

No one who has lived in a large city would deny the importance of privacy and physical separation from others. At the same time, no organizer should expect his or her efforts to be any easier because of them; the western ethic "a man's home is his castle" dies hard, even when some of the castles are filled with cockroaches and many of them need new plumbing. Organizers, rather than quickly uniting people around their buildings' inadequacies, may often first have to shake loose the atomizing assumption that united action designed to improve one's housing is not synonymous with an encroachment on one's right to privacy in his or her own home.

Such problems explain why tenant unions are often found at the final stage of organizing rather than at the beginning. The organizing process develops through a variety of organizational steps, each one manifested in a particular group model. While both external and internal factors interact continually to expedite or impede the organizing process within a building or development, certain distinct patterns present themselves for easy description.

The first and simplest kind of organization is an *ad hoc committee*, a group that usually forms around some specific and glaring problems, e.g. garbage in the halls due to an inadequate number of garbage cans. Its membership may take part in a petition drive, talks with the landlord or public housing administrator, etc., and will usually dissolve quickly once even minor corrections have been made or, equally likely, if the landlord makes conciliatory gestures of a few monthly meetings, a suggestions box in the lobby, or even the hiring of a new management company.

When tenants are left unsatisfied with such responses or if the landlord continues to be indifferent to their grievances, the next type of organization formed is often a *tenant association*. A tenant association can perhaps best be described as a voluntary association emphasizing tenant problems. While concentrating on union-type issues of maintenance and high rents, its inattention to increasing association membership beyond its original size often inhibits the group from developing far beyond the level of a lobbying group with the landlord or housing administration. There are of course obvious exceptions, but the typical public housing tenant association (those begun by management) serves this lobbying function, as do many of the more middle class tenant associations found in parts of Manhattan and the Hyde Park area of Chicago.

Actual *tenant union* formation is often an amalgam of many external and internal developments, but it can perhaps be best understood through a typology describing two organizing methods. The first begins when an outside tenant union (or local community organization) perceives that the tenants of a building(s) would be receptive to the organization's activities. Interested in developing its own power and prestige in the local community, the already-established group will have one or more organizers begin recruitment drives in the buildings. These organizers use informational meetings about the union, "rap sessions" on specific problems within each building (both of which are best accomplished in a friendly tenant's apartment), and leaflets to educate the tenants to the need for and purposes of the tenant union. This type or organizing can begin at any time and has the advantage of being able to link up disparate tenants with a well-developed organizaton. However, outside organizers run the risk of being confronted with tenants distrustful of the union and the notoriety some of its past activities may have created. Furthermore, by being outsiders, the landlord more easily gathers support from other institutions (the law, the press) through cries of "outside agitators" and "rabble rousers," which, however invalid, may lessen the organizers' effectiveness in recruiting.

The second process leading directly to union formation begins when one or more tenants indigenous to the building or development decide that their problems will only be improved through a more intensified, long-term effort. This indigenous organizing, while slower in developing, may have greater chance for success because the tenants themselves will probably have experienced the qualitative differences between short-run, ad hoc issues of inadequate maintenance and the longer range issues of tenant inequity.

Once tenants decide to develop a tenant union, it is necessary to carefully think through the process of organization, for it is probable that the organizing itself will determine the eventual dimensions of the union structure. Problems not uncommon to other grass roots organizations must also be resolved. Leadership training, the need for full-time organizers to maintain the new local group, and continued education around the long-term goals of the union are a few of the issues the tenant union must consider if the newly-organized tenants are to remain active members of the organization.

The tenants' rights movement is still in its awkward adolescence and, naturally, mistakes will be made. Many of them can and have been avoided by drawing analogies to the labor movement's early development. In order to be effective, however, people must concentrate not only on the similarities of past labor union activities but also on the very real differences. As this section will suggest, labor's lessons for tenant organizing will be found in labor laws developed for organization and membership self-defense, not in worker-employer relations.

The organizing process is always involved. The first article in this section, broken into three sections ("The Pre-Organizing of Organizing," "Collecting Information," and "Activating the Tenants") is based on the actual experiences of many tenant groups across the country. Written by the National Tenants Organization and the editor, it is, hopefully, a useful guide to laymen and professionals alike in describing the careful preparations that tenants must undertake if they are to organize effectively a large group of formerly atomized tenants into a cohesive organization.

There are obvious differences between private and public housing tenant unions—including tenant-landlord relationships and the problems of organization. The public tenant union, rather than organizing against a landlord interested primarily in profit, works directly with—or against—a local housing commission or other public officials. At the same time, the public housing administration staff is in direct contact with tenants and often can intimidate or co-opt tenants interested from joining a potentially militant tenant organization. These and other realities are discussed in the N.T.O.'s paper "Organizing in Public Housing."

Once organized, people obviously need some kind of organizational structure to ensure that their efforts are maintained beyond the quickly dissolved, emotive activities of the group's first months. As any organization will reflect the particular dynamics of its own interests, a tenant union, while similar to other advocate organizations in its maintenance functions, will necessarily differ from them with respect to involvement in tenant issues of housing code enforcement, building maintenance, and the like. More specifically, the special organizational requirements for setting up and maintaining a rent strike must be clearly defined within the union structure if the group is to remain responsive to a wide variety of tenant needs. Many tenant unions, born in the throes of a rent strike, face the danger of displacing their larger goals with the limited aims of the strike—essentially the group's major tactic. To enable people to understand the differences and demands of a tenant union from other organizations, Stuart Katz has written an article that clearly delineates the structure of a tenant organization and the roles its membership must perform in order to maintain and enhance the group's efforts. Its contents, previously in booklet form, have been used to establish both public and private housing tenant unions throughout the country.

One final note: these articles have been chosen to provide more than just information on the actual processes of tenant organizing. For people interested in the broader activity of community organizing, but unfamiliar as to what it really "looks" like, they form a composite picture of the way an organizer really organizes. Too often one hears that community practice is all excitement, filled with glamorous moments of militancy, kindness, persuasion, and, of course, eventual victory. Such an image is like the one that surrounds courtroom law; it looks extremely attractive on television, but it bears little resemblance to reality. The work behind the image involves concentrating on petty detail, doing research in stuffy offices, and spending long nights mapping out future contingencies. Hopefully, these few articles will give the reader a glimpse of just how hard this work is if image and reality are ever to be combined.

CHAPTER 8

The Long Process of Tenant Organizing

Stephen Burghardt and National Tenants' Organization

Organizing in the private housing community demands patience and selectivity. This first article explores the careful preparations necessary for a tenant union to develop or expand its organization. Some parts of this piece may seem esoteric to those anxious to get on with the "grass roots" of their organizing. But most of the topics discussed, if not all crucial to a tenant group's initial activities, are eventually important issues demanding expertise—either in negotiations, further tenant union growth, or in strategy formation involving particular landlords.

Part A: The Pre-Organizing of Organizing: Choosing Tenants and Targets

Certain economic and social factors will greatly influence the success of any organizing effort. Not to consider them could be disastrous to the tenant organization. The three most important factors are the conditions of the buildings selected to organize, the type of tenants chosen to work with, and the type of landlords chosen to combat.

A tenant union must first consider the condition of the buildings where organizing is to take place. If they have deteriorated so much that little can be done to improve them short of demolition and reconstruction, they may not be worth the effort. On the other hand, luxurious apartments with no code violations may leave organizers with few tools with which to organize tenants. It must be mentioned, however, that other contextual factors (e.g. the legal system of the state) may constantly affect any organizing effort regardless of building conditions.

Generally, there are three classifications of buildings. The first kind are *standard* buildings. These are buildings with very few housing code violations, and are occupied by primarily well-to-do or middle class tenants. Some lower-middle or poor tenants may occupy such dwellings. Despite their general economic well-being, the tenants may still be aggravated and organizable due to recently increased or exorbitant rents. The successful rent strike in Tiber-Carollsberg Square in Washington, D.C. attests to this potential. Tenants whose income ranged up to $40,000 and whose membership included such figures as Senator Edward Brooke and Rep. John Conyers, were able to roll back proposed rent increases and establish grievance procedures in the building through cohesive action.

A danger to tenant organizing in standard buildings, however, lies in the lack of code violations. In most states where rent strikes are legal, the sole cause for rent striking is housing code violations. Tenants who live in standard buildings place themselves in the jeopardy of immediate eviction if they rent strike. Other tactics—especially those geared to "moral suasion" which might embarass landlords (e.g. picketing, leafleting the landlord's neighbors) —might be used instead both to organize these tenants and to force the landlord into positive responses toward the union.

The second building type can be classified as *substandard*. A greater number of housing code violations no longer places them in the class with standard units, but the buildings have not deteriorated so far as to be impossible to rehabilitate. These are choice buildings in which to organize, for tenants have a legal way of combating the landlord and the very real possibility that their efforts will have highly visible results.

Some of the clues concerning a building's slide toward substandard conditions must be learned from tenants. If they know that the landlord is increasingly reluctant to make repairs, does a poorer job on present work than was done in the past, and totally avoids major repairs (plumbing, etc.), then there is a good chance that the landlord has decided either to sell the building or to "let it go" for a quick, high profit margin. If it appears that the landlord is ignoring his property, organizing will have to be swift and cohesive if it is to keep substandard buildings from further deteriorating into the poorest conditions.

The final category is made up of *dilapidated* buildings. There the tenants have many grievances; housing code violations may be so common that present landlords may have often paid fines in the past. Such conditions may generate enough tenant anger to make organizing relatively easy. At the same time, if buildings are so poorly kept as to be dilapidated, they may be too expensive for any one landlord to repair. But this does not preclude bettering present housing conditions. If tenants recognize the limitations on the repairs to be made, or if they are able to get receivership of such buildings and apply for rehabilitation grants, these buildings can be productively organized.

The next factors to consider are the tenants within the buildings. The number of tenants in a building is of primary importance: generally, the more the better. Small numbers of tenants in a building mean that many buildings must be organized from the outset. This generally requires dealing with many different landlords, different problems, and tenants in the local organization who have less in common. Furthermore, one small building may rely on one tenant to keep the building organized; if he or she leaves, the whole organizing effort is destroyed. In a larger building the loss of one or two tenants would rarely be consequential to the success of the struggle.

One must also consider how transient the tenants are. Highly transient tenants are extremely difficult to organize; they lack interest in ongoing organizations and provide little reliability, in terms of support or cohesiveness, for a newly-developing tenant union. Obviously, large families and couples are the most receptive and helpful to a tenant union.

Finally, the racial or ethnic make-up of a building or group of buildings may be important. If racial differences in a group of tenants have previously bred conflicts, these same animosities may develop during tense periods of the organizing process. While these problems can and have been avoided—as have potential problems in the mixing of middle class and poor tenants—not to consider these realities from the outset may create problems in the future. It may be necessary for different tenant groups and community organizations to first form separately around housing problems and then to build coalitions around highly specified events or issues of benefit to all the groups involved.

The final important consideration involves the type of landlord. Perhaps the easiest fact to determine is the personality and status of the landlord (if these facts are readily available, the economic factors are probably easy to learn also). Unstable landlords make easy targets for organization efforts. If the landlord is highly irrational and emotional at times, tenants may have many reasons for resentment. An entire building of tenants went on strike in Ann Arbor after one landlord beat up a rent-striking tenant and threw his furniture into the street. Other landlords have been known to steal tenant's possessions for back rent. The resulting criminal charges have greatly strengthened the tenant organization's own cohesiveness and the group's legitimacy in organizing against the landlord.

The social position of the landlord is also important. If a well-known and highly respected businessman in the area happens to be a slumlord as well, tenants can exploit this factor easily for their own benefit. Checking out such background characteristics—which may require talking to neighbors, looking over past news clippings, etc.—can be highly rewarding for the union.

Financial characteristics of landlords are equally important for a tenant organization to know, for each type will demand different organizing strategies. In general, there are three categories of landlords.

The wealthiest type is the *absentee professional.* This landlord may be an individual, a group of investors, or a corporation owning many buildings, perhaps as many as 40 percent of an entire slum area. While often difficult to organize against, this landlord type does have the resources to make the changes necessary to improve slum housing.

The difficulties are obvious. The more money he has coming in from a variety of sources, the greater his power to withstand one particular source of economic irritation. In being wealthy, any fines and "tickets" received from the courts can be paid without difficulty. He can also hire a battery of lawyers to stall affirmative actions begun by the tenant union.

But a large pool of resources is equally attractive to a tenant organization's staying power. Knowing that a landlord has the financial ability to improve markedly his buildings can motivate tenants to struggle much harder to achieve success. Furthermore, these "professionals" are attuned to the fine points of economic argument. If they realize that it is economically better for them to sign a collective bargaining agreement than to suffer a prolonged and expensive rent strike, they will sign. A highly cohesive tenant organization may stand much to gain in dealing with this type of landlord.

The second kind of landlord—the *absentee amateur*—while like the professional in his distance from his buildings, owns only a few properties (usually no more than twelve buildings). Many of these landlords are found at opposite personality extremes. They may be concerned, well-meaning people trying to improve their property for their tenants while at the same time making an adequate profit. At the other extreme is the irrational and emotional person willing to steal a tenant's television set in order to meet his mortgage payments.

Either type may be relatively easy to organize against. The "concerned" landlord might feel that a tenant union is a "good idea", especially if the collective bargaining agreement contains provisions for the tenants to help cut down on vandalism or to aid in making some of the repairs. The irrational type landlord may have angered tenants enough to motivate them to prolong any rent strike. Faced with mortgage payments and probably with limited capital, this absentee-amateur type might then capitulate to tenant demands.

But the lack of resources common to many absentee amateurs is also a hindrance in effective organizing. When funding is limited, the repairs to be made may be equally limited. A tenant group would have to decide just how much it must demand before effectively dealing with this type. A close review of the landlord's accounting books (if he is poor, he should have nothing to hide) might be in order if the union decides to narrow its expectations for the landlord's benefit.

The final landlord type is numerically the largest in slum areas: the *owner-occupant*. Owning and living in the same building, this landlord is usually as poor or almost as poor as his tenants. The only reason he does not maintain or better the building is obvious: he doesn't have the money to do so. He probably tries to get along with his tenants, for he has everything to gain from friendly interaction. Because of this, a tenant union would probably be wiser to organize for all the building's occupants by exploring receivership possibilities or other devices leading to collective ownership. If this doesn't appear feasible, a well-organized union may be able to aid the landlord in finding loans for at least some repairs. In this case, most of the benefits in such arrangement would be distributed equitably among all the building's occupants.

Part B: Collecting Information

Information is essential for a group that knows where it wishes to become involved in tenant organizing, or for an indigenous group anxious to find out all that it possibly can about its landlord. To determine the best strategy for a particular landlord, certain economic and social facts must be learned. For example, how irrational is the landlord? How wealthy? Is he using the building for tax purposes or income purposes? Perhaps most important to begin with, who *is* the landlord? The answers to such questions are mandatory if a new tenant union is to grow into a successful one.

There are several sources for information. They range from the obvious to the esoteric; some may be common everyday knowledge, others may be so complicated as to demand professional help. All of them can and should be used by a tenant group willing and able to spend the effort to unravel the facts within them. Once known, such facts will be invaluable.

The easiest source for information are the tenants. They may have frequent contact with the landlord, and they undoubtedly know their management company's operating style. If they have leases, the landlord's name or representative's name will appear.

Another source equally close to home is the janitor. While many janitors will have little interest in your questions, others might be willing to speak freely about their employer. A janitor will know maintenance policies or, if nothing else, can provide a description of his daily tasks which will give clues to the type of work expected of him. Perhaps an even better source are janitors' assistants. Often part-time or temporary help, they have much less stake in protecting the landlord than the janitor does. While his contact with the landlord will be less frequent, his lack of defensiveness may help a tenant union glean interesting information, including name, residences, and personality types.

Another easily accessible source for information is a telephone directory. If a tenant union knows the name of the landlord and the general vicinity of his residence, a brief check of a few listings may locate his exact address. Then, if desired, picketing at his home or leafletting his neighbors can begin. The same process holds for locating business establishments.

One of the most accessible agencies for a tenant group to use for information is the city housing department. If code violations exist, they may be recorded and used for later publicity and in the court. If it is found that there are only a few recorded violations and it is obvious many more exist, the tenant group, through a tenant already in the building, can ask for a reinspection. The new violations can be added to the economic and legal pressure already on the landlord. One can also find out if the landlord has made any recent attempts to secure a permit to make alterations in the building. If he has done so, it is all to the good; if not, the union keeps building a stronger case in the courts for landlord negligence.

The County or City Tax Assessor is responsible for estimating the worth of each piece of property in the municipality. He also keeps a record of who receives the tax bill and pays the taxes. As this information is listed according to address, one can obtain it without first knowing the owner's name. Furthermore, the person or company paying the taxes is undoubtedly in close contact with the landlord—being either the landlord's manager or the landlord himself. Such information can be most helpful in later meetings with the landlord.

Knowing the amount of taxes paid is also beneficial in determining the worth of the particular piece of property. It is equally important to know if the taxes have not been paid. If not, then the landlord may be in poor financial condition or he may be planning to abandon the property altogether. Furthermore, if there are tax liens on the building, a tenant union may want to reconsider the possibilities of buying the property. If they are too high, the group may wish to look elsewhere.

A title insurance company in the area may be as much help as a Tax Assessor's Office. With information located in more accessible form, it can get it to you rapidly and without your own effort. While some firms are more accessible than others, many can run a "title pencil search" for you at a minimal fee. These searches can turn up such facts on a local piece of property as the owner's name, the taxes paid, and the assessed valuation of the property itself.

One of the more subtle ways to obtain information is by visiting local real estate offices. As mentioned by Michael Beckman elsewhere in this volume (in his essay on the realities of multi-unit ownership in an urban setting), slum buildings are put up for sale rather frequently so that landlords can capitalize on certain income tax advantages. There is always a good chance that an organized building will be up for sale. A person presumed to be interested in buying can gather all sorts of information. Most obviously, if it is for sale, then the union knows that any bargaining agreement must cover subsequent purchasers. The real estate broker might also disclose the amount of income presently made on the building. The asking price may also be revealing. All these facts can be used by a tenant group to counter landlord complaints about financial troubles he is faced with in operating his buildings.

If a tenant union knows the name of a building's landlord, the county recorder's office can be a wealth of information. By looking through the recorder's files, one can discover to whom he has mortgaged the property and from whom he bought it. Or, if you know the name of the past owner, you can trace the name of the present owner. Corporate owners may be discovered later after finding out the name of the person who signed a mortgage on behalf of the corporation.

It is equally important to discover all of a landlord's properties so that pressures can be maximized by organizing tenants in all of his buildings. This will not be easy; titles to property can be put in many different names. The most one can do is check all the holdings listed under the name of the landlord, his relatives, or his employees.

If a group is meticulous enough, it can find out approximately how much the landlord paid for a particular property and how much money he originally had to put up. All deeds must have a minimum of $1.10 in federal revenue stamps for every $1,000 transacted. The actual purchase price may be hidden, however, because excess stamps may be bought. No stamps are required for the part of any mortgage which the buyer has assumed from the seller.

Finally, if a tenant union has a legal staff large enough or relatively free from pressing demands, a discovery proceeding in court can be arranged in conjunction with some other legal action brought by local tenants. These proceedings, if used effectively, may uncover a great deal of information concerning profit margins, building income, landlord holdings, and such. The difficulty with these proceedings lies in the potential harm it may do to the tenant involved in the primary case (say, an accident due to faulty steps). A landlord, once he recognizes what discovery might reveal, may instruct his lawyer to use all the delaying tactics possible (there are many in the legal world). For the poor tenant, who may need the potential funds from the case for medical expenses, discovery could prove quite burdensome and unfair. On the other hand, if the suit was designed primarily for discovery purposes, then the tenant group can afford to wait longer to continue its case.

Part C: Activating the Tenants—Initial Organizing and Code Enforcement

The behind-the-scenes work described in the first two parts of this article are meaningless if at the same time tenants are not being actively engaged in confronting their housing problems. As the following National Tenants' Organization paper points out, many of the first public forays will center on better code enforcement. Discussed here are some of the basic organizing guidelines any tenant group must be concerned with if it wishes its organization both to grow coherently and maintain itself as a permanent organization.

Tenant groups usually get started because tenants have specific complaints about poor housing conditions, sudden rent increases, or other objectionable management policies. Tenants talk to each other individually and then get together to discuss what they can do about their common problems. Sometimes an organizer from the poverty program, a civil rights group, or elsewhere will help bring the tenants together to form a tenants council. Usually the whole purpose of forming the tenant organization, at least at first, is to get specific complaints answered.

In the period of initial organizing, timing and the momentum of the newly-formed tenant group are very important. There is danger both in going too slow and in going too fast. On the one hand, meeting after meeting without some accomplishments that the group can point to as the result of its work will lead to lack of interest on the part of tenants. Tenant council members need to be involved in different ways in the work of the council, and the tenants council should concentrate on one project at a time, such as getting a particular maintenance worker hired or fired, or whatever the group wants done. When one project is completed, the tenants council can then point to it as an accomplishment of the organization, which will help attract other tenants to join. Without definite accomplishments, tenants will tend to stop coming to meetings after a while and interest will fall off. Thus the council should not meet just for the sake of meeting, but rather to work on a particular project or plan.

On the other hand, there is also a danger in going too fast and taking on too much before the organization has a solid base and people have shown a real commitment that will last over a period of time. Many groups attract lots of interest in the excitement of starting an organization; they then go after a big victory right away, like going on rent strike or signing an agreement with the landlord. Once the initial excitement has worn off, or the first big battle won, they may find tenant interest wearing off, because it was not built up over a period of time. A sudden burst of interest may also die off suddenly. This happened with some of the Chicago tenant unions in 1966; after they signed agreements with the landlord, some unions then found they didn't have a solid enough organization to make them work. A tenant organization should build up to the big battles neither too quickly nor too slowly.

If tenant complaints involve poor housing conditions which are violations of the city housing code, then a fight for better code enforcement is a good place for the tenant group to begin. Code enforcement has a limited value, however, because it cannot directly do anything about rent increases or arbitrary management policies (aside from the failure to make repairs). Tenant groups which are concerned about other management policies have effectively used the code enforcement effort not only to get better housing conditions, but also to pressure the landlord into changing management policies generally, and giving up some control over them to the tenant organization.

Most tenants tend to be conservative by nature and feel more secure by working through established structures in the beginning. Although, at first, tenant groups may want only better housing conditions, after the lengthy delays and limited response from the establishment, they are often drawn into the broader fight for tenant control over management policies. Therefore, we are discussing code enforcement here as a strategy for both immediate better conditions and for later tenant control. For a successful code enforcement effort, the following steps have proved useful to follow in the past and may be a helpful guide for tenant groups:

1. The City Building Department

The general strategy is to pressure the building department into properly enforcing the city housing code against the landlord; such pressure for code enforcement, begun by the tenants and carried out by the city, may help pressure the landlord into meeting tenant demands.

Tenants representing the tenants council should go to the building department, explain that they are trying to get their landlord to fix up his property, and ask to see the records of any past inspections of the property. Building departments generally have regulations which allow tenants to see the records on the buildings they occupy. If the tenants council is not allowed to see the records, political and legal steps may be taken to get access to the records. The tenants council should talk to friendly officials in the city government or on the city council about getting the records open, if that fails, a lawyer could challenge the policy as unconstitutional. The local American Civil Liberties Union chapter or the local Neighborhood Legal Services program would probably be interested in such a suit and should be contacted.

If there is a record on the building indicating that code violations have been reported, the tenants should then find out the status of the reported violations: whether the landlord has already been given time to make repairs, whether the building department has sent notice of remaining violations to the city's legal office (the corporation counsel) for prosecution of the landlord, and if so, what the status of the court case against the landlord is. The tenants should make it clear to the building department, the corporation counsel office, and anyone else they talk to in the city government that they mean business and that they intend to bring all the pressure they can to get the code violations repaired and, if necessary, the landlord prosecuted.

2. Housing Inspection

While at the building department, the tenants should get several copies of the city housing code and should become familiar with the more common code violations that occur. If possible, a tenant, or a lawyer or law student working with the tenant council, should summarize the important parts of the housing code and mimeograph the summary to distribute to tenants, so they will know what code violations to look for.

If there has not been a recent thorough inspection of the property by the building department and there are a number of existing code violations, the tenants should ask for an inspector to come out right away. They should try to find out when he is coming, and then have a tenant or organizer who is familiar with the code go through the building with the inspector to make sure that he writes down every possible code violation. After the inspector has finished and has turned in his report, the tenants should ask to see the report, on which they may have to take notes at the building department. Tenants should then go through the building to make sure that every violation has been listed.

If all violations have not been listed, the tenants should call or go to the building department at once and ask for a reinspection. If the building department refuses to reinspect, the tenants council should then threaten to call the mayor and the press to demand that the city enforce its housing code. If they still refuse to reinspect, the tenants should make good on their threats. The tenants can probably find allies to join in this demand among other tenants groups, community organization, or civic groups in the city.

(In calling the press, the tenants council should beware of one danger. The press prefers to cover such stories by focusing on the story of one family or one tenant. The press may thus ignore other tenants council members, which can lead to divisions and resentment within the tenant organization. This happened to one group in Vine City in Atlanta. To avoid such divisions, the tenants council should try to see that hard-working members get credit for their work in press coverage of the group's activities.)

If the buildings are reinspected, that reinspection should be checked too, just as the earlier inspection was. If all the violations are still not reported, the tenants then have a case for corruption in the building department and should proceed at once with an attack on the city administration in the press, and on the landlord and the city in the courts. The tenants should demand the removal of officials or inspectors in the building department who were responsible for failing to report violations. This whole campaign will show the building department that at least when this tenants council calls for an inspection, it must be thorough; and it will show the landlord that the tenants are organized and active and are putting pressure on the building department to force him to make repairs.

3. Court Cases

Whatever legal strategies the tenants' lawyers use on code violations, the tenants council should always try to involve the tenants as much as possible in the court case. If tenants are not actively involved, an attitude of "let the lawyers handle it" may develop, and interest in tenant council activities may drop drastically while the court case drags on for months and months, as such cases do except in special situations.

Tenant organizations in Chicago have found it useful to intervene directly into building court cases, rather than waiting for the building department to present their case. They discovered that the officials of the building department did not vigorously present the severity of the violations and the urgency of the situation before the court. They have filed petitions to intervene as a party to the dispute when cases reached the building courts and have been successful in getting the courts to allow tenants to testify. The effect on the courts have always been beneficial to the tenants. In numerous cases the building department representative would testify that the landlord was working to correct a violation and the tenants would speak up to contradict him. In some cases the judge has inspected buildings himself to see what was going on, and usually the judge was "shocked" by the uninhabitable conditions. In some instances judges have ordered that rents be reduced by one-half because of the conditions in the building. None of this would have happened without the intervention of the tenants into the case.

The tenants council should involve tenants both in the court case itself and in other activities during the legal battle. In work on the court case, tenants can help gather information necessary for the legal suit through surveys of housing conditions in the project. If the lawyers or the tenants can find a law student to work with the tenants council, he can be very helpful in involving tenants in some of the legal field work necessary for the case. The law student can also help coordinate tenants' involvement in other ways, such as lining up witnesses, taking tenants to meet with the judge in his chambers if the lawyers can arrange it, or taking tenants to watch the case (or other cases) in progress in landlord-tenant court.

Besides working on the court case, tenants can apply political pressure to go along with the legal pressure of the suit. (They can also apply economic pressure, as described in the section on rent strikes below.) Applying political pressure can take different forms depending upon what the tenants want to do and what resources they have. They can picket the landlord at his place of business or his home, or both, to expose his slum properties; they can meet with, picket, or sit in at the building department and corporation counsel office to protest lax code enforcement; and they can talk to friendly organizations and politicians about supporting them and pressuring the landlord. The tenants may be able to find allies in other tenants of the same landlord (to find out what other property he owns, a law student or tenant can check the city's real estate tax records); or they may band together with other tenant groups of other landlords to demand better code enforcement.

The tenants council should be careful not to be overshadowed by political figures or non-tenant organizations. The council should invite the support of others on its own terms from the beginning, so that its cause doesn't get taken over by others who may then use it to their own advantage and to the detriment of the tenants. This is less true of other tenants organizations which generally agree on strategy and goals; it is more of a problem with politicians or moderate-liberal groups like labor unions, church groups, or civic organizations. Middle class tenants councils are another possible source of support; and they may have useful contacts. But again, the tenants councils should try to agree on strategy and goals at the beginning, to avoid misunderstandings later.

During all of this code enforcement effort, it should be made very clear to the landlord that it is his tenants who are behind all the pressure on him; so that if he wants to stop the pressure, he must go to the tenants and negotiate with them over their demands. He may try to evict some tenants, particualrly tenant council leaders, in this code enforcement fight; but under the *Edwards v. Habib* case, such "retaliatory evictions" are illegal: the landlord cannot evict tenants for reporting code violations to the government. One lower court decision in Washington, D.C., has made an exception to that rule where rent-striking tenants openly stated they wanted to take over ownership of the building. The case is being appealed, but until it is decided, tenants should be cautious about making public statements that they intend to take over ownership. Witnesses should avoid making such statements in court.

This article has attempted to show that organizing is similar to all strategy formation in its attention to detail, membership demands, and, when possible, contingency planning for future needs. Indeed, these initial organizing plans are merely the first steps that any community organization must take if it is to develop successfully into a permanent organization. The next steps— the development of a cohesive organizational structure and the elucidation of staff and membership responsibilities—will be discussed in the next article.

CHAPTER 9

The Organizational Structure and Staff Membership Roles of a Tenant Union

Stuart Katz

(This chapter may be viewed as a manual for organizing grass roots tenant organizations in both public and private housing. It is based on the early history and development of the Ann Arbor Tenants' Union (AATU), an organization which, despite several difficult and unique problems, has made a significant impact on the larger community. The chapter does not take on the structural format of a manual, however. It is not a list of rules which the reader may consult as a statutory code. Rather, it is written historically because the writer feels that this is the only effective way of communicating a real sense for the task of organizing. If rules alone make the skeleton of an idea, it is hoped that what follows will add flesh and life to the idea. Otherwise the nature of organizing cannot be fully understood and appreciated—S.K.)

The early part of tenant activity in Ann Arbor centered around the organization of a rent strike and not the formation of a tenant union. There was, and still is, much debate as to the merits of this unequal emphasis. Nonetheless, it is clear that for the purposes of uniting tenants, an immediate issue, namely a strike, is more dramatically visible than moving directly into the organization of a permanent union. The question here is not which issue is best—clearly the formation of a collective body of tenants capable of controlling its housing is the ultimate goal—but rather how best to develop the movement in a way that will insure maximum interest and participation until the final goal is reached. This is why the strike is emphasized here.

---

*The author, one of the founders of the AATU, is presently an assistant professor of Psychology at the University of Georgia.

There are, of course, other ways of giving an incipient group an initial "push." As the writer will repeat several times in this paper, the particular strategy selected will depend to a large extent on the local conditions and level of consciousness of the participants.

Phase I—Structure During the Early Stages

In Ann Arbor, during late fall of 1968 and early winter 1969, several individuals interested in a rent strike called two meetings which attracted over 100 organizers. These meetings, both of which were well publicized, accomplished several purposes beyond bringing committed organizers together.

First, organizers obtained special kits at these meetings which contained the following items:

1. An assignment giving the number, street address, and name of landlord of the building or buildings the individual was to organize.
2. Pledges to strike—statements pledging to begin withholding rent when a certain number of signatures had been collected. [1]
3. Information on the housing market, including a checklist of housing code violations.
4. Information on the escrow fund—explanation of how the fund was set up and how money should be paid to the Tenant Union (TU).
5. Typical questions and answers to allay common fears and rumors.
6. Posters advertising the TU and TU buttons.
7. Form letters to be signed by tenants and sent to the city housing department charged with the enforcement of the city housing code.
8. Advice on defense against extra-legal tactics commonly employed by landlords, such as turning off utilities, lockouts, etc.
9. A sheet for each striker to fill out giving information such as occupation, phone number, rent, and housing code violations in the apartment and the building.

Secondly, the meetings served as training sessions to acquaint organizers with facts and proper approaches for interacting with the typically frightened and naive tenant. A failure on the part of the AATU was in not expanding this training. It is clear from the experiences of some organizers that the organization should have had at least a week of intensive training workshops. Only later was it realized how damaging a poorly trained organizer could be.

Finally, the meetings served to establish an *ad hoc* central steering committee responsible for coordinating the strike. The original positions that were established for this group—so crucial for any struggling tenant organization's growth—are listed below. For simplicity, they are first defined and then their effectiveness is discussed.

1. Office Coordinator. The duties of this position are: (a) to see that the central office of the TU-RS is manned at all times by people capable of answering most tenants' questions; (b) to keep the office and all the records in an orderly manner so that information is easily and immediately accessible. (This is extremely important because, as learned the hard way, an enormous amount of time can be wasted merely hunting for information. With hundreds of people involved in a rent strike, this kind of inefficiency can be catastrophic, particularly during times of stress common to all grass roots organizations); (c) to maintain a list of people willing to work for the strike. (Every new person who appears in the office should be asked to help out. The names and phone numbers of people willing to work should also be recorded); (d) to insure the security and materials of the office.

2. Research Director. The central requirement of this position is to coordinate research of: (a) all aspects of the housing market (e.g., who owns what and where, profit margins, etc.); (b) interlocking connections between landlords, the judiciary, city officials, and others; (c) projected housing needs of the community; (d) the illegal activities of individuals named above.

With the information obtained, the AATU was able to identify the landlords it wanted to strike, publish facts on shockingly high profit margins, and disqualify two judges in the city who had strong connections with property interests. In addition, the AATU was able to bring an anti-trust suit against certain major landlords for violation of the Sherman and Clayton Acts. This suit, besides having important propaganda value, has real legal merits of its own. A favorable verdict could cost the landlords millions of dollars in damages.

It should be pointed out that the kind of research talked about here is not always easy to carry out. Obtaining important information frequently requires considerable ingenuity; often some piece of informaiton is impossible to find. Yet whatever is learned proves invaluable as a tactical weapon or as a lesson about the nature of political and economic power in this country. Because the job is so time-consuming and often esoteric, this is perhaps an ideal position for any professionals interested in aiding a tenant group.

3. Publicity. The duties of this position are: (a) the responsibility for designing and submitting all advertisements to the news media; (b) constructing large, permanent posters to be located around various parts of the city or neighborhood; (c) creating the various items such as flags and small posters which, through wide distribution, show the solidarity and pervasiveness of the organization. It is an adequate arena for new members of a tenant group still concerned about some of the more demanding tasks such as organizing or researching.

4. Press Liaison. The press liaison must establish and maintain regular contact with the local and state-wide press. Contact with the local media must be closest since communication with the tenants themselves is necessary to sustain interest in the movement. Local media are to be kept aware of all TU-RS activities and should work with reporters to assist them in giving comprehensive and accurate coverage of the myriad of activities related to the strike. In addition, the liaison issues statements and press releases to the papers, radios, and television stations in the area.

The press liaison must also serve as official spokesman for the group. Assigning a single spokesman avoids conflicting statements by members of the steering committee (and others) on unresolved or controversial issues. However, other members are not always silent. The liaison can often refer the media to the steering committee member most knowledgeable about a particular issue of interest to the press. Besides developing confidence and leadership qualities in a wider group of people, this procedure aids the presentation of an impressive, united front to viewers of the media.

Finally, the liaison serves as a contact with other tenant organizations.

5. Liaison with Other Community Organizations. The chief requirement of this position is to gain the support of, and establish connections with, as many community organizations as possible. This is crucial to broadening the group's political base and must receive top priority. The more support garnished—whether from the NAACP, the city human relations commission, or local student groups—the greater substance and impetus of the movement. Outside support also places greater pressure on the landlords and the courts to seek settlements more in line with a tenant union's demands.

6. Legal Defense. This position requires the coordination of all legal research, legal defense in eviction cases, and other legal problems such as conspiracy and the disqualification of judges. Before any of the details of this coordination are discussed, something must be said about why the law is relevant to the strike at all.

Technically, the major strategy of the strike is to exert economic pressure on landlords by depriving them of rents. To this end, any specific action which allows the strike to continue by keeping tenants in their apartments is desirable. The AATU found that making maximum use of a tenant's legal rights allowed them to achieve this goal more effectively. Exactly how to make most effective use of the tenant's legal rights can only be determined by careful research into each state's laws governing landlord-tenant relations.

Typically, legal action involving tenants and landlords, if initiated by landlords, is rarely carried beyond the early stages of the legal process. Landlords are usually granted "summary judgments" against the tenant (i.e. they are granted all they ask for) because the tenant rarely makes an appearance in court. This happens either because the tenant cannot afford a lawyer or does not understand his rights.

If the tenant sues the landlord, as occasionally happens, the landlord has the distinct advantage of being a defendant. He can make use of the broad range of legal technicalities to delay judgment so that the tenant, due to rapidly accumulating legal costs, must drop the suit.

For these reasons, the basic legal strategy in Ann Arbor has been a defensive one: the tenant stops paying rent (thus exerting economic pressure on the landlord) and the landlord is forced to sue the tenant. The tenant has now replaced the landlord as defendant and is able to make use of all the dilatory tactics once considered the sole prerogative of the landlord. Furthermore, in a massive rent strike the effect of a single eviction case is multiplied many times. While the tenant, as part of the rent strike, pays a relatively small fee for legal costs, the landlord must pay much more in litigating each case. But more importantly, the court docket becomes so jammed that the number of judgments reached affects only a tiny fraction of the total number of strikers. Maximum economic pressure through continued occupation by strikers is thus exerted against property owners until they come to terms with the tenant union.

In Michigan, where the landlord-tenant law is relatively progressive, the AATU demanded and received jury trials for each eviction case. These jury trials, each of which usually takes up a full day, have slowed the eviction process tremendously. Of course, in states where the law leaves fewer options for defendants, a rent strike legal staff will have to be more resourceful. But no matter where the strike occurs, it should be recognized that unlike other groups, tenants can wield a great deal of power by prolonging the entire litigation process through established legal methods.[2]

One further point must be made before leaving this issue of general legal strategy. While such a strategy is generally oriented towards forcing the landlords to take the initiative, this does not mean that a tenant organization cannot, itself, take affirmative action. Three such suits in Ann Arbor were the previously-mentioned disqualification of two judges; the anti-trust suit initiated on behalf of AATU members; and criminal charges against certain landlords who had been harassing tenants in ways ranging from mild verbal threats to physical assault. The political, economic, and personal issues raised, while varying in each suit, were of the type crucial to any tenant union seeking to educate tenants throughout the community to the complex nature of their inequitable housing situation.

Let us now look at the specifics of organizing a legal defense group. The steering committee members in charge of legal defense must seek out law students and other people to do the required work. A nearby law school is obviously an ideal source for workers. This is not, however, a prerequisite. Legal aid groups or even the tenants themselves are possible sources of assistance. Since legal research requires some expertise, such research will probably have to be done by law students and lawyers. However, the actual paper work involved in preparing legal answers for eviction cases can, with a bit of training, be done by almost anyone. The coordinator should not have trouble in assembling a team that can accomplish most of the legal tasks except actual appearances in court. (Court appearances can only be done by practicing lawyers in most states.)

A few words must be said about hiring lawyers. The most important criteria should be: (a) the lawyer's record of dependability; (b) his readiness to state *at the outset* precisely what he is capable of doing and how much he is willing to do for it; (c) whether he is willing to work until the strike's conclusion; (d) whether he is willing to consult with the group regarding tactical decisions. These points are emphasized because the experience of the AATU taught them the bitter lesson of not reaching an understanding on these issues. Their first lawyer, who had represented tenants in past rent strikes, agreed to work for the AATU without realizing the potential scope of the strike and the time required to spend on it. While he was slowly discovering the extent of the commitment demanded of him, his law firm kept exacting additional sums of money. When he finally realized how large the strike had grown to be (1200 strikers and a $150,000 escrow fund), he began to vacillate about his commitment and finally withdrew completely. By that time, the AATU had paid his firm $5,000. Such an amount exhausted the strike funds allocated for attorneys' fees. They managed to survive during a very critical period after his departure by finding several lawyers willing to donate their time on a temporary basis. Since that time, the AATU has been able to hire two young lawyers to handle the eviction cases and two well-known lawyers to handle the conspiracy charges brought against the group by local landlords. Thus, AATU was able to continue the effectiveness of the legal strategy. This experience, however, was a hard way to learn a simple lesson—thoroughly probe your potential lawyers about what they are willing to commit themselves before any strike action begins.

7. **Administrator of the Escrow Fund.** Careful attention must be paid to the administering of money from tenants and other sources. This is the duty of the person in charge of the financial books of the tenant union. More specifically, the requirements of this position are to establish and maintain an escrow fund of rent monies paid by striking tenants and to keep track of all other fees, contributions, and such. If the steering committee member is not an accountant, one should be consulted at the beginning and periodically thereafter to see that the fund is in good order.

An escrow fund, in the technical sense, is simply a fund administered by some third party until certain conditions are fulfilled. In the AATU situation, the fund is controlled by the TU-RS (obviously an agent of the tenants), thereby assuring that the "third party" will be acting in the tenants' interests. The fund itself serves four basic functions:

(a) to keep money away from the landlords. The AATU located their escrow fund in a Canadian bank. This provided maximum security from the long arm of the courts. A foreign location for the escrow fund is strongly recommended or if this is not possible, another state or county.

(b) to demonstrate to the landlords and to the courts that the money has been paid and will be available if and when the goals of the strike are reached.

(c) to aid tenants in saving their money so that they can pay their rent when a court judgment is reached in an eviction case.

(d) to help financially the tenant union by earning interest which might otherwise accrue to the landlords.

The escrow fund was established in three different accounts: (1) a savings account where the bulk of the rents were placed; (2) a checking account which allowed them to pay out money to tenants wanting their rents back for whatever reason; (3) an AATU strike fund checking account, which consisted of money belonging solely to the AATU. It was created by collecting ten percent of the first month's rent of all striking tenants and through fund-raising events.

Tenants paid into the escrow fund either by writing personal checks to the AATU or by writing out money orders or bank drafts to themselves which the AATU held in a safety deposit box. This latter form of payment—allowed because some tenants felt uneasy about making direct payments to the AATU during its formative stages—was later eliminated because it created considerable accounting problems.

8. Coordinator of Information. The main requirement of this position is to provide written materials for leaflets and information sheets. Since there are frequent new developments in the strike, such sheets are indispensible in helping tenants adapt new strategies. For example, one sheet, concerned with the problem of subletting, was distributed to describe a number of options for avoiding payment of rent when a lessee had to move for one reason or another but was still bound to the old lease.

Perhaps the most important product of an information coordinator's work is a tenant union newsletter, which keeps strikers and other interested tenants tuned to the heartbeat of the union. Because this is such an important communications link, a newsletter should be established as soon as possible after the union's inception.

9. General Coordinator. The major requirement of this position is to oversee the work of other steering committee members so that all tasks are accomplished on time and without duplication. The coordinator must also allocate new tasks as they come up, especially when it is not exactly clear whose responsibility they are. In sum, he or she must be both a leader and a trouble shooter par excellence, someone who knows what is generally going on at all times and who, at the same time, can pay attention to the smallest details. Obviously, much responsibility rests with this person and careful thought should be given to his or her selection.

There was one final responsibility each steering committee member held during the initial stages of the rent strike. Each member was a group leader for approximately ten organizers of the strike itself. They each scheduled meetings for his or her group, at which time all organizers worked out any problems. Each group leader then brought any serious issues to the steering committee meetings where further discussion and consolidation of ideas took place.

There are, to be sure, other possible ways of coordinating the grass roots organizing. For example, a separate steering committee function could have been established to accomplish this task. Experience has shown, however, that the full participation of all steering committee members permits maximum dialogue on the problems of organizing. In this way, a group can maintain a sensitive feedback mechanism essential to a new organization with relatively little knowledge of how potential members are responding to its program.

The actual period of organizing tenants in Ann Arbor lasted until almost all the tenants in the "target buildings" willing to commit themselves to withholding rent had signed pledges to go on rent strike. Since these strikers were anxious to begin, the period of initial organizing amounted to a mere five weeks, after which rent was formally withheld and placed in escrow. During this time, the AATU came to know tenants rather well. The organization found that they were initially very fearful, naive about their rights, and diffident about their ability to change things. This was expected—the real problem was how to convince them to be otherwise. The following rules of thumb were developed during this first period of organizing and seemed to help solve the problem:

1. The organizer must know all the general information that is available.

2. The organizer must exude confidence when talking to the tenant and should never express doubts or give in to the tenant's unfounded fears. This rule requires practice, and is why a program of extensive training sessions for organizers is needed. The better these skills are learned prior to actual organizing, the fewer the tenant casualties.

3. At the same time that he is "tough," the organizer must also be absolutely honest and not convey certainty about any information known to be wrong. If the tenant asks a question which the organizer cannot answer, the organizer should say so and try to get the information. When he gives uncertain information he should explain the uncertainty. Nothing is more destructive to a tenant's confidence (and ultimately to a movement) than the tenant's perception of the organizer as a con artist.

4. Despite the fact that the organizer will have much work to do, he must not be perfunctory in his relationships with tenants. If he feels that a tenant might strike, he should try to spend as much time as necessary with that tenant, yet not do it at the cost of time spent with others. He should definitely plan on visiting every tenant *at least twice* prior to the strike. He should also leave his telephone number and address with each tenant. In the experience of the AATU, very few tenants signed after the first contact, but after talking with the organizer at least twice, and also among themselves, many did sign.

Phase II—The Consolidation Period

The AATU experience revealed that once the actual withholding of rent began, the character of the tenant union changed from one of rapid growth to consolidation. This happened for a number of reasons, the two most important ones being that (a) the organization was approaching an upper limit to the number of actual strikers it could enlist, and (b) the legal action taken by the landlords began, as might be expected, when tenants stopped paying rent. In future rent strikes, the neat temporal dichotomy which developed in Ann Arbor will probably not be so clear. Legal action, in the form of preliminary injunctions, conspiracy suits, and damage suits, may well come during the earlier phase.[3] Landlords are unlikely to take future movements lightly

given any success of an organization's original rent strike. With this understanding then, the second phase will now be described.

It is obvious that some administrative positions do not decrease in importance and must, therefore, be fully maintained. These include the positions of
general coordinator, press liaison, liaison to community organizations, information, publicity, legal defense, and finance. For the most part, these functions operate in the same way that they did in the earlier phase.

Legal defense assumes greater importance because of the greater amount
of work required in filing legal answers to court summonses served by landlords on tenants. In dealing with summonses, the legal defense team must not
expect that they will come in at some moderate and constant rate. What will
happen is that the landlords will serve all of the summonses at once; it is
easier for them to do so and moreover they know that it places a great strain
on the legal staff of the tenant union. In addition, since a person cannot ordinarily have a money judgment assessed against him unless the court has obtained personal jurisdiction, the landlords will try to serve the summonses to
strikers before they leave their apartments. For these reasons legal defense
must be fully prepared in advance for intensive periods of interviewing
strikers (in order to prepare their defense) and writing legal answers. This can
only be done by having large numbers of people on call at all times. In Ann
Arbor, the AATU ran into difficulties simply because it was not always capable of handling the legal onslaught, particularly at the end of the academic
year. Such a problem, however, should not be as severe in other communities.

An additional tactic that the legal defense team and a tenant union should
encourage at this point is for strikers to prepare and defend their own cases
with the guidance of lawyers and law students. This can ease the burden of
the legal staff and will help tenants to understand the law more clearly—as
well as demythologize it.

Most of the basic legal research should be done at this time. However,
there will occur all sorts of problems arising from attempts by the landlords
and the courts to speed up the litigation. This will require continuing research, often on very short notice, to prevent any precedents which could
crack the dike which holds back a flood of pending cases.

Other legal action by landlords (such as preliminary injunctions, conspiracy and damage suits), are also very likely at this time. In early spring of
1969, landlords in Ann Arbor brought a conspiracy suit against ninety-one
tenants in an attempt to put an end to the growing threat to their control of
the housing market. Although the suit could have posed a threat to the
AATU in the future, it gave the movement a boost inasmuch as it brought
to the fore important political issues such as the right to organize and public
versus private ownership of property. These issues, raised by the landlords
and not by the tenants, have been primarily responsible for rallying community support to the tenants in exposing how property owners respond to demands for decent housing (and to legal methods for achieving those demands) when profits are threatened.

The Structure of the Tenants Union

One of the basic premises of an organization of this type is that for a rent strike (or any tactic directed toward a single issue like housing) to have meaning, a long-term, permanent organization of tenants and consumers must emerge. This is asking a great deal of any movement, yet to fail to set such a goal makes a rent strike politically and practically absurd. Immediate demands may be attained, but long-term needs become irrelevant without continual pressure on the landlords. Moreover, the possibility of expansion to other issues, purely economic or purely political, can never be realized without a permanent organization. For these reasons, the AATU began, even before withholding rent, to work out plans for the formation of the tenant union itself. This plan is set out below. It should be treated with more than ordinary caution because it arises from a very specific context and may be inappropriate for other tenant organizations. The real value in the plan is that it provides an example of a representative, democratic structure responsive to constituents.

1. Organization of the base. Each building or buildings with a certain number of members (depending, of course, on the size of the tenant union) constitutes a basic unit. Each unit should be organized on the basis of proximity—members of a unit should live as close together as possible. Every unit elects by majority vote one representative from among themselves to a Council of Representatives. To ensure that he or she adequately represents the group, the following procedures are constituted:

(a) all council meetings are open to the public.
(b) each representative must give all minutes of all meetings to the base unit within a relatively short period of time.
(c) local representatives can be recalled by majority vote of the base unit at any time.

Each local representative has the further responsibility to do all of the following:

(a) keep tenant union records at the local level, collect checks during rent strikes, and distribute information about the organization to members.
(b) contact new tenants on behalf of the tenant union, i.e. serve as organizers.
(c) initiate meetings at the local level and participate in the activities of the union at the building and community level. (Other tenants are of course urged to participate at both levels also.)

2. The Council of Representatives. This second-level body has the ultimate responsibility for deciding on the structure and the future activities of the organization. The Council is divided into small groups of approximately ten individuals. The exact lines along which the division is made cannot be fixed in any simple way for the reason that no single rule or set of rules would allow for equal partitioning of groups or, in some cases, fair representation of certain interests. This problem can be partially solved by initially partitioning the Council according to landlords and membership within each local. It is clear that a number of arbitrary decisions will have to be made to achieve equal divisions.

Each of these subgroups will elect, by a majority vote, one group leader who will be a member of the steering committee. He or she will be assigned one steering committee function.

The Council of Representatives will sometimes meet as a whole or sometimes by sub-groups depending upon the specificity of the issue and the pragmatic requirements of efficiency and rapidity of actions.

3. The Steering Committee. This third-level group must be responsible for the following tasks:

(a) perform the normal administrative duties of the union.

(b) carry out policies established by the Council of Representatives.

(c) be responsible for the distribution of any proposal signed by at least a minimum number of Council members or tenant union members to the Council of Representatives.

In the earlier discussion it was pointed out that with the passing of time certain steering committee posts are likely to increase and others to diminish in importance. It is also probable that new positions will be required to meet needs that did not exist at the beginning of the strike. Two of the most important to consider are fund raising and tactical mobile defense.

The biggest source of income for a rent strike is from the tenants themselves. A fixed percent or flat sum taken from one month's rent (or from each month's rent), along with interest accumulating from the escrow fund, should provide a sizable source of income with which to meet unavoidable expenses (legal, secretarial, etc.). The AATU, however, found that these sources of income over time were inadequate. It became necessary to establish a fund-raising position.

Some of the fund-raising efforts which have taken place in Ann Arbor included a benefit dance, a bucket drive, solicitation of funds from sympathetic citizens and organizations, and a booth at a local art fair. These efforts have on the whole been rather successful. Besides raising funds, these tasks have given publicity to the AATU and have involved many people in them.

Considering these successes, it is tempting to pursue fund-raising right from the outset. However, the experience of the AATU has shown that money pressures can be handled with considerably less effort by restructuring the manner in which membership fees are collected. Since 10 percent of each striker's rent was collected for only a single month, the need for supplementary sources was greater than if fees had been collected on a regular basis. This latter process would eliminate much of the need for most *ad hoc* fund-raising activities. [4]

An issue quite distinct from fund-raising concerns harassment by landlords. Obviously, intimidation by landlords can be a harrowing experience for most tenants. Because of this, a Tactical Mobile Defense Unit (TMDU) should be established which can protect tenants and reassure them after they have been hassled by their landlord. The tasks required by the TMDU include putting locks on doors at the tenant's request, getting such utilities as water and gas turned back on, and physically preventing landlords from forcibly entering the apartment of a striker, a task to be handled with sense and sensitivity. The steering committee member in charge of the TMDU keeps people on duty day and night and makes certain that these people know how to deal with each kind of intimidation.

During the course of the rent strike in Ann Arbor, harassment became a common occurrence, especially among the smaller, less sophisticated landlords. In some cases, the landlord smashed down doors and destroyed furniture (damaging his own property), assaulted tenants, and damaged and dragged out into the street property belonging to the tenant. The TMDU helped defend the tenant in every case, recovering the tenant's belongings when they were removed and expelling the landlord from the apartment. The defense unit became an important source of security for strikers.

Some Final Remarks

There remain three brief points to discuss. The first is an imperative and concerns the practical issues relating to mass organization. The second and third are observations of the effects of the TU-RS on its participants.

The Mechanics of Organizing

Given the correct preconditions, there are two simple pragmatic axioms for organizing within a social movement: work hard and work efficiently. Working hard means that many individuals must commit themselves to an intensive effort over a long period of time. Without a large source of energy, no situation, however ripe in other ways, can be developed into a radical movement. The AATU represents thousands of hours of labor, yet each participant knows that each hour spent was necessary for the organization's success.

Working efficiently means intelligently tapping the energy source to accomplish the most tasks with the least duplication or waste of effort. The group must plan ahead, be quickly responsive to change, delegate authority as much as possible, and pay careful attention to details. There must be concern with the seemingly banal problems in an office, such as the filing of legal answers or keeping orderly financial books.

These rather obvious points are emphasized because too often they are not realized in modern social movements and grass roots organizations. Radical leadership has continually eschewed these simple practices in favor of rhetoric and charisma. But the relatively brief life of these contemporary organizations underscores that there can be no substitute for an intense, creative, and long-term commitment.

Changes in Political Efficacy

As noted earlier, the AATU discovered in the process of organizing tenants to strike that tenants initially felt helpless about their situation. This sense of impotence was present everywhere. The strike, however, had a very positive effect on the tenants. They outgrew their passivity and began to participate actively in the AATU activities as well as to take a more militant stand on other issues. But how did the AATU get participants to commit themselves in the first place?

It was decided that by emphasizing the nitty-gritty questions which concern the tenant ("Will I be thrown out?" or "What can they do to me if I don't pay rent?") and minimizing rhetoric, the tenant's fears would be reduced; the organizer began to appear as someone with whom the tenant had a common problem. The success with this approach led the AATU to conclude that when the individuals being organized do not feel that they can exert very much control over their social environment, one must first deal with their feeling of helplessness before raising more abstract political issues. This can be done only by organizing around the real needs of the people, and initially sticking to the more material issues. Harangues will simply not be understood and will only alienate the tenant from the organization.

Political Education

While organizing must be based on the material needs of the people being organized, it does not mean that they will fail to learn political lessons. Once they are involved in the movement, the political basis of their oppression can be easily demonstrated. In Ann Arbor, the disqualification of judges, the conspiracy suit against the AATU, the physical harassment of tenants by landlords, the exposure of an interlocking economic relationship between landlords, judges, and bank officials provided important lessons on the nature of capitalism. These lessons and others meant something to tenants. This was something different than the diatribes often directed at them by self-styled community leaders. Any tenant group should be able to go beyond the purely economic goals of the organization in the future, because the tenants will understand that other more abstract political issues are directly related to their own housing problems.

The above observations grew out of an incomplete experience. There is more to be learned and there are more obstacles to overcome before the AATU is fully established as a functioning political and economic force in the community. But many of the lessons learned in this setting were painfully and expensively bought; they need not be relearned again at such cost. The AATU experience will have been worth while, if only to have made less arduous the birth of other tenant unions.

1. The AATU picked a figure which was both arbitrary and unnecessarily inflated. Any group which chooses to set a minimum figure should think it through carefully. Otherwise, failure to attain the goal could give the unfortunate impression of initial failure.

2. In many states the law so overwhelmingly favors the landlords that legal delays are impossible. In these situations, extra-legal tactics may be the only way to maintain occupation of the apartments.

3. For further elucidation of these and other Legal points, see Thomas Jennings, Chapter 3 herein.

4. See Stephen Burghardt's "Building a Permanent Organization" for further discussion on the problem of a small organization's fiscal base.

CHAPTER 10

Organizing in Public Housing

National Tenants Organization

This paper is designed to clarify the significant differences between public and private housing organizing. The process of organizing is the same, the variations occur in the structure of the public housing sector itself.

There are four general differences in organizing tenants in public housing. First, there are many tenants for just one landlord—the local housing authority. The potential strength of a mass movement of tenants is therefore greater, although other factors to be discussed below should not lead one to believe that the work is easier.

Secondly, political pressure for change aimed at HUD and the local housing authority is often more effective than such pressure against private landlords, for the simple reason that public officials are at least in theory accountable to the public. Because of such pressure, HUD and local authorities have recognized to some degree the validity of tenants rights and tenant involvement in running projects. The problem in public housing is to get such concepts applied in practice. In private housing, generally there is still as much work to be done on concepts as on practice.

Thirdly, public housing, which in theory exists to help the poor, is distinct from private housing where the landlord clearly and by definition exists for his own profit. The private housing landlord makes a less formidable enemy. No one, not even the landlord himself, can argue that his reason for existence is to help the tenants. Thus it is much easier to organize tenants against a target that openly exists for its own benefit, not for theirs. Public housing administrators who insist that their purpose is to help the tenants are not only a more elusive target, but sometimes they can also be a more stubborn one. Often they are so self-righteously convinced that their way is best for the tenants that they are harder to change than a private landlord who is often willing to change when he starts losing money.

Finally, many housing administrators are so convinced that they are right that they will sometimes try to win tenant support for their views by organizing rival, management-oriented tenant groups. This rivalry can create tremendous problems for a genuine tenant group which has grown out of real tenant grievances, not the proddings of management. (The above charge of self-righteousness and of organizing rival groups also applies to officials of non-profit housing organizations.)

The main organizing problem unique to public housing concerns the situation outlined above of housing officials not being a clear organizing target. For example, there are many more black administrators and managers in public housing than in private housing. Some of them are shrewd politicians who know how to cool off angry tenants without really meeting their demands. This can make the tenant union's job more difficult. To organize and arouse tenants to action, there is nothing better than an irate individual on the other side who over-reacts and makes extreme, offensive statements. The housing authority in Washington, D.C. once had a black official who had donuts and coffee ready for the tenants when they stormed into his office. By the time the snack was over, the tenants often had lost their appetite for satisfying their demands.

The Washington housing authority also hired a full-time black organizer to work with tenants in housing projects where militant tenant groups were active. The organizer had access to recreation equipment for children and authority facilities generally. Most important, he had the status and legitimacy that many tenants still associate with the housing authority, particularly more middle class tenants who may be offended by the militant rhetoric of the altruist tenant group.

Management-oriented tenant groups have existed for years in many cities. Though always mild and generally inactive, they still have the legitimacy of seniority. The old divide-and-conquer rule can be very damaging: public officials are quick to use the existence of rival groups as the excuse for inaction; different groups can cause embarrassment in the press too.

Because such rivalries and divisions can be so harmful, militant tenants starting a new organization should make a special effort—before feelings harden and rivalries are established—to involve leaders of the old tenant association who still live in the project. Even though the old tenant group may seem weak, tenants and organizers should keep in mind that housing authorities have a way of bringing them back to life. When this happens, the chances for a united tenant movement are destroyed or seriously damaged. One possibility is to offer leaders of the old group positions of leadership in the new group, or to use the old group's constitution as the model for drawing up a new one.

All this can be carried too far. Tenants and organizers will have to decide how much they want to involve more conservative tenants in their group. There is surely a risk of weakening it to the point of being ineffective either by too much involvement of conservative tenants or by excessive division among rival tenant groups. The best approach is to talk at length to the more conservative, middle class tenants at the beginning and try to win them over. The experience of working with a tenant organization almost always makes people more militant as they go along. Tenants who appear quite moderate at first may not remain so after a few frustrating experiences with the housing authority and other public agencies.

Tenants cannot organize around code enforcement efforts in public housing as they can in private housing; city housing codes are not legally enforceable against public housing authorities because they are considered agencies of the federal government. Tenant groups in Washington, San Francisco, and Oakland have brought legal suits to challenge the failure to enforce local housing codes against housing authorities. Some suits have been settled when the authority agreed to repair the properties.

In Washington and perhaps elsewhere, the city building department has inspected public housing projects, delivered code violation notices to the housing authority, and then stopped short of going to court to enforce the citations. Tenant groups might try to get copies of such reports of code violations, which they could at least use to embarass the housing authority, and to prove to the public and the press their charges that housing conditions are bad in the projects. Even if the legality of nonenforcement is upheld by the courts, presumably there is nothing to prevent the city building department from simply making inspections when tenants ask for them. One would think that even the housing authority would like to know for its own purposes whether its buildings contain code violations.

The discussion of rent strike strategies for private housing generally applies also to public housing, the main differences being in the kinds of demands made and the ability in public housing to appeal to HUD prior to and during the rent strike.

Demands

Public housing tenants have often undercut themselves in rent strike situations by demanding too little. Usually such demands have centered around specific grievances, such as getting window guards, rather than around the larger issue of whether residents should control the housing. In recent years, as tenant groups have begun to communicate more with one another, demands which bring about more dramatic changes in rents, conditions of the property, and the status of the tenant have been common. Among the frequently used demands are the following:

1. That tenants have a majority on the Board of Commissioners who set policy for the Local Housing Authority. Tenants in the East Park Manor Tenants Council in Muskegon Heights, Michigan, demanded this (see Chapter 2 herein). After their long rent strike they now select three of the five members of their Board of Commissioners.

2. Establishment of a Tenant Affairs Board. Such a Board, composed entirely of tenants and patterned after the one in Detroit, would be larger than the Board of Commissioners, thus allowing tenants from each housing project to participate, and would have the power to veto actions of the Board of Commissioners.

3. A new Director for the Housing Authority. This demand was granted by

the Mayor of St. Louis when it became apparent that the rent striking tenants there could not and would not relate to the previous Director.

4. A training program so that tenants may move into the jobs now occupied by managers who do not live in public housing.

5. Free office space and telephones, a demand granted by the Philadelphia Housing Authority to the Residents Advisory Board there after they held up millions of dollars of modernization funds by complaining to HUD.

6. Dues checkoff. A precedent of sorts exists in San Antonio where the Housing Authority grants its tenant councils fifty cents per year for each tenant in that council's housing project. Why not make it more?

7. Fairer methods of determining a tenant's income for the purpose of setting rents.

8. Lower rents. No comments needed.

Appeals to HUD

Public housing tenants have long complained about arbitrary and unfair admission, eviction, and general management policies of housing authorities. However, in February, 1971, HUD announced the successful arbitration of both a model lease and grievance procedures for all tenants living in public housing. The National Tenants Organization, which was active throughout these negotiations, felt that both the lease and procedures were "real victories" for tenants, as long as they were enforced.

The most crucial sections of the lease demanded that the management show cause on a tenant's violation of the housing contract and that separate legal processes be used to collect monetary claims other than rents. In the past, local housing administrators had the leverage to evict arbitrarily tenants. By forcing such eviction proceedings and other monetary issues to be settled outside the offices of the housing administrators, the leverage of tenants has increased substantially.

The grievance procedures established are of great importance for the public housing tenant. In the past, there was little that the tenant could do if he or she had grievances, for the hearing (if there was one) was held by those who were being complained about—the public housing officials. This has been rectified by the establishment of an outside arbitrating panel for all grievances. Tenants have also been guaranteed the right to all information concerning the case before the trial, and standard grievance proceedings common to labor are in practice.

Public tenants cannot gloat over such victories, however. As mentioned earlier in the paper, many local public housing officials firmly believe they are right in their decisions, and this new power for tenants has bothered many of them. The outcome of their dislike for increased tenant power was the federal suit filed in July of 1971 in Omaha, Nebraska on behalf of ten housing authorities. In short, their argument is that the increase in tenant equity (as manifested in the model lease and grievance procedures) will lead them into bankruptcy. There appears no foundation for this fear. As the same documents on which the model lease and grievance procedures are written (Renewal and Housing Management document numbers 7465.8 and 7465.9), it states that the financial responsibility for such added expenses will come from the federal government through HUD. That these local officials choose to ignore these directives and instead attempt to undermine these steps toward greater equity, only reinforces the notion that even greater tenant control in public housing is a necessity.

Finally, the regulations for the modernization program within the HUD manual (section 1.9 of the Management Manual) call for involvement of the tenants "in the plans and programs for the modernization of the project, changes in management policies and practices, and expanded services and facilities." The regulations emphasize that modernization of housing projects means not only improving physical conditions but also changing management policies, such as involving tenants in the modernization program as quoted above.

The language is quite general and broad, but it was successfully used as the basis for an appeal to HUD by Philadelphia tenant groups which resulted in the wide-ranging written agreement with the authority discussed below. The tenants filed an administrative complaint with the Secretary of HUD asking him to hold up a HUD grant for the Philadelphia authority's modernization program because the authority had not involved the tenants in the planning of the program, as required by HUD regulations. Under this threat of not getting its modernization funds, the Philadelphia authority negotiated an agreement with the tenant councils providing not only for tenant involvement in the program, but for many other tenant demands as well.

This tactic of appealing to HUD was spectacularly successful here because the local authority was threatened with the loss of its modernization grant. It might well work in other cases too, particularly where a HUD grant is involved. Even if the appeal fails it provides the basis for a later court suit, since courts generally require plaintiffs to exhaust their administrative remedies before going to court. As in other actions, tenants themselves should be involved in the appeal to HUD as much as possible; that means traveling to the HUD regional office or to Washington, which is often not possible. If it is not possible, tenants should insist upon a full report from the lawyer and tenant leaders who do make the appeal to HUD.

Rent Strikes

Both in private and in public housing rent strikes, it is very important that the tenant organization be strong enough to withstand the pressures of a rent strike before beginning one. Good legal help and political support are important in public housing. Political pressure is more important in public housing than private because it is generally more effective: public officials are naturally more susceptible to political pressure than private landlords. Such pressure should be applied through meetings, picketing, sit-ins, and political support contacts both before and during a rent strike (and afterwards if neccessary). It should be applied not only in the form of appeals to HUD, as discussed above, but also at the local level. The tenants' group should pressure local housing officials and city government officials to take action. Local officials can change management policies, put tenants on the housing authority commission, and even raise money to reduce rents, as they tried to do in St. Louis. A permanent solution to the problem to high rents will have to be a national solution set by Congress and HUD. Several housing authorities appear to be on the verge of bankruptcy; only much larger subsidies approved at the national level will save them and prevent higher rents.

The same problems of continuing a rent strike exist in public as in private housing. If anything, the problems of rivalries between tenants and tenant groups are greater in organizing and continuing a public housing rent strike. This is true partly because as described above, housing authorities can foster divisions among tenants. It is true also because, although tenants have a common landlord to unite them, they live in different parts of the city and in different housing projects which have somewhat different problems. Rivalries can crop up between tenant groups in different projects, as well as among tenants in one project. Again, from the beginning tenants should prevent such rivalries from getting established, because they are so destructive and time-consuming. Many public housing projects have groups of welfare mothers organized into local chapters of the National Welfare Rights Organization. Tenant groups should make every effort to work together with such welfare groups on their common problems. The basic activities of the tenant organization, however, will generally follow those discussed earlier in private housing.

Part IV

STRATEGIES AND TACTICS

Introduction

The problems of strategy development, while crucial for every community group, are often magnified for the newly-developing organization. Like children, these new groups are high in energy, low in expertise, more often involved in the excitement of moving than in arriving anywhere. Like children, they sometimes neglect to plan for the future. This is more than unfortunate, for the crucial difference between the young child and the tottering community organization is that the former's elders are concerned with its welfare and growth; the latter's are not. Organizations develop out of some perceived or real need in a community; their presence implies that established groups are not meeting it. Birth signals competition, not nurturance, and the new organization desiring to be effective in the future must quickly move on from the pleasure in being alive to consider the work which lies ahead.

The first strategic distinction an organization must make is over means and ends. That distinction has at least two underlying dimensions. The first concerns organizational issues related to goal attainment. It is most often discussed in terms of task goals and process goals. Task goals relate to the end results desired by a group; individual needs are secondary. Process goals are often developed to maintain group solidarity and organizational efficiency. An example here of a task goal would be tenant management of buildings; a process goal might be a rent strike designed to attract discontented yet atomized tenants to a tenant union.

The second, less frequently discussed dimension of the means-ends debate is more subtle than goal distinctions. It concerns the scope of membership participation in and the style of strategies used by an organization to achieve either its task or process goals. Machiavelli eliminated the need for this kind of discussion by suggesting that only the ends mattered; Alinsky has pointed out that to the victors belong not only the spoils but the right to determine if one's means have been moral or not. Such analyses make strategies rather easy to implement. Unfortunately, "Do It!" has an existential quality to it that, however transiently attractive, is of little worth for those with long-term effectiveness in mind. In short, on how much principle will a strategy lie? And how democratically will that strategy be developed and run?

The former question revolves around both individual situations and the general on-going activities of an organization. It demands consideration of the degrees of humaneness, honesty, and justice the group will try to employ in whatever it does—as well as when such principles can or should be compromised. It is perhaps the most agonizing set of questions an organization will face. Sometimes the questions appear too trite and hackneyed for much deliberation. Often they involve procedures only amorphously recognized as part of an organization's overall strategy—such as the degree of militancy used at city hall or the manner in which office phones are answered—and are easily lost in the excitement of a rent strike or during the tiresome negotiations with a landlord. What each organization must decide is how much of its change effort is weakened by such losses.

Problems involving the scope of membership participation in strategy development are no less difficult to resolve. The ideal is that everyone takes part; reality has shown that mass participation often dissolves into chaos. Most American trade unions resolved the problem of democratic participation versus organizational efficiency by centralizing decision-making within the leadership cadre. Trade union centralism ensured the development of an efficient organization capable of securing monetary (and much needed) reforms for its membership. At the same time, union leaders have grown distant from the membership and, as even *Time* and *Fortune* magazines have pointed out, rank and file alienation from their work place has remained at best unchanged. To some, the increased alienation was too large a price for efficiency and a few more inflated dollars in the pocket; to most, it was not. Whatever, as the above example suggests, the tension in maintaining both strategic effectiveness and organizational efficiency will remain a significant factor in any community organization's strategy formation.

These issues concerning moral and democratic principles are crucial for those groups dedicated to long-term social change. They raise the very real possibility for those organizations that goal achievement, if accomplished in a manner no different from that used by organizations which impede social progress, may indeed by very hollow. For example, many members of the tenants rights movement have long dreamed of replacing landlords with tenant management. However, if that tenant management then proceeds to exploit tenants through arbitrary behavior and intimidation, only the hands of power, not its shape, have changed. Such victories become meaningless.

Thus, before beginning activity, an organization should consider its task goals, its process goals, and the political and moral values by which it will attempt to achieve them. This, of course, is often difficult to do, especially for groups which spontaneously form around a particular issue and then develop into on-going organizations. No one would suggest that groups forming so quickly should first pause and look over this long list of organizational, political, and philosophical musings. To do so would undermine the energy which helped create the group in the first place.

However, an organization usually goes through some event at some early point in time which signifies its desire for permanence in the community— the election of yearly officers, the drawing up of a constitution, or even the renting of a store front office. This period, while obviously filled with more salient issues, can also allow a group the opportunity to consider not only what goals it hopes to accomplish, but the manner and spirit in which it hopes to accomplish them. It is an opportunity that once lost rarely can be regained.

There is no easy method to strategy formation. There are too many contextual factors surrounding an organization's activity—antagonisms from other groups or institutions, membership expectations for activity, the responsibilities for keeping up with the office work—to allow it to fully develop all the strategies, tactics, and methods of operation that it should. However, if an organization first decides purposefully what its long term goals are, then develops strategies to fit both future aims and present realities, there is little reason why the group should wind itself into irrelevance. All short-term goals—even those with "task" functions—would be seen as helping the organization develop its capability to achieve its final ends. For example, squat-ins become more than just a means to secure housing for its participants; it is also a dramatic tactic used to education other people to the seriousness of the housing problem and to the role tenant groups must play in ending that problem. (It also keeps the tenant union in the public's eye.)

Adapting a developmental approach to all of one's activities calls for a great deal of patience, a limited commodity in those living in degraded and unsafe housing. Such ideal approaches are found more frequently by far on the well-ordered pages of books than in the turbulence of one's community. They are mentioned here more as a typology for tenant groups to orient towards than as an easily operationalized model of strategy formation.

The articles in this section are presented developmentally, starting with the immediately specific tactics of importance to a new tenant group and proceeding to those strategies only useable by well-developed tenant unions. The first part concerns "short-term" strategies that concentrate on the education of the community, the involvement of membership in the organization's activities, and the formation of the initial rent strike group. Tony Henry and Ted Parrish, in two separate articles, present strategic analyses of the tenants' rights movement two most glamorous tactics, the rent strike and the squat-ins. Nancy Romer Burghardt, in an analytical review of the organizational, political, and education functions of various tactics, presents other creative tactics open to both tenant unions and other grass roots organizations.

The second section contains a group of articles dealing with longer range strategies. Stephen Burghardt, in looking at the latent dysfunctions of overly large rent strikes, goes on to discuss some of the financial responsibilities of small yet permanent organizations. Myron Moskovitz and the Earl Warren Legal Institute staff give a thorough review of potential collective bargaining agreements which tenant unions must consider before taking over or managing buildings. The then go on to discuss economic alternatives for the union as well. Finally, Thomas Anton and Roger Lind present a policy paper on potential funding for more public housing which is highly adaptable for tenant groups to consider in their own advocacy for more and better housing. It serves as an example of advocacy planning open for tenants to develop in other areas as well.

CHAPTER 11

Rent Strikes

National Tenants' Organization

Rent strikes are the ultimate weapon tenants have to force acceptance of their demands. In the past few years, as the tenant movement has grown, they have been used more frequently and more effectively than ever. This chapter considers the best strategies for running a rent strike. It covers five topics: preparing for rent strike, evictions, rent money, pressuring mortgagees, and ending the rent strike.

Preparing for Rent Strikes

Rent strikes usually lead to legal suits, attempts to evict tenants, and other strains on the tenants and the tenant organization; it is important that the tenant organization be strong enough to stand up under such pressures. Tenant leaders and organizers should determine whether there is enough interest among tenants in taking collective action. If interest is lacking, the group should concentrate on meeting the individual tenant's needs. Tenants' collective action should not be pushed into before they are ready. Those who see the need for collective action should of course express that opinion, which may persuade others. But the pressure to undertake a rent strike should not be so strong that tenants are pushed into it before they are really committed to it.

Some tenant groups, in order to gauge their support, have had tenants sign statements that they are willing to withhold rent if a certain number of others agree to do the same. In Muskegon Heights, Michigan, tenants even committed themselves to going to jail before releasing their rent money if that became necessary. (See Chapter 2 herein.) This method has the advantage of giving the leaders a clear idea of the amount of solid support they have before they begin. It also reassures the participating tenants that they will not be deserted by their friends when the going gets rough, a prime fear among tenants. It has the disadvantage of reducing the number of rent strike participants at the start. Rallies and meetings have been used to get verbal commitments from tenants, while giving the tenants a more secure feeling of mass action.

In addition to having a strong tenant organization, other preliminary steps to a rent strike can be taken. A code enforcement effort is a good beginning. If, however, there is no interest in this tactic, pressure on the landlord can be applied through meetings, picketing, bad publicity, and other political pressure. These preliminary steps should not be dragged out too long if the tenants are willing to withhold their rent and the landlord has not met their demands. The rent strike should then begin. The value of the preliminary political pressure is that it helps build up and test the strength of the tenant group, and it may give the tenants a more favorable position in the press by presenting the landlord opportunities to settle before a strike.

The strategy to develop political support for the tenant group is similar to what one would do during a campaign for better code enforcement. Law students or college students working with the tenants, or the tenants themselves, may want to check real estate tax records to find out the landlord's other properties and businesses for a possible link with his other tenants or business employees (especially if they are already organized in a sympathetic union).

More detailed research about the landlord can also show who the real owner or owners are, who the mortgagee is, and other information about how vulnerable the landlord may be economically and politically. If there is a particularly stubborn management company running the property, the tenants should investigate further to discover, for example, who its other tenants and property owners are.

Good legal help is important and should be arranged before the rent strike starts. It is important to get an attorney who not only knows the law, but also is politically aware and sympathetic to the tenants' view of their struggle. This means an attorney who is not afraid of the idea of rent strikes (which are not strictly legal in most cities), the threat of evictions, or the politics of confrontation. A lawyer seems to have special status in our society, and tenants tend to give a lawyer's viewpoint a lot of weight. Thus, a lawyer can have great influence over a tenant group by what he says, the way he says it, and what he reveals about his own political or tactical views. A good lawyer, sympathetic to a militant tenant group, can help inspire and bolster the morale of the tenants; a bad one, acting or sounding overcautious, can divide a militant tenant group and seriously damage its effectiveness.

In short, the tenants should be very careful about which lawyer they get; tenant leaders and organizers should try to sound out the lawyer before he takes the case. Often tenant groups will have to choose a Neighborhood Legal Services or Legal Aid Society lawyer. There may be a choice among different lawyers working in one office of such agencies, and tenants should try to find out who the best lawyer is for them, both in terms of legal ability and in terms of temperament and political persuasion.

Evictions

Eviction is the landlord's major weapon in fighting tenants. There are some court decisions and state laws which provide tenants some protection against eviction, but the threat of eviction is still a serious one for tenant groups generally. There are two kinds of defenses against evictions: one political and the other legal. Both are usually used, in varying degrees and in different ways; the tenants may have to choose which one should take priority.

The political defense against evictions is patterned after the civil rights movement's experience in confrontation politics. Part of the political defense includes rounding up support for the tenants from liberal-moderate elements like labor, church, civic, and political organizations which may have some influence with the established power structure. But that kind of support is not always easy to get, and it may not be enough to prevent evictions and have tenant demands met.

More important is the strategy of confrontation politics which uses dramatic tenant issues such as evictions to build up community tension and thus force the government into direct conflict as it attempts to defuse the situation. It is almost never clear in advance just what government officials will do in such a confrontation. One factor affecting their decisions will be the number of people involved, large numbers being essential for the tenant union's success. Another will surely be the degree to which meeting tenant demands helps them politically. Thus it may be harder to win a victory through confrontation in a generally conservative city, or one with a conservative administration, where politicians have little to gain from meeting tenant demands. This does not mean that confrontation tactics are always bad in such situations. Conservative opponents can also help solidify the tenant group. In addition to the politics of city officials, consider their personalities. There may be some indications in their past record as to how they will react to a confrontation.

The most successful example of confrontation tactics used by tenants was in the small town of Muskegon Heights, Michigan, where a public housing tenants union decided not to fight their lower court eviction orders in court and pledged to go to jail if the city tried to evict. As community tension mounted with the prospect of 89 families being jailed, the Mayor settled the strike with a last minute agreement to the tenant demands, the main one being the removal of three of the five housing authority commissioners and selection of their replacements by the tenants union. The decision not to fight the eviction cases but to use political confrontation instead was probably the main factor in the tenant union victory; there were other important factors, as well, such as the town's 52 percent black population, the Mayor's sympathetic approach to the problem, the housing authority's overreaction which solidified the tenants, and the mediation of the Michigan Civil Rights Commission.

The legal defense against evictions varies greatly in different cities, depending upon state and local laws and court decisions. Where there is a danger of eviction, the usual legal tactic is to delay as long as possible to give the tenants time to work out a political solution with the landlord and the city. The danger in the legal defense is that it may defuse the situation and fail to dramatize the issues enough for either the tenants or the city administration to be aroused to action. Although the legal defense is essential as a first step to prevent evictions and provide the tenants much-needed time to get better organized, it should usually be subordinated to the political defense when the tenants seek major changes. The Muskegon tenant union clearly chose to subordinate legal action in deciding not to appeal the lower court's eviction orders. Whatever legal defense is undertaken, it is very important to involve tenants as much as possible. Too often the "let the lawyers do it" attitude has drained the vitality of tenant groups, just at the time when they need the most active support of members.

About fifteen state rent strike laws of various kinds provide some protection against the retaliatory eviction of rent-striking tenants. In many cases, however, such laws are more trouble than they're worth because of complicated court escrow arrangements, other legal procedures, and extensive delays. Such laws make it harder for tenants to take the initiative and to control their own fight, which weakens the spirit of the tenant union. In some cases the building department must first find code violations to permit a rent strike, and in others the court, not the tenants, controls the escrow account of rent money.

In addition to these laws which allow for some collective tenant action, three states—New York, Illinois, and Michigan—provide for welfare agencies withholding rent when housing code violations exist. And five western states—California, South Dakota, Montana, North Dakota, and Oklahoma—have repair and deduct statutes under which tenants can have repairs made and deduct the cost from their rent, up to a limited amount.

In states without rent strike laws, where rent strikes may be technically "illegal", there are still ways of preventing evictions. In some areas, a few favorable court decisions can have the effect of a rent strike law, or an even better situation, since most actual laws are complicated, time-consuming to operate, and thus self-defeating to the development of a strong tenant organization. In Washington, D.C., for example, lawyers for tenants have won two or three key court decisions which now protect against evictions in almost every situation. The Washington strategy has been to combine a broad decision prohibiting retaliatory evictions (*Edwards v. Habib*) with another decision declaring that code violations at the time of the rental make a lease invalid (*Brown v. Southall Realty Co.*). These two decisions are similar to some state laws, except that they are not as definite and specific in saying what is permitted, and therefore allow tenant groups more freedom of action than would state laws.

In the absence of state rent strike laws and favorable court decisions, it is still possible to prevent evictions through a combination of political and legal defenses that provide delays long enough to allow alternate settlements of the conflict. Legally, eviction orders can be delayed by continuances, appeals, and demands for jury trials. Politically, the landlord can be pressured and then negotiated with on the condition that a moratorium on evictions be declared. Direct action is another delaying tactic that has been used effectively in Chicago. Evicted tenants have been moved back in by the tenant group after the police have left. The landlord was then forced to file a civil suit for trespass, which was many months coming to trial because of the backlog of cases, by which time the landlord had dropped the case. In another Chicago case, the tenants met the sheriff's bailiffs and physically prevented them from evicting, which meant re-scheduling the eviction and thus more delay.

Rent Money

The issue of what to do about rent money during a strike is a very important one. Whether to collect rent money and put it in escrow or to allow tenants to keep it is the first decision to be made. Obviously, tenants need the money themselves for other things and would rather not pay rent, which is usually a large percent of income. Also, the fact that some rent-striking tenants do pay their rent to an escrow account while others do not can lead to serious divisions within the tenant organization. If the tenant organization decides to collect rent money and put it in escrow, the question then is how to deal with tenants who don't pay rent and refuse to put their rent money in escrow. Should such tenants not be considered part of the organization? Should they be defended by the tenant's group lawyer? Should the landlord be told who they are if he asks?

If there is a general widespread agreement among the tenants that the rents should be paid to an escrow account, then the divisions created by a decision to collect rent may not be great. But if it looks as though a decision to pay rents to an escrow account would seriously divide the tenant organization, then the best solution may be for the group to establish a fair rent schedule, or what the tenants would charge if they owned the building. If the tenants can agree on such a schedule—and if they make allowances for tenants who can't afford to pay—then collecting rent money might actually strengthen the tenant organizaton rather than divide it. Tenants who don't pay the agreed upon rent because they are not committed to the group would not be considered part of the group and would not get such benefits as legal assistance. It may be a good idea, however, not to give the landlord the names of such tenants, leaving them the chance to join the strike later (unless they are so destructive to the group effort that the group wants them evicted).

In spite of the trouble involved in collecting rent money, there are some important advantages to an escrow fund. First, it provides an important bargaining tool in negotiating with the landlord; the landlord will be more likely to agree to tenant demands if agreement means some of the collected rent money can be used for repairs. Also, judges look much more favorably on the tenants' cause if they have been collecting rent money while on rent strike. Increased support from the public and the press may be gained if rents are collected in escrow. After the strike is settled, a portion of the money may be used for repairs, recreation facilities, hiring an organizer, or whatever else the tenants want to do with it.

An escrow fund also offers some advantages in developing a strong on-going organization. It provides the least fallible way of knowing how many people are withholding rent. More than one rent strike leader has learned in a crisis that not all of the people who told him they were rent striking were doing so. (In one instance, a leader thought she had her whole building on rent strike, only to learn that she was the only one.) Collecting rent money forces the leaders of the strike to get out and relate to people on a door-to-door basis and justify the strike each month. This keeps people informed and maintains the momentum of the strike. Otherwise, there is a natural tendency to avoid the hard work involved in such communication. The holding of the rent money also makes most tenants demand that the leadership of the strike remain responsive to them. If you have their money, they will let you know if they don't know about or don't appreciate what you are doing. Without such feedback the leaders may never learn of tenants' dissatisfaction with leadership decisions.

Where to keep the collected escrow money is another important issue. To be able to best use the money as a bargaining tool, the tenants should have as much direct control over it as possible. In Philadelphia, under the state law, the tenant organization itself can be the escrow agent that keeps the rent money. In other areas, both with and without rent strike laws, the courts tend to be (or to want to be) the escrow agent and have control over deciding who gets the money when the strike is settled. This puts the tenants in a weaker bargaining position.

Several methods are used for keeping withheld money. Some groups have the tenants write out money orders to the organization and then deposit the money in a bank. The tenant then has both his money order stub and his receipt from the tenant organization to show the amount he has placed in escrow. Other groups have the tenant write the money orders to themselves and place them all in one safe. This method eliminates possible allegations that tenants' monies have been lost or misused, since no one can use the money order but the striking tenant. It also eliminates the possibility of a bank account being attached by the courts.

To reduce the likelihood of the landlord getting the funds being kept in an organizational bank account, at least three techniques have been used. One is to use an out-of-state bank, which at least makes it more difficult to get to the money. Striking tenants in Ann Arbor, Michigan, even used a foreign bank, depositing their money in nearby Canada. Another method is to open an individual account for each person withholding rent that only he can draw on. In this system the bank statements should be mailed to the organization so that it can verify how much money is in each account, if a checking account is used. If a savings account is used, the bank books should be reviewed regularly. By using this method, the landlord is forced to sue each tenant individually, a time-consuming and costly process. A variation on this approach is to require two signatures to withdraw any funds, one being the signature of the tenant and the other the signature of a representative of the organization. This guards against the possibility of a person withdrawing from the strike without the knowledge of the organization, while it protects the tenant against misuse of his funds and the organization from a single, mass suit.

The charge that rent strike funds are being misappropriated or lost will almost inevitably be made by either worried friends or malicious enemies. For this reason it is absolutely necessary that money be properly collected and handled, leaving no opening for criticism. Organizers and lawyers working with tenant groups should intervene vigorously on this point since many new leaders cannot forsee the problems which lie ahead and may be willing to handle money informally. Under no circumstances should cash or checks written to individuals ever be accepted for an escrow fund. The amount given is always open to challenge, regardless of receipts. Money orders and cashiers' checks are not as subject to question since the originals can always be traced or, in the case of money orders, the tenant has a stub.

Pressuring Mortgagees

The mortgagee who financed the housing project for the landlord can play an important, although usually unseen, role in a rent strike. Mortgagees are banks, mortgage companies, life insurance companies, or savings and loan associations whose loans on low-income housing are usually insured by a federal agency (either the Federal Housing Administration [FHA] or the Federal Savings and Loan Insurance Corporation [FSLIC]).

Mortgagees who are closely tied to the landlord, as they often are with low-income housing, sometimes will suspend payments on the mortgage which the landlord owes during a tenant rent strike. Thus, just as the tenants are trying to put as much economic pressure on the landlord as possible, the mortgagee can remove much of the pressure simply by suspending mortgage payments. If this happens, tenants and their supporters should talk to, picket, and otherwise pressure the mortgagee not to suspend payments owed by the landlord. Mortgagees should, if possible, be shown that it is in their own economic interest to pressure the landlord to meet tenant demands, because poor maintenance and continued landlord-tenant fighting can only be bad for their investment. The tenants must convince the mortgagee that they will continue to fight if their demands are not met.

If the mortgagee is somewhat sympathetic to the tenants' approach, the tenants could go one step further and urge the mortgagee to negotiate directly with the tenants over their demands. This will put more pressure on the landlord; and if the mortgagee decides to foreclose, the tenants may be able to get the mortgagee to refinance the mortgage to the tenant organization as the owner.

There has been one example of such direct negotiation between tenants and mortgagee. In September, 1967, FSLIC signed an agreement with the tenants association of Coronet Village in Harvey, Illinois, outside of Chicago. The agreement provided for substantial repairs and rehabilitation of the property, guarantee of certain tenant rights, and the establishment of a grievance procedure for future disputes between the tenants and FSLIC which had foreclosed on the landlord and taken over ownership. The agreement did not provide for tenant ownership or direct control, but it did result in much improved housing conditions—an important first step.

Ending the Rent Strike

Unless the tenant group is well organized, there can be problems of continuing a rent strike over a long period of time. A tenant group, like any kind of group, needs projects for its members to get involved in, and it needs to make some progress in its work to keep its members' spirits up. Rent strikes can be and often are a long, slow process with little sign of progress at times. If this happens, the tenant organization should try to take on some other projects in which it can involve tenants, such as work on a recreation area, action for better police protection, or other tenant grievances.

In any tenant organizations, tenants should be involved in the group's activities as much as possible, and the group's leadership should be as broad as possible. This is especially true in a long rent strike. If a few tenant leaders have done most of the group's work, they may simply (and understandably) get tired of the extra burden after a while and decide to move away, or some of them may get evicted. Without broad group leadership, the loss of one or two tenant leaders can ruin the whole tenant effort.

Rent money can also be a factor. If tenants have not paid rent money into an escrow account, but instead have kept it, they may be more likely to move away if there seems to be little hope for rent strike progress. Not having paid out rent money, they can more easily afford to move. One way to alleviate this problem is to ask those tenants withholding rent to agree at the start of a strike to contribute one-fourth of the rent to the organization if they move.

In deciding whether and when to settle with the landlord through negotiation of an agreement, the tenants should consider several things. First, of course, is what the tenants can and want to do. If their main concern is better housing conditions rather than tenant control, then they may want to negotiate an agreement whereby the property is fixed up but still owned by the landlord. If the tenants are getting tired of the emotional strain of the rent strike and the tenant organization seems to be weakening, then the tenants should try to negotiate an agreement with the landlord while the organization is still strong. Secondly, the attitude of the landlord is a factor. If he is willing to give up some control to tenants as well as repair the building, then the tenants may be more willing to sign an agreement with him than they would with a landlord who will give up no control at all. Finally, the availability of a better alternative to private landlord ownership is a big factor in the decision whether to settle. The main alternatives to private landlord ownership are ownership by a tenant cooperative, a non-profit tenant corporation, or a non-profit housing development corporation. These alternatives are just being developed, and in many areas they are still not readily available. If one of these alternatives is possible and the tenants want it, then they should keep up the pressure on the landlord and continue the rent strike until the landlord is foreclosed or is forced to sell to whatever group the tenants want to own the building. If no such alternative is available, then the tenants may want to negotiate an agreement with the landlord . . . A tenant group that has progressed this far with its landlord will be interested in the next developmental state of strategy formation—tenant management or control of the building. This subject is discussed in Chapter 15 herein "Moving Toward Tenant Control of Housing" by Myron Moskovitz and the Earl Warren Legal Institute staff.

CHAPTER 12

The Housing Crisis and Squat-ins

Ted Parrish*

Similar to other sections of the country, Boston's housing crisis continues unabated. When people complain about the crisis they often cite factors such as tight money, the Nixon Administration's cutbacks on housing programs, diversion of available funds to luxury housing, the dearth of activity in construction of public housing, the out-moded construction methods and the limited manpower in the construction industry. This chapter focuses on squatting—one confrontation method used by the National Tenants' Organization (NTO) and its members to help end this crisis.

A squat-in is, very briefly, a move-in, stay-in, and live-in of a poor family aided by a tenants' organization. The family may be moving from nowhere, from a bus station, a friend's overcrowded apartment, or simply a sub-human living accommodation. Once a family in such desperate housing need is found, and after full briefing on the ramifications, jurisdictions, and uncertainties of the technique, they are helped to squat. Obviously, the new accommodation—whether it is in public housing, private housing, an unused office building, or federal properties—should have better facilities than the situation from which the family has just come. The family or families should be prepared to pay up to 25 percent of its weekly income for the new, standard living unit.

There are several compelling reasons for use of the technique. Foremost is that a squat-in can beat the slum-janitor and housing officials in delivering a standard unit. Whereas the housing inspector, court, and slumlord team may take years to get an apartment up to code, and then only through repeated, effective and consistent pressure, a squat-in can end the critical housing crisis. In the selection of families at this early stage of the squat-in movement, care should be taken to choose families whose previous living situations cry out for attention. This will help convey the housing crisis much better than the case of a family whose apartment is quite livable, but just slightly

---

*Ted Parrish has long been active in the tenant's rights movement. Presently, Parrish is a regional coordinator for the National Tenant Organization. This article, originally written for *Tenants Outlook* was composed by the author while serving a 30-day jail sentence for his squat-in activities in Boston.

cramped. For example, a mother and child sleeping in a bus station, and on the waiting list of the public housing authority, will usually win the sympathies of most people. Public consternation at recalcitrant public and private authorities is more likely where the squat-in family is carefully chosen. Also, careful selection of the site for the squat-in enables the tenants' organization to dramatize the contradictions characteristic of certain real estate dealings and personalities.

For example, one landlord against whom The Boston Area Congress for Tenant Rights (BACTR) squatted was all of the following: a slumlord; a president of a non-profit housing group; a speculator in real estate for his own private interests; a member of the American Civil Liberties Union; a member of a well-known liberal law firm; in private, a rehabilitator of houses for middle class people; a recipient of government funds, used for private rehabilitation of houses for middle class people; a community resident who had displaced several poor families to house his own family.

One can raise questions such as the following about such a person: In view of his exploitation of poor people, why is he president of a non-profit housing group which is supposed to build houses for the poor? Why at a $20,000 a year salary as a lawyer and landlord does he get government subsidy to build profit-making houses for middle class people? Why do poor people get government 312 loans so much less often than people in this slumlord's income bracket? Why have the Housing Inspection Department personnel moved so slowly against such a man?

The squat-in is a bold technique well calculated to force confrontations, for it attacks many of the foundations of American life. Squat-ins run counter to all that is sound and proper, legal and acceptable, sacred and constitutionally guaranteed. A squat-in states that human rights take precedence over property rights. Thus, in modern America, confrontation is inevitable.

Finally, a squat-in requires teamwork; no one or two people can successfully accomplish it. Someone has to work on strategy; someone has to contact the communications media. One person arranges transportation while another selects families and still others worry about organizing support and so on. Such teamwork helps foster the tenants and squat-in movements, which in and of itself is one justification for use of squat-ins.

Since the foregoing has alluded to some of the tasks which must be done to achieve a successful squat-in, it would be well to briefly describe this procedure.

Some serious thought should be given before an ongoing tenants' organization attempts a squat-in in its own name. It may be far too dangerous if that organization expects to encounter a particularly serious confrontation. It may be wiser to establish a neighborhood or city-wide ad hoc coalition of blacks, browns, and whites. There are several reasons for this. First, such a broad coalition points out that the housing crisis is not confined to blacks and browns. Second, authorities may hestiate to take action when protesting whites are involved. Third, there is some value in having blacks, browns, and whites provide the supportive activity to desperate black, brown, and white squatters to the same building.

Once a coalition is formed around this crisis, it should be possible to do a few small things that can give some cohesion to the squat-in: a meeting with public housing officials to discuss leased housing for desparate families; a few supportive actions for individual tenant organizations' efforts; a talk by a NTO representative regarding confrontation tactics employed around the country. Once these things have been done and the group is ready to take the plunge, a strategy committee can be brought together. Care should be taken to select a functional strategy committee which reflects the composition—racial, ethnic, and geographic—of the coalition. This strategy committee, which might consist of eight to ten persons, must deal with a number of basic questions before the full coalition can get down to the nitty gritty of a squat-in.

(1) What is the most logical site in terms of the owner's vulnerability, building defensibility, and likelihood of subsidy from public sources?

(2) What types of families should be moved in to enhance the chances of success; black, brown, white or some combination of the three?

(3) When is the best time for the squat-in to take place: Should it be a Friday afternoon when police forces are thin or involved with other things, so that you have at least two days of success without a great deal of police manpower? Or should the squat-in take place around a holiday when the police force is light and the neighborhood population is at its height?

Once these issues are dealt with and plans have been made to complete research on the landlord's points of vulnerability, a meeting of the coalition can be called. There the following committees can be put to work: transportation; fund-raising for paper, flyers, bail money, and incidentals; communications; family selection; legal defense; publicity; organizational and individual support and program.

While most committee functions are obvious, several specific functions should be noted. Besides establishing a telephone list, the communications committee should draw up the most convincing flyers possible and see that they are distributed throughout the city, e.g. at sympathetic community organizations, at colleges, to grassroots folks. The flyers may have to be written in various languages and styles. The organizational support committee might plan convincing talks at the National Welare Rights Organization, the Black Panthers, Students for a Democratic Society, unaffiliated tenants' groups, and any other groups which might provide functional support.

The coalition itself should be responsible for delivering between forty and sixty people to carry out the squat-in operation. That means around-the-clock surveillance for the first few days, until it looks like the landlord and city will accept the "transplant."

The strategy committee should be the final authority on the minute details of timing of the move, diversionary tactics, when the families would be informed of the move, when the media would be called, or what kinds of programmatic supporting activities are most appropriate. The latter point is crucial. While political movies might be a good thing, to have people painting signs directly on the building might not. In order to be fully accountable, the strategy committee must make final decisions.

While it is clear that squat-ins make a dramatic confrontation tactic, there can be serious problems and consequences. Police surveillance of the building will heighten police and community tension. Outside supporters may bring possessions to the building which could endanger the project if they were taken in a raid by the police. New families may also have difficulty getting along with strangers who speak another language. The latter problems can be handled by arranging several house meetings at the first opportunity. Before the squat-in, families can be briefed about the racial, ethnic, and family mix. At later meetings, day-to-day house problems (who takes care of the garbage, who cooks, etc.) can be handled.

More important than these items are the following kinds of concerns:

1) How to select a set of spokesmen from the coalition who can speak to the same theme, who can alternate with each other and who are available for as long as is necessary—perhaps up to two or three weeks.

2) Whose names will be used in event of a court injunction?

3) What do you do with the families if the squat-in is busted?

4) How do you find a law on which to hang a defense if supporters get busted?

5) How do you deal with the police who are often more intimidated than the landlord?

Our experience suggests some methods or solutions to be considered. In Boston, we chose the coalition chairman to speak to the press. Whenever he was unavailable, a first or a second spokesman was available. All three were members of the strategy committee and the latter two lived within minutes of the squat-in site. Incidentally, the latter two also served thirty days in jail for trespassing.

The same person's names were used in the press and with the police. Consequently, restraining orders were taken out against these men, plus a few of the squatters. Whenever squatters faced contempt, they were moved and the tenant organizations that supplied the families assisted them in finding new facilities. Hence, no families have been busted.

Since the lawyers involved with the squatters have not found a law that has significance in our existing courts, trespassing convictions can be expected if the landlord wishes to force the issue. In order to avoid a major confrontation in Boston, the Boston Housing Authority (the landlord) and the BACTR reached an agreement. Still the establishment felt that an example had to be made of the squatter leaders, and the police brought a charge of assault, which was thrown out of court after a week-long jury trial. However, the maximum sentence for trespass of 30 days was handed down by the judge— despite this being our first "offense."

This problem, coupled with potential racism of the police and other public officials, will not make squat-ins an easy task. But they can succeed. Unlike almost any other tactic, a squat-in not only forces public officials to react, it points out the severity of the U.S. housing problem. When other groups and individuals see how bad conditions really are for some people, they may be galvanized to pressure politicians and landlords to seriously help tenants acquire housing.

CHAPTER 13

More than Just Rent Strikes: Alternative Tactics

Nancy Romer Burghardt*

An organization is judged in good part by its tactics, for it is through a variety of imaginative tactics that an organization attracts attention, organizes members, and gains real power. Choosing a timely, appropriate tactic requires that a group balance its organizational resources against the purposes of the action. Three main purposes or functions are analyzed here: (1) building the organization; (2) educating members and nonmembers; and (3) favorably altering the political environment. While a specific tactic may engage only one or two purposes, all of them must, at some time, be attended to in order to keep the goals and structure of an organization alive and working.

Building the Organization

As Saul Alinsky asserts, most people join community organizations out of self interest. A tenant may join the tenant union because he or she is angry at a rent increase or poor maintenance. What the tenant may not realize is that these particular problems are endemic to the present landlord-tenant relationship. The job of the tenant organization, then, is to help its members understand this relationship and how it can be changed through group action.

A person's commitment to the goals of the group is often related to the amount of contact he or she has with it. A wise organization will familiarize individuals with the organization so that this commitment may begin to take root. Members who show interest in increased participation can be offered a series of opportunities in which they can become involved. It is ludicrous to expect the average new member to engage in political arguments at a steering committee meeting or to disrupt a city council session, for these activities demand a great deal of personally internalized commitment to the group. A

---

*Nancy Romer Burghardt, a doctoral student at The University of Michigan in the Joint Program in Education and Psychology, was an organizer for the Ann Arbor Tenants' Union.

union can, however, offer the new members the chance to participate in a variety of activities in which they can feel comfortable, such as leafletting and getting signatures on a petition to the landlord. Community experience, and organizational commitment can grow out of a series of such well planned tactics. As members work together, they will develop trust in each other and in the organization. New members should feel that the opportunity to grow is present without the pressures of having to be completely involved all at once. Some tenants are willing only to affix their names to a petition; others are willing to go to jail for the organization. But between them stands the vast majority of members who should be helped into extending their relationship with the group.

Some may accuse the notion of "levels of involvement" as elitist, but a clearer look will reveal just the opposite. An organization that immediately demands a great deal of sophisticated participation from all "active" members (such as participating in many nightly political meetings) will soon find their numbers dwindling. Members must feel comfortable to attend or not attend without comment. Hopefully, they will realize that they are welcome and able to join in on all the activities of the organization without being required to do so. They must feel they can influence the general organization without having to dedicate every evening to it. One minor way of achieving this is to announce all meetings and keep them open to membership participation. Demanding too great a commitment too soon will scare off many members and will, in the long run, leave only the diehard politicos to make decisions.

Educating Members and Nonmembers

Education is referred to here as political growth on an organizational and personal level. It is important to remember that political growth must occur on both levels. A well-versed political theorist may know nothing about running an organization, how to get the media to cover a demonstration, how to publish a newsletter, how to talk to the city housing commissioner, or how to talk to tenants. On the other hand, an efficient organizer may not be able to make sense out of power relations in city, state, or federal governments.

As many members as possible should become acquainted with the functioning of the union office. Participation in writing up the amended answers or legal briefs for their rent strike cases increases a member's understanding of the work and of the political implications in our legal system. A good number of members should learn all the steps involved in planning an "action," including calling the press, making up and using telephone lists, making placards, and getting people to participate. Members will need help in their organizational lessons, but they must be allowed to be independent students, regardless of an occasional mistake. Tenant groups have also found it important for many members to know how to give a talk on the tenant organization to another group, or how to chair a meeting. If the same people take responsibility for these tasks over and over again, the organization will probably not be able to perpetuate leadership within its ranks. The many "unsophisticated" members will remain dependent on the few leaders, a situation which is organizationally and politically disastrous.

The more active a member is, the more educated he or she will become; but political education may continue on many levels. The members who attend each steering committee meeting and each "action" will quickly learn about the political machinations of the organization. But for the less active member, the newsletters, leaflets, and organizing "raps" will be the main vehicle for their education. Presenting the facts on how the legal relationship between government and business adversely affects the housing conditions of the poor can lead to a greater understanding of the housing problem. When the rent strike cases first began to appear on the court docket in Ann Arbor, Michigan, many people were shocked to learn that several judges, once challenged by the Union, had to be disqualifed from presiding over the cases due to their extensive business dealings with the landlords in question. What if the Union hadn't challenged the judges? How just would their decisions have been? Much research must be done on each landlord, judge, management agency, government housing official, and others, so that interrelations may be found and exposed. The facts are often quite radicalizing.

Members must, finally, learn the ethic of collective action. They know how isolated and impotent they are alone. They must be shown the political and social clout of an organized group of people with common goals. This points to motivating away from merely individual achievement and in the direction of group achievement. In short, this entails developing group consciousness. Tactics emphasizing group effectiveness should therefore be used as often as possible.

The goals for political growth of members will, of course, be more extensive and important than for nonmembers. It should not be forgotten, though, that among the huge contingent of nonmembers lie future members, sympathizers, and public opinion. Through any available publicity (newspapers, T.V., radio, posters, leaflets, actions) the union should try to explain its goals and purposes. The organization may use a creative tactic or communication to demonstrate some of the political realities facing tenants. For example, a tenant group may pitch tents on the lawn in front of the housing commissioner's house to show that while he lives in luxury, they live in slums barely better than tents. They may run a muckraking campaign designed to make people question the "goodness" of "good government."

While one cannot expect to educate people thoroughly by one or two tactics, a union can offer them opportunities to participate with or learn more about the organization. A wise organization will always add to any of its communications a number to call or address to write to for more information. They may also display the date of the next meeting or action, and the bucket drive for spare change will always be effective. Nonmembers, like members, will relate to the tenant group on many levels of interest and participation and these opportunities should be available to them.

Affecting the Political Environment

The real purpose of a tenant organization is not just to improve maintenance or to keep the rent from rising. These may be among the initial reasons for getting a group together, but the underlying problem is one of political power and privilege. In a rental situation, the lone tenant has neither the political power nor the legal privilege to jockey effectively for his own position. Any tactic, or more broadly any tenant union, should seek to change the existing power relation so that the tenant begins to reap the returns. Andre Gorz summarizes the optimal purpose of a tenant group or community organization interested in social changes in the concept of "structural reform:"

> "Structural reform" is by definition a reform implemented or controlled by those who demand it. Be it in agriculture, the university, property relations, the region, the administration, the economy, etc., a structural reform *always* requires the creation of new centers of democratic power . . . structural reform always requires a *decentralization* of the decision making power . . . (p.8, *Strategy for Labor,* Beacon Press, Boston, 1968)

Although that is a lofty and optimistic view of what a tenant organization may accomplish, it is important to maintain this notion of structural reform as a political goal. Each tactic may gear itself toward a particular, small goal, but the group must not forget its ultimate direction. For example, picketing and rent striking may ward off this year's rent increase, but who will guard against a rent increase two years from now unless the tenants have a major role in the decision making? Inattention to this purpose undermines any coherent political function of the tactic, however militant it may be.

A tenant organization should also try to develop itself as a mass-based political organization which derives its strength from its active constituency. Sometimes a tactic that masses people together and gives them a feeling of strength and solidarity can be both politically intoxicating to the tenants and downright frightening to the landlord or city housing authority. This reinforces the reliance on group action for the tenants and presents the tenant union as an influential advocate for better housing in the eyes of the public.

Political coalitions with other groups offer an interesting alternative. Many tenant unions throughout the country have joined with their local branch of the National Welfare Rights Organization and/or Southern Christian Leadership Conference in undertaking a particular tactic or action. Other unions have joined with radical and liberal political organizations for mutual help. This increases the influence of both organizations and builds an even larger power bloc in the community while allowing for trade-offs in personnel, expertise, and finances. Moreover, it helps people to see the tenants' rights struggle as part of a larger struggle. Experience has shown, however, that it is wise to make coalitions on a temporary basis, e.g. for carrying out a specific tactic. It is best not to join with another organization for permanent, day-to-day functioning, since the tenant group must concentrate on its own growth in the beginning of a movement.

Tactics

It is important to choose the right tactic for the right group, since each special group has its own attributes, liabilities, and expectations. For example, a middle class tenant group may have more money and expertise, allowing them to use more expensive and legalistic tactics than a union of mainly poor people could. However, the poorer group may be more militant, with greater solidarity and class consciousness. It may also have less invested in the system and thus be more willing to act to change it. Distinctions in tactics must be made between groups of young people and old people, families and individuals, blacks, whites and browns, religious and non-religious, women and men, public and private housing tenants. Each group should make an accurate assessment of its own needs, styles, and resources in order to choose the appropriate purpose. It is also important to examine the type of city the organization is in. A small city allows tenant groups to get greater coverage by the media. Such cities are also often more receptive to small pressure groups. On the other hand, a larger city may have the advantage of more resources and may contain an increasing variety of political coalitions vying for larger constituencies. The political leanings of a city is an important factor to look at for tactical direction also. New York City is far more liberal than Dallas; tenants should plan their strategies with that reality in mind.

Tactics can be modified in an almost infinite variety of ways. Clearly, three major factors involved in deciding upon a tactic are the resources needed and available, the characteristics of the group involved, and above all, the purposes of the tactic. Before we proceed to a listing of suggested tactics, a word of caution: Do not do too much too fast. Too many tactics at once may scatter and weaken the effectiveness of the organization. It is best to choose one or two tactics at first and build organizational strength along the way. Build on your successes, as small as they may be at first. Once a firm foundation has been established through a few successful tactics a plethora of creative tactics are available for use.

Below is a listing of tactics that have been used by tenant organizations in the past. Most of these tactics have also been used by groups outside the Tenants' Rights Movement. They are typical of militant organizations with few resources and much creative energy. Almost every tactic listed here may be carried out in either a militant or moderate manner, depending on the slogans or posters, the specific actions, and press statements of the members. Undoubtedly many good tactics have been left out of this discussion due to poor communication. Often, a tenant group will use a fresh idea but no one will recognize its ingenuity and thus the word will not spread.

Petitioning is a good way of changing the minds of tenants who believe that the landlord or housing authority would change "if they only knew the problems." It's a good first step to organize and radicalize tenants. This helps build the organization and educate the members. In Houston, a tenant group petitioned the landlord for repairs and rat extermination. The reaction of the manager was to send out eviction notices to the organizers of the petition drive. This triggered a general rent strike and the birth of a tenant organization.

Leafletting the local area has been used mainly as a publicity and educational tactic. It can be a preparation for "more to come" or used simply as support for another tactic.

Letter Writing Campaigns to public officials have been used to change existing laws. In New York, the Community Council on Housing, led by Jesse Gray, sent rubber rats in letters to Governor Nelson Rockefeller, demanding his support of legislation providing emergency repairs in slums. A group of tenants in the Muskegon, Michigan Tenants Union wrote letters to the mayor demanding the removal of the allegedly racist housing board commissioners. They finally succeeded, through many activities, to place some of their own members on the board instead.

Picketing is an old stand-by; its uses are infinite. The Ann Arbor Tenants Union used it to protest thefts by a slumlord of the property of rent-striking tenants. The AATU picketed his luxurious home, rapped with his neighbors, and built snowmen with pithy placards on his lawn. In Muskegon, picketing underscored the rent strike; the city administration building was picketed every Friday afternoon for the duration of the strike.

The Telephone-In is used primarily to harass a particularly obnoxious landlord or housing official. It consists of just a few persistent members taking turns—all day for several days—at calling the party concerned. This effectively cuts off any and all business usually conducted by phone.

Boycotting an especially bad landlord is a good educational tactic. People who live in an area are encouraged *not* to rent apartments from the target landlord, who is then left with no tenants. While this can strengthen a well organized tenant group, it may be hard to do if the housing market in your particular city is very tight. It has been used very successfully by the Madison, Wisconsin Tenants Union.

Marches can be extremely effecitve if they are well organized. Brief marches may be used to publicize and show group solidarity; lengthy marches show, in addition, the seriousness and dedication of the tenant group. Members of the New Orleans Tenants Union marched one hundred miles to the state capitol in Baton Rouge to protest a 42 per cent welfare cut. The six-day venture started with one hundred fifty marchers, had fifteen at its lowest point and ended with a rally of three hundred on the steps of the Capitol Building. Meetings and benefits were held in towns along the way.

Rallies are used primarily as support for other tactics. They build publicity and group solidarity among other things. One of many examples is the Boston Area Congress for Tenants Rights which held a rally in support of their squat-in (described in the previous chapter herein).

Public Hearings have been used to express tenant opinion on specific legislation being considered by city or state government. For example, a group of Washington, D.C. tenants spoke at public hearings on a "Tenants Rights Regulation" bill which would have restricted the right to rent strike. Other groups have used the Public Hearing to get better housing codes and housing code enforcement. This is a particularly important tactic for cities and states in which the right to rent strike has not been granted or where housing codes are either non-existent or unenforced. It has the potential for altering the power structure through legislation, but one should not expect much more than pure education for union members for a long time.

Guerilla Theater is a particularly creative way of portraying the landlord-tenant relationship. A group of tenants who enjoy and are sufficiently skillful at theatrics can really get a lot of educational and political mileage out of it. This has been used widely in student communities but may, as yet, be too avant garde for most groups.

Preventing Eviction is a very general category for a variety of tactics. Earlier, in Chapter 9, Stuart Katz dealt with the formation of a tactical defense squad which helps tenants combat landlord harassment or eviction. These squads help the tenant see concrete ways the union can benefit him. Aiding one member can result in organizing a good number of neighbors. The most common way of preventing eviction has been to bodily block the proceedings. Several hundred members of a housing group called the Contract Buyer's League in the Lawndale area of Chicago's South Side came to the defense of a family about to be evicted. Through a series of counter-harassment techniques, the tenants got the sheriffs and security guards to leave the building. Many of the black guards left the building with clenched fists raised in solidarity with the tenants. The sheriff's department estimated the cost of the unsuccessful eviction to be $25,000 including the salaries of two hundred deputies and guards.

"Break the Bank" was a tactic used by the AATU to protest the garnishing of striking members' bank accounts. Landlords, with permission from the local courts, were simply taking their back rent by putting liens on tenants' accounts. One bank in town was notably helpful to landlords in providing lists of their account holders and the amount of money in their accounts. After much publicity, hundreds of members and their supporters withdrew over $200,000 on one Friday afternoon. This tactic exposed the cooperative effort of the courts, banks, and landlords against tenants, increased Union membership, gathered statewide publicity for AATU and its demands, and made the bankers look ridiculous, since they didn't have enough cash on hand to make their payments.

Sit-ins have been used by many groups as a tactic that demands a response. If a large group of people take over an office, something must be done to get rid of them or the original occupants must go on vacation. This can be quite educational; political changes can be affected through the ensuing negotiations. In New Orleans, the Tenants Union—in coalition with the local Welfare Rights Organization—invaded the welfare department offices and demanded that if their welfare checks were being reduced by a certain percentage, so should their rent payments.

Tent-ins are a variation of the sit-in idea. It is usually quite dramatic to see a bunch of tents pitched on the city housing administrator's lawn, on the university's main campus, or on a new construction site. The AATU pitched 25 tents on the central campus of The Univeristy of Michigan for one month. The group provided housing for people unable to find apartments to live in and protested the housing shortage in town, due in large part to inadequate University housing. As students and staff walked to class, they received a bit of political education. However, in order for this tactic to remain effective, it will be necessary for the organization to maintain control of the tent-in. If the camp site becomes filthy or people unconcerned with the tenant group's goals begin living there, this attractive tactic can become a nightmare.

Disruptions of "official" meetings, e.g. state hearings, city councils, have been used to press the urgency and extent of tenant dissatisfaction. In Washington, D.C. the local Housing Authority handpicked a few nonmilitant tenants to serve on a committe to develop a tenant advisory board. Active tenant groups in the area, angered by the anti-union selection, disrupted each meeting of the group, finally forcing the group to hold a public election for tenant representatives. All twenty-two seats on the advisory board were won by the slate endorsed by the coalition of tenant unions in the area.

Some of these tactics may sound exciting and romantic. Some may sound like a good deal of fun, and they are—on the day they occur. But it is preparation for each action that will decide whether it succeeds or fails. An organization that does not do thorough advance homework, invites its members to a series of debacles. It is also important for an organization, fresh from the glow of a successful political battle, to maintain some momentum for the future. Each of the three purposes—building the organization, education, and political change—must be attended to. The group must be aware of its needs and choose its activities accordingly. For it is out of the day-to-day struggle, punctuated with exciting tactics, that an effective organization grows.

CHAPTER 14

Rent Strike or Tenant Union? The Building of a Permanent Organization

Stephen Burghardt

Like most small community organizations, tenant unions face a series of problems in gaining a permanent foothold in the community. Often, larger organizations try to intimidate and coopt these groups. However, other problems may lie in the original organizing strategies of the new organizations themselves. There are at least five interrelated problems for tenant unions to solve: (1) the failure to move beyond the militancy of the rent strike which first coalesced the group; (2) a misuse of the legal system for social change; (3) the inability to develop an independent resource base; (4) the dominance of self-interest issues over ideological issues—or the reverse; (5) a misapplication of membership skills within the community.

Moving Beyond Militancy

These problems, unlike those brought on by other institutions, can greatly be controlled. Furthermore, by controlling these problems, the new organization may defend itself against outside hostile forces as well. This article will describe each of these strategic errors, show how they can be avoided, and finally, present positive alternatives for individual tenant unions to use to gain permanence within the community.

If tenants are upset enough, there is no easier way to organize a group than through a rent strike. The withholding of rent (e.g. for better maintenance) creates a clear, crisp division between landlord and tenant interests that is rarely achieved through any other tactic. It has the glamour to attract the press—large membership lists often follow news coverage. And, perhaps most importantly of all, a rent strike can threaten a landlord in a fundamental way that no petition ever could. The more money withheld in a rent strike, the greater the chance that a tenant union's demands will be attended.

But rent strikes are dangerous, too. A common problem with most militant tactics is that their glamour often mesmerizes social activists into confusing situational cohesion with on-going unity. Sometimes, the militant tactic is escalated solely for its own sake as tenant union organizers become so excited with the opening success of a strike that they then try to build larger and larger rent strikes.

The logical conclusions of extended rent strikes are painfully illustrated by the following two examples. In Ann Arbor in 1969, a group of tenants were involved in building both a tenant union and a rent strike. They had over twelve hundred tenant union/rent strike members, were actively influencing the outcome of the city council elections that year, and were developing sophisticated legal suits against local landlords which, if successfully carried through the courts, would have had far-reaching effects across the country as important legal precedents. However, a year later the entire full time staff—one paid lawyer, two paid secretaries, and at least seven to twelve volunteers—worked fifty hours a week to keep up with only the rent strike paper work. Others worked lesser amounts. Everything else—the political work, the legal advocacy, etc.—was forgotten.

A few years earlier in New York City, large rent strike groups soon gathered enough influence to force through one of the first legislative packages allowing rent withholding. One of the first rat control bills came about through their efforts. People were talking in terms of new, important political alliances being drawn from the militant tenant ranks. Less than two years later all such discussion was stilled. Organizers had instead concentrated on building more and more rent strikes—the whole political effort had suddenly collapsed.

What do such results mean? In each case, goal displacement had occurred; the rent strike, rather than aiding the organization, had *become* the organization. In Ann Arbor, union members began to neglect the development of negotiating procedures for more equitable contracts. The organizers instead sought air-tight rent strike cases for the court's favorable disposition. Organizers on the Lower East Side in New York also forgot about developing strong local unions to back up their political demands; they sought to justify their group's existence in a larger, better strike. In both instances work continued at a frantic pace, but as the months wore on, even the short range goals of reduced rents and better maintenance procedures remained as distant as they had ever been.

Implicit in the rent strikes was a fateful paradox—their increasing size and strength was their own undoing. Having lived by the rallying cry of "the landlord is the enemy," the tenant group members justified their large rent strikes, and all the energy demanded in their upkeep, only on the initial discomfort they had brought to landlords. In turn, they ignored the question of a strike's *continued effectiveness* in achieving a wider degree of tenant rights and activity in the community.

The organizers had overlooked an important fact: a rent strike, for all its trappings of militance, creates large bureaucratic demands because it is a *legal, defensive* tactic. Unless the group itself is so cohesive that it decides either to withhold the money permanently or not to return the money when demanded to do so by the court, the union will eventually use the strike to legally defend its members from eviction while they are temporarily withholding their rent.

As a statement, a rent strike may sound hostile; as it is intrinsically organized, it is legal and efficient. For every night of excitement in gathering rent strike pledges, there are days and days of researching, filing for pretrials with the court, establishing an efficient filing system for escrow payments (and making sure they are prompt), and other, minor bureaucratic demands. The structures of the strike which force a group to run it effectively (i.e. win court cases leading to rent reductions and improved maintenance) constrain an organization to devote all its energies to that end. While delaying rent collection to create economic hardship for the landlord is a potential aim of many strikes, the only goal within most organized strikes is very limited: provision for individual improvements through either minor rent reductions or easily avoided repairs. Such narrow benefits atomize each tenant into looking at his or her own case. Concomitantly, no collective tenant union consciousness can maintain itself within such divisive self-interests.

Unless a tenant group is so antagonistic toward landlords that it can withstand all attempts at intimidation or cooptation, a rent strike obviously cannot be used as an all-inclusive weapon. Once it has served the important purpose of uniting a group, the strike should be narrowed and deepened by the tenant union for maximal organizational effectiveness. Thus, instead of ramming rent strike pledges down a large number of interested tenants' throats—usually manifested by letting them know how much of a rent reduction they would receive after rent striking—organizers should be given a small number of new apartments to organize. With less work and the same amount of time to devote to it as in the larger strike, these tenant organizers will be able to explain more fully the political nature of the tenants movement, as well as the needed services available to organized tenants. In short, by narrowing and deepening, organizers would stop collecting pledges for a rent strike and would instead concentrate on developing a tenant union.

Such narrowing and deepening serves many functions not possible with a large rent strike. First, and most obviously, it clearly distinguishes a rent strike from a tenant union. The former should only be used to aid the latter's goals for ameliorating inequitable housing conditions. If it is overemphasized, it will displace that basic goal, and the scenario in a tight housing market will proceed from initial excitement to frantic bureaucratic involvement to irrelevance.

Secondly, organizers can concentrate on both the short- and long-term goals of tenant action which are often blurred after the early stages of militancy. Working in carefully selected buildings owned by target landlords, the organizers would not force membership in the union through rent striking. It would be left as an option if a majority of tenants in the building decide to use the tactic, but its limitations as a political lever would be emphasized so that people could avoid involvement in the narrow self interests which a rent strike can provoke.

A tenant union, rather than using a rent strike as the only tactic for change, could explore the existing channels of tenant-landlord procedures for any possible results. Only when the landlord remains unresponsive would the tactics be escalated in militancy. More importantly, this gradualistic process serves as an educating lesson for all tenants in the area. By publicly focusing on the difference between tenants and landlords throughout the agitational process, parallels could be effectively drawn for those who initially resist the professed militancy of the rent strike. This combination of education and action should help increase tenants' consciousness throughout the area.

A tenant union must also work more directly on its longer range goals. Ironically, one of the arenas demanding more attention is the courtroom—not as a place to defend one's actions, but as a platform from which to advocate greater tenant equity. For example, why does the burden of proof in grievance procedures fall on the tenant and not the landlord? What determines "fair rent"? Is it some national or local standard? Or what the landlord considers to be a "fair profit"? To prepare affirmitive suits around these and other issues will hardly be easy. Present housing law, based as it is on English common law, still greatly favors the *owners* of property over the *renters* of property. Such a long tradition of inequity will understandably mitigate against immediately effective legal advocacy. However, it is certain that tenant union lawyers cannot even present affirmative suits around housing inequities if they are immersed in analyzing the city housing code for its applicability to a dozen rent strike cases on next week's court docket.

Building a Resource Base

Restructuring an organization's rent strike tactics and concentrating on affirmative rather than defensive legal actions are only two roles which a tenant union must develop. Perhaps the most important function demanding organizational attention is the building of an independent resource base. While extremely difficult to maintain in areas already choked with poverty, an independent source of fresh funds, no matter how limited, will allow any community organization to consider a much wider range of strategic alternatives. Its importance cannot be overestimated.

Some groups find that the tasks of mounting a coherent daily presence in the community and paying their bills are often conflicting. Part of this problem relates to their inability to combine the actual interests of the local community with the organization's political goals. Some of the groups are too amorphous in their stated actions (a self-help project) or too removed from salient community functions (such as a sectarian socialist group) to be attractive to any large constituency. Unable to interact effectively with a broad base of community members or unable to attract others' resources, most of these groups either die or remain small and without influence.

But a tenant union is in an extraordinary position to build a permanent community presence because of its obvious concern with issues of self-interest. "Housing" and its problems are a constant source of concern to a neighborhood. A tenant union can capitalize on this inherent identity with community concerns if it structures a service arena within its own organization. Within this service component, a union can attract new members by providing services not available elsewhere—explaining contract clauses, finding available housing and aiding in relocation, or serving as an emergency repair service for small but important jobs (fixing broken outside doors, mailboxes, windows overlooking fire escapes). Not only could this initial service attraction begin educating tenants to the more political nature of the tenants' rights movement; it also might be able to create enough financial support to pay its own expenses and to finance the research costs of the smaller rent strike and the previously-mentioned affirmative suits.

At the same time, this does not mean that a service arena should dominate the workings of an organization. It is assumed that if an organization's final goals are political—that is, concerned with the restructuring of political and economic institutions for greater power equalizaton—then all organizational strategies will be designed towards that eventual political success. Pragmatically, services cannot dominate the organization; instead they must be used both to attract new, politically disinterested constituents and to help economically maintain the group itself.

Thus, a repair service would not be set up just to fill the union's coffers or to correct the plethora of code violations for which management is responsible. Instead, it would draw up a list of "emergency" repairs—such as those mentioned above—which the union would perform for a small fee. In order that the political problems are understood, the tenant and the union could fill out readily available forms to be filed with the housing authority before the repairs begin; if possible, pictures of the problems affixed with a notary seal should be taken. The results are that the tenant union has received money for its work, the tenant has been aided *and* educated in his or her problem, and the landlord has another mark on his record. While minor in scope, the benefits could be mulitplied greatly over time. If the union is able to perform these and other services—advocacy legal aid, speedy relocation—its resource base and legitimacy in the local community will be greatly expanded.[1]

A tenant union would now be using its members in three arenas: organizers doing political and educational work within the refined rent strike; its legal staff involved in advocacy and legal aid; and other members doing service work within the community. Another role which tenants could serve would be as advocates to city and state governments for both improved legislation and more low-cost housing.

To be effective advocates, however, local tenant groups must be willing to use professionals and students interested in better housing and more equitable housing conditions. These two groups are often ignored by small advocacy organizations. Sometimes their antipathy has been justified; it is understandable that local members are aggravated by condescending outsiders who try to dominate store-front groups with a presumed universal expertise. Yet under the firm direction of a tenant union, professionals and students can perform valuable tasks, particularly in research and planning. Given a narrow enough mandate, these two groups can gather the necessary information on the potential and need for increased housing expenditures, ways of reallocating resources, plans for development, etc. [2]

Though these efforts are not as exciting as gathering new members into a rent strike, a tenant union's voice, backed up by hard facts and figures, can expect to be heard when priorities are reordered in the local area. For example, AATU documentation and publicity on the lack of low- and moderately-priced apartments in the city led to increased interest in housing by local officials. The city's mayor was quoted early in 1971 that the local April referendum on land annexation "was assured passage" with the union's backing. While other political factors undoubtedly were involved in such a statement, it was obvious that the legitimacy of the union's position did not develop through mere emotional appeal. There is no reason why other tenant unions, serving as "experts on need," could not have similar effects.

Coalition Building

Tenant groups cannot hesitate to build political coalitions either. Small community organizations can do only so much alone. Eventually, their issues will relate to broader community problems involving welfare, educational needs, and other services important to large segments of the community. But coalition building can be a tricky business. If done too often and for every remotely related cause, the groups involved may lose credibility with their more immediate constituency. For example, a "people's movement" of tenants, students, anti-war activists, and women's rights advocates may sound theoretically attractive, but *operationally* they can do little together. The alignment may result in a tenant group's constituency becoming bored with what it perceives to be a lot of abstract political talk.

Tenant unions must also try to avoid one of the classic problems in coalition building: the division of groups by more powerful forces. It is far easier for local political officials to invite a coalition's leadership into its good offices (at a hefty salary for all) than it is to capitulate to the growing movement's larger political and economic demands. If that doesn't work, it is still easier to provide favors for only one segment of the coalition. This attention to distinctive interests may lead to division within the entire coalition itself, as smaller groups begin competing for equal treatment. This was a common problem throughout the sixties within the OEO's Community Action Program; perhaps it can never be entirely avoided. Clearly one way to at least minimize these outside, divisive interests is to make sure that as many organizations as possible within the coalition have their own independent sources of income.

There are three other operational factors which a tenant group should consider if it wishes to maximize its political leverage in coalition building: (1) the geographic proximity of the groups involved; (2) the political districting of the area, to minimize local ward or district splitting and thus maximize political clout in the area; (3) and the similarity or complementarity of the constituencies involved, so that all material concerns aren't forgotten. Here, a coalition between a tenant union and a welfare rights group in the same neighborhood is obvious; a coalition of tenants and an anti-war group across town is not. Once again, this approach attempts to intertwine both political demands with constituency needs. If differing constituencies are helped to recognize the similarities within their political and material interests through coalition building, the gains for each individual group are increased accordingly.

We have tried to suggest in this chapter that it is indeed possible to go beyond the unifying militancy of an early rent strike. Surely if any community organization is in a position to capitalize on the self-interest of its constituency, a tenant union is. If it uses effectively this latent interest to offer legal, planning, and political strategies to its constituency—and to develop its own resource base—the group cannot help but grow in to an influential community organization.

---

1. Another income-producing alternative for tenant unions to consider is a union furniture and household goods cooperative. Organized similarly to those run by Goodwill Industry, the organization could help tenants by selling needed furniture at reduced prices.

2. For example of the kind of document professionals could prepare, see Thomas Anton and Roger Lind's proposal for increasing housing expenditures, Chapter 16 herein.

CHAPTER 15

Moving Toward Tenant Control of Housing

Myron Moskovitz and the National Housing and Economic Development Law Project*

A tenant union will often work from the assumption that the landlord has the financial resources to meet the union's demands. This is the premise upon which a collective bargaining agreement or similar agreement is usually based. This approach can be successful—especially in the early stages—when used against landlords whose operations are particularly vulnerable or profitable. However, this approach has only limited applicability. Quite often the landlords with whom the tenant union must deal suffer from all the problems of slum ownership. Landlords in such a position are either unable or unwilling to absorb the costs of improving the housing condition of their tenants.

It is here that the often-drawn analogy between a tenant union and a labor union begins to break down. In a labor-management conflict the bitterest battles are often fought over recognition or jurisdiction. The economic issues are usually settled more easily because costs of such a settlement can often be passed on to the consumers in the form of higher prices. This simple expedient is not available in a tenant-landlord dispute. Landlords usually feel that they are being called upon to absorb the costs of rent reduction or rehabilitation. Thus, once a landlord has absorbed such costs in meeting the tenants' demands that will bring his rate of return down to a normal or acceptable level, any further success may depend upon the tenant union's ability to find some other method of financing the additional costs. In cases where the landlord at the outset is making an inadequate return on investment, even an initial success in repairing the building may depend upon the tenant union's ability in this regard. The most likely strategy that a tenant union will adopt at this point will be to reach an agreement with the landlord by which the ten-

---

*This material is adapted from *Handbook on Housing Law;* Volume II: *Landlord-Tenant Materials,* by National Housing and Economic Development Law Project; copyright 1970 by National Housing and Economic Development Law Project, Earl Warren Legal Institute, University of California; published by Prentice-Hall, Inc., Englewood Cliffs, New Jersey.

ant union will assume some—if not all—of the risks and prerogatives of ownership. This step has been taken by several of the more successful tenant unions in the country.[1] The following paragraphs examine the form that such "control agreements" can take or have taken.

Other strategies are possible. The tenant union could continue to make demands and back these demands with rent strikes, etc. The object of this strategy would be to force the landlord out of business and force the government to intervene. If the governmental response was a normal one, such as an action for a receivership, a tax sale, a condemnation action, etc., the tenant union might attempt to gain control of the building by buying at the sale, having itself appointed receiver, etc. In such case this strategy ultimately reverts to the previous strategy, the difference being that the tenant union is dealing with the government as owner of the building instead of with the original landlord. On the other hand, the strategy of the tenant union may be to push for a "political" response to the problem: by forcing a large number of landlords to the point of abandonment the tenant union hopes that the political and business establishment will intervene with injections of money to prevent a general collapse of the slum economy. This type of strategy will be discussed in a later section.

Management Agreements

A management agreement seems to be the natural next step beyond a collective bargaining agreement. In practice, the borderline between the two types of agreements becomes blurred.[2] A management agreement has an immediate practical advantage over a collective bargaining agreement since the tenant union itself performs the actions necessary to correct the tenant grievances. It therefore tends to eliminate many of the frictions and delays arising out of the need for meetings, bargaining, cooperation, etc., with the landlord that are inherent in the typical collective bargaining relationship.

Another advantage of a management agreement is its enforceability. A collective bargaining agreement might not be enforceable if a majority of the tenants of the particular building are not members of the tenant union. Therefore, any turnover in tenants throughout the lifetime of the collective bargaining agreement might jeopardize the agreement unless the new tenants are recruited to union membership.[3] This problem does not arise with a management agreement, since management services are frequently performed by companies that make no claim to represent the tenants of a building. Of course, it is always desirable from a practical, if not from a legal, point of view that all of the tenants of a building be members of the tenant union.

The functions that a tenant union can undertake under a management agreement vary from small, specific tasks to virtually all of the prerogatives of ownership. The most important decision is whether the tenant union should confine itself to physical management of the building or whether it should undertake to collect the rents and pay the expenses as well. If the tenant union manages the finances of the building, it is in a good position to set aside an adequate amount of money for maintenance and repairs. There is always some risk, however, that the tenant union will take on the role of the landlord in the eyes of the tenants and become the object of a rent strike or some other tenant action. Despite the risk, the tendency seems to be for tenant unions to move in the direction of total management of the building or buildings.

A management agreement can be attractive from a landlord's point of view. If the tenant union assumes the risks of vandalism and deterioration, it eliminates from the landlord's point of view two of the factors that contribute to high rents and low maintenance in the slum economy. Of course, the risks are not eliminated entirely, but merely transferred to the union. In exchange for the assumption of these risks, the tenant union should be able to bargain for lower rents or for the diversion of a portion of the existing rents into a fund for repairs. In some instances, tenant unions have bargained for the temporary diversion of all or nearly all of the rents into a maintenance fund. The landlord in such cases probably relies on the increased resale value to offset his decrease in rental income because of the repairs. This type of bargain is optimum from the point of view of the tenant union, but it is obviously not obtainable in every instance. It should also be pointed out that what appears to be an assumption of an economic risk by a tenant union often is not. The tenant union often reserves the right to cancel the management agreement and thus runs no real risk of loss if it fails to halt the deterioration of the building. Theoretically, the right of cancellation should greatly decrease the attractiveness of a management agreement to the landlord, but if a particular landlord is in a weak enough position even a cancellable agreement may prove attractive.[4]

Master Leases

A master lease of an apartment building would seem to be the next logical step for the tenant union. However, we know of no instance where this form of agreement has been tried. Under this type of arrangement the tenant union leases the entire building from the landlord and sublets the apartments to the tenants. A lease has certain advantages by virtue of being a normal commercial instrument. Thus, the rights of a lessee are usually well-defined as to successive purchasers, creditors, public agencies acting under eminent domain, etc.[5] A master lease also gives the tenant union a property interest in the building. Thus, if contributions to the tenant union are tax deductible because of the organization's charitable status, contributions for improvements that benefit the leaseholder should also be tax deductible.[6] A lease of an apartment building or buildings is a planning tool that gives the tenant union a predictable supply of apartments at a fixed rent. A planning tool of this sort may be essential when some tenant movement is necessitated by the nature of the repairs and rehabilitation to certain buildings or by the need to group certain tenants in the same building or buildings for the purpose of qualifying under certain federal programs.

A long term lease with a tenant union might in some cases enable a land-lord to refinance an existing loan or obtain an otherwise unobtainable con-ventional loan. Refinancing on better terms will, of course, result in a reduc-tion of the monthly debt service expense, and this savings could be used for repairs, maintenance or rent reductions. The tenant union's obligations un-der the lease would provide additional security to the lender and could, there-fore, influence his decision to make the loan. Of course, this security is only as good as the credit of the tenant union, and a fledgling organization is un-likely to have any impact on a lender's decision. However, a lease coupled with a guarantee from a tenant union with a record of success and strong fi-nancial backing could prove important in helping the landlord obtain a loan.

A tenant union is likely to find a "net lease" the most attractive for its pur-poses. Under a net lease the tenant union assumes virtually all of the eco-nomic risks in the operation of the building, such as vandalism, deteriora-tion, vacancies, costs of eviction, etc. Therefore, since the landlord's risks are considerably diminished, the tenant union should be able to rent an entire building for an amount that is considerably less than the total of the existing rents on the apartments in the building. It could then pass on the savings as a fund to cover vacancies, repairs, etc. As with a management agreement, the risks that the tenant union assumes under a master lease do not disappear.

Coupled with the economic risks are the psychological risks. A tenant union operating under a master lease has clearly passed over the line and be-comes a landlord in the eyes of the tenants. This needn't lead to failure if the tenant union maintains the confidence of its members and does not promise more than it can deliver.

Option to Purchase

An option to purchase, when coupled with a lease or management agree-ment, gives the tenant union maximum flexibility in planning for the use of the property. An option, first of all, can be used by the tenant union to cap-ture any increase in the value of the building arising out of its efforts at re-pairing the building or upgrading the neighborhood. Thus an option may help boost tenant morale and could serve as a potential source of money. If the value of the building increases above the exercise price of the option, the tenant union could exercise the option and immediately resell the building at a profit or it could sell the option itself for a profit.

An option can also be used by a tenant union to purchase and rehabilitate a building with the aid of a federally subsidized loan. From the tenant union's point of view, an option for this purpose is preferable to a straight purchase of the building or an agreement to purchase. The tenant union is able to get direct experience with the building before committing itself to the building's probable value, i.e. its feasibility for rehabilitation or the long range problems in ownership. An option points to a sufficient enough inter-est in the building to permit the processing of a loan under the federal programs, and it therefore does not cause any additional delay in securing such a loan.[7]

An option would normally be drafted as part of the lease or management agreement. From the landlord's point of view, an option is usually of no advantage over and above the value of the lease or management agreement itself. In situations where the resale market for a slum building is particularly weak, the landlord may sense some advantage in an anticipated, if not obligated, sale of the building. However, under normal circumstances, he is likely to feel that he is being asked to give up in advance any increase in the value of the property that may result from the efforts of the tenant union during the term of the lease or management agreement. In such a case he is likely to consent only if (1) the exercise price for the option includes the anticipated increase in value or (2) a substantial price for the option itself is included in the rent. In the former case the option loses much of its value; however, it is probably still worth obtaining for the purpose of planning and of preventing speculative profits in the case of an extreme increase in value. The latter case may require careful judgment. Is the immediate cost of a rent level that is higher than the level that could otherwise be negotiated without an option likely to be offset by an increase in the value of the property or the option itself? In making this judgment the tenant union must consider the effects of any improvements to the buildings that it is likely to make during the term of the lease or management agreement, any savings in operating costs, any upgrading of the neighborhood as a whole and the likelihood that the building may be feasible for rehabilitation under a federal program.

In some cases the tenant union may be able to negotiate for the application of all or a portion of the rental payments against the purchase price if the option is exercised. This would naturally represent a substantial savings to the tenant union in the form of a lower purchase price and should therefore be a serious item of negotiation where there is a good likelihood that the option will be exercised. Of course the landlord is likely to demand some increase in rents to offset this advantage. But the correspondence need not be an even one in all cases: in situations where the landlord's resale market is particularly weak, he may himself attach some value to this type of an arrangement since it increases the likelihood that the option will be exercised.

Agreement to Purchase

A lease or management agreement with an agreement to purchase at a later date is likely to be preferable to an option from the landlord's point of view because it gives greater assurance of a buyer in a weak resale market. Under a lease with an agreement to purchase, the tenant union has assumed every economic risk except the insolvency of the tenant union itself. Accordingly, the tenant union should be able to negotiate a very substantial rent reduction during the term of the lease or management agreement.

A lease or management agreement with an agreement to purchase is useful where the tenant union intends to purchase and rehabilitate the building.

Since a tenant union is not likely to be able to make a downpayment, it will have to obtain a loan under a federal program or some other non-conventional source that can provide 100 per cent financing. Hence, the agreement should probably be made contingent upon obtaining such a loan. Although such a contingency reduces the landlord's assurance of a sale and may cause a corresponding decrease in the tenant union's bargaining position for a rent reduction, nevertheless the tenant union is not likely to want to assume the risk of being obligated to an agreement for which a loan cannot be obtained.

An agreement to purchase at a future date could be used as a device to prop up the resale market and, thus, as a bargaining tool to obtain a lower rent level, for example, a ten-year lease with an obligation to purchase at the end of the lease term. The tenant union would either have to purchase the building itself or find a buyer to whom it could resell. The tenant union would, in effect, be gambling on a stable or rising resale market due to its efforts in the building and the neighborhood during the lease period. Other types of agreements with a variety of conditions are possible, such as, the tenant union agreeing to use its best efforts to find a buyer for the property. The value of such agreements as negotiating tools can only be determined from the peculiar needs and expectations of the individual landlords.

The applications of rent payments to the purchase price is an item that is negotiable in purchase agreements as well as in the case of an option.

Purchase

A straight purchase without an intervening lease or management agreement is probably not advisable when dealing with a federally subsidized loan program. The approval of such a loan and the closing of the transaction is likely to take many months.[8] Without a lease, management agreement or some other form of agreement, the tenant union has no control over the property during the intervening period. It would seem to be a rather simple expedient to negotiate an intermediate agreement at the time the purchase was negotiated.

Access to New Money

The responsibility for control undoubtedly means a search for more money. An agreement, no matter how advantageous to the tenants on paper, is meaningless—and may prove harmful—to them if they do not at the same time have economic maneuverability. We now turn to the economic alternatives available to tenant groups.

A tenant union's access to new money for repairs, purchases, administrative expenses, etc., is one of its main sources of strength and one of the reasons why it may succeed in improving slum conditions where individual landlords fail. This does not mean that the tenant union itself is a source of capital. It is, almost by definition, an organization of relatively poor individuals who do not themselves have the financial resources to improve their own environment. A tenant union can, however, be a catalyst for funds from other sources. These sources may be considered under three general headings: conventional financing, federal financing, and other loans and contributions.

Conventional Financing

The purchase and rehabilitation of property through conventional financing is generally not a viable alternative for a tenant union itself because a downpayment is usually required by the lender. If a tenant union were to attempt to purchase buildings on any meaningful scale, it would have to tie down large amounts of money in individual down payments for individual buildings. A tenant union with sufficient capital to make a large down payment could probably make better use of such money in a trust fund designed to guarantee its performance of master leases on several pieces of property. The object of this strategy would be to create a fund that would induce lenders to re-finance the indebtedness of the existing owners on terms that will allow repairs to be made to the property.[9]

A conventional purchase of a slum building by a new private investor in a different economic position than the existing owner could work to the benefit of the tenant union. A new owner with good financial resources could obtain a loan on more favorable terms than an owner who relied merely on the security of the property, and the savings on the loan payments could be passed on to the tenants in the form of repairs or lower rents. A new owner in a higher tax bracket could benefit from the tax advantages of ownership, while the old owner has passed the point where continued ownership can have any tax benefit.[10] This could take the pressure off rents as the principle source of profit. A tenant union could assist the transfer to a new owner by exerting pressure on the old owner to take back a large second mortgage or to lower his sale price below the appraisal value set by the lending institution.[11] Either of these tactics, if successful, could result in decreasing the down payment that the new owner would have to invest.

Efforts by the tenant union to secure new conventional investment are likely to produce only minimal results initially. Although a new owner in a higher tax bracket may benefit more from his investment in slum buildings than the existing owners, still his investment might not compare favorably with a comparable investment in non-slum apartments. Thus, the decision to invest is not likely to be made, or if it is, it is likely to be made for political or social reasons. Fortunately, the mere existence of a tenant union is looked upon as a favorable factor by some landlords or potential landlords. Moreover, if the tenant union is successful over a period of time in making its other programs work, the economy of the former slum may begin to function more normally. At this point an investment in the area, although still no better than an investment in a non-slum area, may not suffer from any disadvantage. Thus, the tenant union's inducement of conventional purchases of slum buildings by new owners on a large scale is likely to be the last step in the conversion of an area from a slum economy to a non-slum economy.

Federal Financing

Financing by federal subsidy clearly provides the most promising method by which a tenant union can make a substantial impact on the rehabilitation of a slum community. The tactics discussed up to this point have involved either the assumption of certain economic risks by the tenant union or the inducement of more conventional capital into the slums. Both of these tactics can have an impact as part of an overall program. However, the central element in an effective program is the full use of federally subsidized programs, because only these programs can provide the large sums needed for major rehabilitation. Several tenant unions are now using these programs.[12]

The focus of this section is on purchase and rehabilitation under Section 236, a program enacted as part of the Housing and Urban Development Act of 1968 and administered by FHA.[13] This program is one of the most likely to be applicable to the situations faced by a tenant union. Other related programs will be referred to as the occasion warrants.[14] This section is not intended as a full or detailed explanation of these programs but rather as a discussion of how they may be applicable to the situation faced by a tenant union.

Section 236 (Non-profit sponsorship). A Section 236 loan enables a tenant union or other non-profit sponsor to purchase and rehabilitate slum apartments—in many cases with little or no rent increase to the tenants. Under Section 236, the tenant union borrows 100 per cent of the amount needed to purchase and rehabilitate the building or buildings by means of a 40-year conventional loan at the market rate of interest. FHA guarantees the loan and subsidizes it by paying to the lender the difference between the monthly payment necessary to amortize the loan at the market rate of interest and an interest rate of 1 per cent (this is often referred to as the "interest differential"). This is the maximum subsidy, and it will decrease if tenants with incomes near the upper limits of income eligibility are included in the program.

In order to be eligible for a Section 236 loan the project must meet the following requirements:

(a) The income level for most tenants within the project may not exceed 135 per cent of the maximum income level for eligibility for public housing within the particular area.[15] However, some tenants in a project may have income levels in excess of this amount but not in excess of 90 per cent of the income levels set by the Secretary of HUD for eligibility under the Section 221(d) (3) program.[16]

(b) Each tenant must pay 25 per cent of his income in rent. If the income of the tenant increases, the tenant must pay 25 per cent of the increased amount up to the fair market value of the apartment.[17]

(c) At least 20 per cent of the requested financing must be for rehabilitation.[18]

(d) The building when rehabilitated must be brought up to the minimum building code standards set by the FHA.[19]

(e) The total cost per unit (i.e. purchase price plus the cost of rehabilitation) may not exceed $11,600 (no bedrooms), $16,312 (one bedroom), $19,575 (two bedrooms), $24,650 (three bedrooms), or $27,912 (four bedrooms).[20]

The strictness of these requirements can be mitigated in several ways. First, several buildings in the same community—even in non-contiguous sites—may be combined together and the cost per unit taken as an average. This allows the tenant union to include some units within a project loan even though the percentage spent on rehabilitation of such units is below the minimum level or the total cost of such units is above the maximum level. These costs must, of course, be averaged out by costs of other units in the project that are well within the acceptable limits.

Secondly, in computing the cost of rehabilitation per unit (which must equal at least one-fifth of the total cost) the tenant union may include the amount of reserves necessary to finance certain future improvements, for example, if a new roof will be needed within five years, the tenant union may include the annual amount placed in reserve for such purpose when calculating the amount spent on rehabilitation.[21] The effect of this is to lower somewhat the minimum dollar value of initial rehabilitation per unit that is necessary to make the project eligible.

Thirdly, the project ". . . may include such nondwelling facilities as the Secretary deems adequate and appropriate to serve the occupants and the surrounding neighborhood . . . ." However, the project must be "predominantly residential" and the non-residential features must contribute to the "economic feasibility" of the project giving ". . . due consideration to the possible effect of the project on other business enterprises in the community . . . ."[22] Partial use of a structure for business or service facilities can help lower the portion of the total cost allocable to the dwelling units, thereby bringing these units within the limitations on cost per unit under the program.

Finally, up to 20 per cent of the units in any project may be occupied by tenants receiving assistance under the Rent Supplement Program or may be leased by local public housing authorities under the Section 23 program for rental to persons eligible for public housing. This is a very important aspect of the Section 236 program.[23] The subsidy under both of these programs is roughly equal and is deeper than is otherwise available under the Section 236 program.[24] This deeper subsidy allows the tenant union to include persons in a project whose income levels are so low that they would otherwise render the project not feasible. The Section 23 program requires coordination with another federal agency (the Housing Assistance Administration) and with the local public housing authority, hence it may entail greater administrative difficulties.

The Section 23 leasing program could, however, be used for an entire project apart from its use with a Section 236 project. This type of project seems feasible where all the tenants or potential tenants of the building have incomes low enough to be eligible for public housing. The respective rights of the tenant union and the housing authority would be defined by agreement; however, the tenant union would normally retain the right of tenant selection.[25]

Practicability for Low-income Tenants. It can be seen that a Section 236 loan is generally available only when a moderate amount of rehabilitation is needed. If the rehabilitation is not so substantial as to amount to one-fifth of the total cost, the project is not eligible. If, on the other hand, the necessary rehabilitation is very extensive and very costly, the total cost per unit will probably exceed the eligibility limits. It has also been stated that a Section 236 project is only feasible for tenants with a moderate income level (that is, $4,000 to $6,000 per year).[26] This is undoubtedly true as it pertains to new construction, but it may not be correct for rehabilitated housing.

The cost of new construction contains relatively few variables, and the rent levels necessary to pay off a loan—even with the FHA subsidy—run at predictably higher levels than the hard core poor can generally afford. The same generalization does not apply to rehabilitated housing because there are several variables to consider. The purchase price of the existing buildings is likely to fluctuate, especially when a tenant union is the potential purchaser.[27] The cost of rehabilitation will vary because the condition of different buildings varies and because the rehabilitation industry is far less structured than the home building industry. Finally, the terms and the amount of any existing indebtedness on slum buildings may vary widely.

The existing indebtedness on the property has a particular importance that should be examined more closely. A large debt means large debt service costs, which the existing rents have been made high enough to cover. A large indebtedness on terms and conditions typical for a slum area may indicate that a substantial amount of money can become available for rehabilitation simply by refinancing the existing conventional loan with an FHA loan under Section 236.[28]

Two problems with the approach should be noted. First, the present tenants may not be eligible for the federal program utilized to rehabilitate the building. They may not qualify because their incomes are too high or too low, or because they do not satisfy other criteria prescribed by the program. Second, rehabilitation will increase the value of the building, thus causing an increase in taxes. As a result, there will be an added expense reflected in the rents, thus decreasing the amount of rehabilitation possible by refinancing without raising monthly rents.

Administrative problems. A Section 236 project involves administrative difficulties, expenses, and delays. The average processing time from initial application to occupancy of the building is probably on the average not less than 19 months.[29] Funding is a problem. Section 236 and other federal programs depend upon annual appropriations by Congress that are often inadequate. The tenant union as a sponsor faces the problem of "seed money" necessary to cover costs incurred before the loan is obtained. These costs usually include costs in securing the land, advance fees to architects, contractors, consultants, etc. This is largely a cash-flow problem, since the cost of such expenses will be reimbursed to the tenant union out of the proceeds of the loan. Administrative difficulties can arise if the tenant union is unfamiliar with FHA procedures and a professional consultant has not been retained. This has important implications for the structuring and staffing. If a tenant union plans to undertake such projects, it will probably want to retain a competent professional consultant or will want a working arrangement with a housing development corporation or similar organization.

Section 236 (limited-dividend sponsorship). Section 236 projects are not limited to non-profit sponsors, since "limited-dividend" companies are also eligible to participate. Limited-dividend sponsors can only obtain 90 per cent financing (as opposed to the 100 per cent financing for non-profit sponsors), and they are limited to a 6 per cent return on the equity invested.[30] Although the rents in such a project must be sufficient to cover a new item of expense (the 6 per cent profit on the owner's equity), this expense is offset by the decrease in the loan amortization expense (the amortization is based on a 90 per cent loan instead of a 100 per cent loan). Therefore, the rents in a limited-dividend project need not be any higher and may even be lower than rents in a non-profit project.

Limited-dividend projects have a practical advantage in that they usually require less FHA scrutiny. A non-profit sponsor must show certain ties with the community to assure the FHA that the organization will maintain a continuing interest in the project and the loan. With a limited-dividend company the 10 per cent down payment usually speaks for itself.

It is probably not practical for a tenant union to sponsor a limited-dividend project, because the down payment—even a 10 per cent down payment—would normally be out of its reach. A limited-dividend sponsorship is, however, a practical form of investment for a private investor, particularly because of tax advantages attractive to wealthy investors. A tenant union will probably want to encourage and facilitate such investment. Sponsorship of rehabilitation projects by limited-dividend companies may eliminate many of the problems of delay, seed money, and expert personnel that a tenant union might encounter if it attempted to do all of such projects itself.

The success of a tenant union in obtaining new investment in limited-dividend projects largely depends on how attractive such projects are when compared with a comparable investment in non-slum conventional apartments. The question of a comparable investment must, first of all, be made clear. In a Section 236 project the investor puts up a 10 per cent down payment; in a conventional investment a down payment of about 20 per cent is often required. Hence, an investment under Section 236 may generate a loan and a project roughly double in value to the loan and project generated by the same amount of money in a conventional investment. Therefore, since the accelerated depreciation is computed on the full value of the building, the tax deduction for depreciation may often be twice as large for a Section 236 investment as for the same investment in a conventional project. A Section 236 loan that is twice the size of a conventional loan is likely to require loan payments 2/3 to 3/4 the size of the loan payments on such conventional loans. Thus, the interest deduction for a Section 236 project will be less than for a comparable project under conventional financing. Although a larger percentage of each monthly payment goes towards equity build-up, this larger percentage is computed on a smaller monthly payment. Hence, there may be no appreciable difference in the equity build-up in the first ten years of a Section 236 project as compared with a conventional project. Normally, a smaller monthly loan payment would add to the profitability of a project by reducing the expense of debt service, but this is not the case with a Section 236 project because profit is limited to 6 per cent of the equity invested. This 6 per cent limitation is generally considered to be somewhat low.[31]

In terms of the factors just discussed, a Section 236 investment would seem to compare rather well with a conventional real estate investment. However, comparative resale value must also be considered. The demand for both types of apartments will probably remain high for the forseeable future, so there is probably little difference on this point. However, the FHA does not permit refinancing of a limited-dividend project until 20 years have elapsed, and as a result the resale value of such projects is poor as compared with the profitable resale market for non-slum apartments. This factor obviously weighs against a Section 236 investment.

Another factor to consider is that the investor may not always be a passive investor. In the case of new construction under Section 236, an investor-builder or investor-architect may realize a combined profit on the investment and construction so as to make the project more attractive. In such a situation the actual cash make-up of the owner's equity may be quite a bit less than the 10 per cent of cost. This is quite advantageous to the investor.[32] In rehabilitation—as opposed to new construction—the attractiveness of this may be lessened somewhat by the fact that a small percentage of the total cost of the project will go for construction and repairs. On the other hand, it may be enhanced by the fact that federally subsidized projects are among the few projects large enough to permit economies of scale in the rehabilitation process.[33]

The biggest deterrent to limited-dividend sponsorship of rehabilitation projects may be the fear that the apartment buildings will fall victim to the cumulative effect of the deterioration on the surrounding slum neighborhood. A strong tenant union can help offset this fear by making some impact on halting or reversing the deterioration of the neighborhood.

The tenant union could also help reduce the operating expenses of the project. The FHA calculates a rent schedule based upon a vacancy factor of 7 per cent of gross rents and a management fee of from 3 to 8 per cent of gross rents. Any savings on these projected amounts in the actual operation of the building can be used to repay the mortgage, increase operating reserves, finance improvements or reduce rents. A tenant union may have better control over vacancies and management costs because of economies in its scale of operation. For these reasons, it may be that a strong and cooperative tenant union would tip the scales in favor of a decision to invest in a limited-dividend project.

A limited-dividend project is also possible where the original owner retains his interest in the building. In such a case the owner transfers his equity interest to a limited-dividend company of which he retains control.

Rehabilitation by the original owner under Section 236 seems limited in its usefulness. Rehabilitation would not provide the same tax benefits that a purchase and rehabilitation by a new owner would generate since the old owner is likely to have exhausted any depreciation advantages. Moreover, in most instances, rehabilitation by the original owner would not permit the grouping of several buildings into one loan package so as to obtain the minimum number of units required, average out the cost differences, and simplify the administrative procedures. However, a Section 236 loan to the original owner might prove useful in one instance. If the owner insists upon a price for his equity that is so high as to put the cost per unit above the FHA maximum, he may be persuaded to transfer his interest to a limited-dividend company for an assigned value that is within the FHA cost limitations. The owner in this situation would be limited to a 6 per cent return on the assigned value of his equity, but this might prove attractive to an owner in some situations.[34]

Loans and Contributions

A tenant union can always use money, and it is probably superfluous to say so. However, it is worth considering briefly how non-commercial money (money that is not usually attracted into the real estate market) can be attracted by a tenant union and how it can best be utilized.

A tenant union could increase its attractiveness for loans and grants by qualifying itself as a charitable entity. Charitable status may be an absolute requirement in attracting contributions from charitable trusts and corporations.[35] It may be just as important in attracting gifts from non-charities, since charitable status is necessary to make such gifts tax deductible for the donor.[36] However, charitable status may require restrictions on the tenant union's political activities. For this reason the most practical way to achieve the same result is for the tenant union to establish or to affiliate with another organization that qualifies as a charity.

Gifts of money without limitation as to its use are, of course, ideal from the tenant union's point of view. However, gifts limited to specific purposes such as loan funds and improvements to certain buildings can also be valuable. Low interest loans can also be valuable. Gifts and loans are important not only for meeting the expenses of the union but for bolstering its balance sheet, thus adding to the belief that it will be able to meet the financial obligations it undertakes.

There are other, less obvious forms that private economic assistance can take. Some of them are:

(1) A guarantee of the tenant union's performance on a master lease or leases. A guarantee by an organization with solid financial resources would not only increase the attractiveness of such a lease to a landlord but may also increase the landlord's ability to obtain refinancing of this property on more favorable terms through conventional sources. Such refinancing could result in reduced rents or money for repairs to the structure.

(2) A loan fund for tenants. When a tenant union leases a building, it assumes the costs of vacancies and evictions, many of which are caused by a tenant's temporary inability to pay rent. A loan fund on attractive terms would enable individual tenants to meet such emergencies and would help the tenant union by cutting down on vacancies and evictions.

(3) The loan of employees. A successful tenant union requires several employees with a variety of skills. A financial backer could lend employees with specialized skills to the tenant union permanently or temporarily when they are needed. This would obviously lower the administrative expenses of the tenant union considerably.

(4) Co-sponsorship of federally subsidized projects. By lending its name and prestige to an application for federal funding (such as a Section 236 loan), the financial backer that is familiar with FHA procedures can facilitate the granting of such a loan.[37] Either co-sponsorship or sponsorship through an entity formed jointly for such purpose is a possibility.

All of this raises the question of financial dependency. A tenant union must obviously assess any risk to its independence and guard against it. However, a judicious use of private funds is likely to be an important adjunct of its success.

---

1. Four Tenant unions that have achieved some success in this regard (described in subsequent references) are: Cleveland - Hough Tenant Union, 7811 Hough Ave., Cleveland, Ohio; League of Autonomous Bronx Organizations for Renewal (LABOR), 1309 Boston Road, Bronx, N.Y.C., New York; Lawndale Union to End Slums, 3322 W. Roosevelt, Chicago, Illinois; United Tenants for Collective Action, 7641 Linwood Ave., Detroit, Michigan.

2. The Cleveland Hough Tenant Union operates under a collective bargaining agreement but performs some functions that are similar to those of a management agreement.

3. Davis and Schwartz, "Tenant Unions: An Experiment in Private Law Making," in *Housing for the Poor: Rights and Remedies*, 111 (1967).

4. A management agreement with a mutual right of cancellation is similar to a normal, commercial agreement to manage property. The latter is merely an employment agreement in which the manager is paid a percentage of gross rentals. See Everett, "Apartment House Management," in *Real Estate Encyclopedia* 606 (1960).

5. See, generally, Tulley, "Lease Contracts," in *Real Estate Encyclopedia* 775 (1960).

6. Internal Revenue Code, §170.

7. Interview with John J. Boyle, Director, Low- and Moderate-Income Housing Branch, Federal Housing Administration, San Francisco Regional Office.

8. *Kaiser Commission Report*, 87.

9. For example, a tenant union could establish a trust fund from rent savings, contributions, etc., for the purpose of curing any default on a mortgage or deed of trust by a landlord or landlords with whom the tenant union has a master lease. Whether such a fund would have any influence on a lender's decision would probably depend on two factors: (1) the size of the fund in relationship to the size of the mortgage or mortgages, and (2) the number of mortgages that are guaranteed by the same fund.

10. George Sternlieb, *The Tenement Landlord*, Rutgers University Press, p. 102.

11. The practice of appraising property at a higher value than the sales price is a method used by lending institutions to finance a higher proportion of the purchase price. This is often done to attract borrowers when money for loans is plentiful.
See Wallace F. Smith, *The Low-Rise Speculative Apartment*, 23 (1964). Presumably, a tenant union could accomplish the same thing by forcing the old owner to sell at a price below the appraisal price, thereby allowing the new owner to purchase the property with a smaller down payment. However, lenders will almost always require some cash investment by the purchaser to deter him from abandoning the property in case it becomes unprofitable.

12. For example, Lawndale Union to End Slums, United Tenants for Collective Action.

13. 12 U.S.C. §1715z-1.

14. Sec. 221(d) (3), enacted as part of the Housing Act of 1961—the predecessor of the Sec. 236 program [12 U.S.C. §1715 1(d) (3)]
Sec. 235, enacted as part of the Housing and Urban Development Act of 1968—a homeownership program parallel to Sec. 236 [12 U.S.C. §1715z.]
Sec. 235(j), enacted as part of the Housing and Urban Development Act of 1968—a program for the rehabilitation and sale of homes to moderate-income families [12 U.S.C. §1715z(j)].
Sec. 23, enacted as part of the Housing and Urban Development Act of 1965—a program enabling local public housing authorities to lease units in a privately owned structure [42 U.S.C §1421b].
Sec. 101, enacted as part of the Housing and Urban Development Act of 1965—a program for providing rent supplements to low-income persons [12 U.S.C. §1701s].

15. 12 U.S.C. §1715z-1(i) (2). Eligibility for public housing varies from area to area. In each area the public housing authority must demonstrate:
. . . that a gap of at least 20 per centum (except in the case of a displaced family or an elderly family) has been left between the upper rental limits for admission to the proposed low-rent housing and the lowest rents at which private enterprise unaided by public subsidy is providing (through new construction and available existing structures) a substantial supply of decent, safe and sanitary housing toward meeting an adequate volume thereof . . .
United States Housing Act of 1937, §15(7)(b)(ii). This requirement is mitigated by a $300 allowance for each minor child. 12 U.S.C. §1715z-1(m).

16. 12 U.S.C. §1715z-1(1)(2). No more than 20 per cent of the tenants in the initial rent-up of all Section 236 projects may have incomes within this higher category. However, this is a limitation on the entire program—not on any particular project. Hence, a project can theoretically be approved even if all of the tenants are within this higher category of eligibility. However, the FHA is directed to administer the program ". . . so as to accord a preference to those families whose incomes are within the lowest practicable limits for obtaining rental accommodations in projects assisted under this section."

17. 12 U.S.C. §1715z-1(f).

18. Boyle interview, *supra* note 7. This is an informal administrative guideline based on the FHA's interpretation of §236, which directs that the project shall ". . . comply with such stan-

dards and conditions as the Secretary may prescribe to establish the acceptability of the property for mortgage insurance. . . ."

19. *Ibid.* This is also an informal administrative guideline and generally consists of the higher of (1) the local building code, or (2) the FHA Minimum Property Standards for Urban Renewal Rehabilitation (1963). The latter standard, which technically only applies to urban renewal projects, is used informally in this context. It consists of two parts, one of which is mandatory and the other of which is recommended. See McFarland, "Residential Rehabilitation: An Overview," in *Residential Rehabilitation* (1965).

20. §221(d)(3)(ii) [12 U.S.C. §1715 1(d)(3)(ii)] as incorporated by reference into §236(j)(3) [12 U.S.C. §1715z-1(j)(3)]. The limitations stated in the text are 45 per cent higher than those stated in the code. The FHA has authority to use the 45 per cent higher cost limitations where the ". . . cost levels so require; . . . ." Information provided to the Kaiser Commission by the FHA indicated that in many major cities the purchase and rehabilitation of housing units is feasible within the FHA cost limitations. *Kaiser Commission Report,* 101.

21. Boyle interview, *supra* note 7. This can be very important for small buildings since a minimum of five units is required for a §236 project. (12 U.S.C. §1715z-1(j)(5)(B).) *Kaiser Commission Report,* 102.

22. 12 U.S.C. §1715z-1(j)(5)(A).

23. The authorization for including up to 20 per cent of the tenants within the Rent Supplement program is set by statute. 12 U.S.C. 1701s(h)(1)(D). The inclusion of a §23 lease within a §236 project is authorized by administrative practice only. In general, the FHA will follow a similar 20 per cent limitation on §23 units within a §236 project, however it is not required to do so. Boyle interview, *supra* note 7.

24. *Kaiser Commission Report,* 64-65.

25. 42 U.S.C. §1421b(d)(1).

26. *Kaiser Commission Report,* 65.

27. Both the Clifton Terrace Tenants' Association and the Lawndale Union to End Slums have had success in driving down the purchase price of buildings.

28. "An examination of the present debt structure on properties in the rehabilitation area is also an important clue to feasibility. It has often been found that where existing debt on properties is for short terms and at relatively high interest rates, existing debt plus the cost of rehabilitation can be refinanced under §220 terms, with little or no increase in existing debt service charges." McFarland, "Residential Rehabilitation," in Essays in *Urban Land Economics,* 121 (1966). See also *Kaiser Commission Report,* 101.

29. *Kaiser Commission Report,* 87-88.

30. *Ibid.,* 82.

31. *Ibid.*

32. *Ibid.,* 81.

33. *Ibid.,* 108-109.

34. A tenant union could perform a very useful function merely by disseminating information about the federal programs that are available. Quite often homeowners and landlords who would benefit from such programs fail to do so because they are unaware of their existence. *Kaiser Commission Report,* 97.

35. See Uniform Supervision of Trustees for Charitable Purposes Act.

36. Internal Revenue Code, §170(c).

37. The Kate Maremont Foundation to End Slums has done this by creating a non-profit corporation in conjunction with the Union and using this corporation to sponsor such projects.

CHAPTER 16

A Plan for More Public Housing Funds

Thomas Anton
Rober Lind*

Sooner or later, all proposals for the achievement of large-scale social objectives encounter the hard question: how are such social programs to be financed? For a variety of reasons—the financial strain of Vietnam, overburdened tax structures, etc.—answers to that question have increasingly been found unsatisfactory in recent years, even as new and greater demands on the public purse have been made. One answer that deserves more attention than it has yet received is the use of idle general revenue funds and public employee pension funds to support desirable public programs that are otherwise underfinanced. Illinois has recently begun such a policy, with excellent results. In this chapter, we investigate the possibility of adopting such a plan elsewhere, focusing particular attention on the problem of low income housing. While the situation in Michigan provides our data, the potential of the program is not limited by state boundaries. Since other states are similarly endowed with pension and idle general revenue funds, what we argue here is clearly applicable on a national scale.

Tenants' unions and other housing groups (commissions, officials, etc.) aware of this potential may well play a role in persuading public officials of a policy-oriented use of public monies. Their own projects might also qualify for support under any new programs which develop.

Informed observers agree that the shortage of adequate housing for low and moderate-income families in the United States is critical. The national dimensions of this crisis were made clear when the Congress, in the 1968

*Thomas Anton is an Associate Professor of Political Science and Roger Lind is a Professor of Social Work; both at The University of Michigan. This paper was prepared with the assistance of the following participants in the 1969 Social Welfare Policy Seminar, the School of Social Work: Charles Chomet, Henry Dooha, Barry Giller, Suzanne Ginsberg, Suann Hecht, Harriet Lancaster, and Lynn Morris. The authors also wish to acknowledge the valuable comments and suggestions of Professor Arthur Bromage.

Housing Act, committed the nation to a policy of building 26 million new housing units by 1978. Its local dimensions have been apparent for decades in the slums of most of our large cities—and recent rioting in those cities has underlined the obvious in a particularly threatening way. Yet, apart from laudable statements of goals, very little has been done to provide decent housing for those most in need of it, and it is increasingly apparent that very little will be done in the immediate future. Periodically high interest rates have siphoned money away from the housing industry to such an extent that new units are now being produced at a rate which falls short of our national goals by more than a million units per year. The Congress has failed to appropriate much more than token sums for low-income housing. And, while there is much talk of finding ways to mass-produce inexpensive housing, industry has failed to take up this challenge, restrictive building codes and union practices continue to create barriers, and money, once again, is difficult or impossible to find. Here, as in other areas of public policy, we have talked a fine game, but we play it very badly indeed.

The easiest response to this situation, perhaps, would be to abandon the hope of making a noticeable dent in the housing shortage. We think that this response is now widespread, but we also think that it is premature, for there exist a number of opportunities for public action that have not yet been attempted. The existence of close to two billion dollars, primarily in public employee pension funds but also including general revenues, constitutes one major opportunity, since these monies are not now being extensively used to support socially-useful programs such as housing, though they can be so used. To do so, existing practices and policies will have to be changed. We know that such changes are not easily accomplished, but we hope to make a persuasive case for the changes we advocate. That case includes the fact that substantial sums of additional money are available without additional taxation; the belief that such monies, in combination with other state resources, can materially affect the housing crisis in Michigan; and the hope that the present political climate in Michigan is ripe for some new approaches to old, but serious problems.

The Availability of Untapped Funds

Governments in Michigan generate enormous sums of money in tax revenues and in contributions, from public employee salaries to various trust funds. Most of the revenue funds are expended rather quickly to support authorized public programs, but for various reasons surprisingly large cash balances exist at any given point in time. Revenues are collected weekly or monthly while expenditures for various purchases—such as construction projects—frequently are not made until months or sometimes years after they are authorized. These cash balances, though large, are dwarfed by the amounts deposited in trust or pension funds whose annual expenditures constitute a small fraction of their huge and growing deposits. Exact amounts will vary from month to month, depending on expenditures, but a reasonably good idea of the magnitude of these monies can be obtained from Table I (drawn from State of Michigan and City of Detroit sources).

TABLE I—MAJOR REVENUE AND PENSION
FUNDS AVAILABLE, STATE OF MICHIGAN
AND DETROIT 1968

Fund	State of Michigan	City of Detroit
General	$326,000,000	$200,000,000
Pension		
State Employees	222,000,000	
Municipal Employees	63,000,000	
Public Schools	561,000,000	
Police and Fire		150,000,000
City Employees		188,000,000
Totals	$1,172,000,000	$538,000,000

Grand Total: $1,710,000,000

Not all of these monies are "available" in any permanent sense. For example, the $200 million general fund total for Detroit represents an estimate of monthly transactions involving, for the most part, investments in short-term treasury notes. And cash balances are required by law for pension funds, thus reducing the availability of these monies. On the other hand, we have confined ourselves to the largest state and city of Detroit funds only. There are many other trust funds which, if added to our figures, would add significantly to our totals. Thus our estimates are probably reasonably fair. Furthermore, our figures are drawn primarily from 1968 reports. Since contributions to both general and pension funds increase as taxes and employee contributions increase, it seems safe to conclude that our figures represent sums that will continue to grow. The certainty of further growth in already huge sums of publicly-generated money underlines the increasing importance of asking whether Michigan citizens are well-served by the present uses of these funds.

How These Funds are Used

Disposition of idle cash funds held by governments in Michigan is authorized and regulated by both Constitution and law, but the limitations thus imposed are not notably severe. Article IX (Sec. 20) of the Michigan Constitution of 1963, for example, merely prohibits the deposit of state funds in banks . . . "other than those organized under the national or state banking laws" and further prohibits such deposits in amounts exceeding . . . "50 percent of the capital and surplus of such bank." Moreover, the State Treasurer, authorized by law to serve as custodian of state funds, is granted wide discretion in determining the rate of interest to be required from state depository banks—limited only by his judgment of the rate he "shall deem best for the interest of the state"—and can, in addition, invest state funds in both U.S. Government notes and prime commercial paper. State law is somewhat more restrictive regarding investments of Detroit funds, limiting such investments to certificates of deposit in banks, municipal bonds, or treasury notes. According to the City Charter, investments of city revenues are made by the Controller's office, with the permission of the City Council. However, each year the City Council authorizes the City Controller to make investment transactions on his own authority. The Charter also authorizes the City Treasurer to place general revenue funds in bank time deposits. Officials authorized to handle idle state and city funds are thus relatively free to dispose of those funds within rather broad and flexible legal limitations.

The manner in which state officials use their discretionary authority can be seen in the Department of Treasury's preliminary report for fiscal 1968 which indicates that of the $326 million held on June 30, 1968, some $109 million was invested in prime commerical paper, $73 million in short-term U.S. Government securities, and $144 million in time and deposits in Michigan banks. We were unable to obtain precise figures from Detroit, but discussions with officials there revealed that most of the City's idle cash is currently being invested in short-term treasury notes which city officials feel offer the best rate of return for city funds. Curiously, however, no attempt is made to compute the actual rate of return on these city investments. Thus, government notes, bank deposits, and commercial paper, in that order, are the primary sources of investment of idle state and city of Detroit funds.

Statutory regulations governing the investment of public employee pension funds are more restrictive, and rightly so, for these monies are held in trust to support public servants in their retirement years. Though such funds have broad investment authority—including, since 1965, authority to invest in common stock—both the nature of the investments made and the proportion of total fund assets to any given investment are subject to precise limitations. For example, such a fund may not "have more than 10 percent of its capital and surplus invested in or loaned upon the securities of any one institution, nor to any one person, corporation or firm . . ." (Sec. 908). Similarly, fund investments in common stocks are "limited to an amount not to exceed 25 percent of its total assets . . ." and stocks purchased "(1) must have paid dividends in at least five of the past seven consecutive years during which period net earnings shall have exceeded dividends paids, and (2) shall be registered on a national securities exchange." (Sec. 2 of P.A. 279 of 1968). Given the desirability of financially sound retirement systems, such restrictions do not appear unreasonable.

Table II indicates investments in real estate and other obligations by the three largest state pension funds and the two Detroit funds. As shown there, real estate comprises a substantial portion of pension fund investments, particularly for the largest fund, the Public School Employees Retirement Fund. Compared to the state systems, the two city funds invest a proportionately much smaller share of their resources in real estate. We were unable to get precise details on the nature of these real estate investments, but it appears that the bulk of state mortgage investments are devoted to F.H.A.-insured loans for multi-family dwellings, and relatively little invested in single-family mortgages.

TABLE II—REAL ESTATE AND OTHER
INVESTMENTS OF LARGEST PENSION FUNDS, 1968

Fund	Real Estate	Other	Total	Percent Real Estate
State Employees Retirement Fund	$ 72,452,000	$145,689,000	$218,141,000	32
Municipal Employees Retirement Fund	13,264,000	48,794,000	62,058,000	21
Public School Employees Retirement Fund	179,789,000	368,794,000	548,583,000	32
Detroit City Employees Retirement Fund	21,555,000	166,646,000	188,201,000	11.5
Detroit Police and Firemen Fund	13,834,000	136,921,000	150,755,000	9
Totals:	$300,894,000	$836,844,000	$1,167,738,000	26

Criteria of Decision

Since legal provisions allow investment officials a fair amount of discretion in disposing of their resources, it is apparent that an explanation of the pattern of investment sketched out above requires some understanding of both who the relevant officials are and the criteria they use in deciding what, where, and when to invest. Officially, at least, the structure of decision-making appears complex. At the state level, the Treasurer is responsible for investing idle cash funds, but the three major pension funds are each governed by seven-man Boards. The Treasurer, however, is a participant in each of these Boards, and in practice the Treasurer monopolizes the investment decisions of the three funds with the aid of a small staff. Informally, then, the State's investment decision-making structure is quite simple. In Detroit, as we already have pointed out, idle cash is invested by the City Controller. Ten and eleven-member boards, some members elected, govern the City Employees and Police and Firemen Funds in Detroit but, as in the case of state funds, a single civil service employee, aided by a very small staff, dominates investment decisions. Probably because of the small size of the staff, each of these funds retains the services of a large bank to counsel it on potential investments. The Detroit Bank and Trust Company has performed this service for the General City Employees Retirement Fund, while the National Bank of Detroit has been investment counselor to the Police and Firemen Retirement System. We shall have more to say about these arrangements shortly, but for the moment, it is most significant to emphasize the simplicity of the decision-making structure handling state and city investments. Probably not more than a half-dozen officials, of whom the State Treasurer, the Detroit City Controller and the Executive Secretary of the two city pension funds are certainly the most important, control the investment of nearly two billion dollars in publicly-generated funds.

Our discussions with these officials made it clear that a single criterion dominates their investment choices—achievement of the highest possible rate of return consistent with safety of investment. This criterion is viewed as a form of "keeping faith" with public employees, whose contributions have built up the pension funds and who deserve the assurance that their money will be handled in a financially sound manner. It is also viewed as sound public policy to generate as much "profit" as possible from idle cash funds. Thus, the city of Detroit prefers Treasury notes to bank deposits because of higher returns; city and state pension funds prefer high-grade stocks to mortgages for the same reason; and in real estate, the funds prefer secure and safe investments to "chancy" possibilities such as housing units in ghetto areas. Such investments are made, but at higher-than-normal interest rates to compensate for the greater risk involved.

To say that one criterion dominates, however, is not to say that other criteria are not involved. Let us examine some of these other criteria used in investing idle cash and pension fund monies.

Bank deposits of idle public funds enlarge bank reserves, at least temporarily, and thus enable banks to generate additional profits for themselves. In making such deposits, the State has followed a policy of placing up to $300,000 with any qualified bank at a rate of 5½ percent. To obtain additional funds, qualified banks are required to pay 6¼ percent, closer to current market rates. The differential between these two rates can be thought of as a state subsidy, paid, according to officials, as a reward for the services provided by banks to Michigan citizens. Not all Michigan banks apply for these deposits, but close to 300 banks received them in 1968, thus revealing the popularity of such subsidies among bankers. The State, it should be noted, requires nothing of banks receiving the lower interest money: they may use it as they wish, according to their own interests, subject only to repayment on demand. In effect, then, the State rewards "service to the public" but it makes no effort to define the nature of the services that qualify for its rewards.

In somewhat similar fashion, the City of Detroit attempts to maintain an established pattern of distributing city funds among various banks, not so much to reward public service in general, but to reward bank cooperation in purchasing the City's tax anticipation warrants—which are not always easy to sell. Or again, the recent shortage of cash among city banks led the City Controller to propose shifting more cash into bank deposits to improve "general city welfare", though such a shift would have been accomplished at considerable expense to the City government. Powerful as the desire to maximize financial return is, then, State of Michigan and City of Detroit officials both follow policies that produce something less than a maximum return on cash investments. And they do so to reward what they view as some forms of "public" service.

Pension fund investors appear to be more strict in demanding the highest possible financial return for the money at their disposal. As noted earlier, this attitude discourages investments in mortgages, except for those backed by F.H.A. guarantees, which constitute the bulk of fund mortgage investments. Conventional mortgages are carefully scrutinized in terms of interest to be paid, length of mortgage, type of project, potential growth of the area, and community characteristics such as vacancy rates. The additional security of geographic diversification is also sought, with the result that a good deal of Michigan money is invested in California, Florida, New Jersey, and other states.

For mortgages especially, the demand for financially secure investments has the effect of imposing penalties on organizations interested in achieving something in addition to profit. The state funds will not invest in multi-family housing units in ghetto areas unless additional interest of almost one percent is paid, and the city funds demand an interest rate one-half percent higher than the current rate on triple A bonds, even for F.H.A.-supported mortgages. Thus the managers of public money in Michigan freely grant public subsidies to banks, simply because they are banks, and at the same time, impose financial penalties on organizations involved in attempting to solve some of our most serious housing problems.

The Need for A "Public" Policy

The situation we have outlined briefly here represents, we think, a mixed bag of accomplishment. Entrusted with large sums of publicly-generated money, state and city investors have performed with some success: some profit has been made on idle cash reserves, the various pension funds have developed investment portfolios adequate to the demands likely to be made on them, and the funds have even put some of their money into useful housing projects. But there are several reasons for concern. One is that, at a time when money to finance housing is extremely scarce in Michigan, a great deal of Michigan money is being invested in other states. Another is that public investors who claim to be pursuing a policy of "highest return" on idle cash investments seem neither to have any very precise idea of what that return is nor to follow any rationalized guidelines for deviating from that policy. A third is that present practices seem to us to subsidize organizations that have no need for state subsidies while penalizing organizations whose need for state assistance is very great indeed. Though it is possible to place other interpretations on these conditions, we believe that, in essence, they reflect the absence of any coherent public standards for utilizing the public funds available to the State and the city of Detroit.

Let us recall again that investment officials claim to be interested primarily in maximum returns from secure investments. To be sure, this criterion is frequently violated, with uncertain results. But even if it were followed perfectly, we think it would be deficient, for in that case it would make of government a mere handmaiden of market forces. Indeed, we think that such a result is precisely what is now achieved with distressing frequency, for many public investment decisions are in fact made through the initiative of the stock and mortgage brokers employed by the various Michigan funds. The State, with its own staff, relies on Moody's Investment Service, while Detroit, with almost no staff, relies on banks to give investment advice. By these means, investors of public funds become locked in to national mortgage and stock markets whose brokers provide information to officials about property or stocks considered attractive and information to financiers about the availability of money from Michigan funds. This surely helps to explain the investment of Michigan funds in other states, as well as the reluctance of investment officials to expand their vision of what is socially useful beyond the first dollar sign. We do not quarrel with the brokerage function, which is and will continue to be essential for public fund managers. Our quarrel, rather, is with the lack of public purposes which permits the broker to assume a role that properly belongs to policy-determining public officials and that can only be played when such officials have goals that reflect public as well as financial policies.

What, then, might such policies be? We propose to give a number of answers to this questions, using as our model, the highly successful program formerly operated by the then-Treasurer of the State of Illinois, now Senator Adlai E. Stevenson III. Through what he called a "linked deposit" program, Treasurer Stevenson developed policies for investing the $600 million idle cash balance available to the State of Illinois every year in banks showing a record of useful community service, including the support of low-income housing.

Soon after Stevenson became state treasurer of Illinois in 1967, he initiated the linked deposit program. That is, he set up policies which stated that the state's depository funds would be distributed to banks in two ways. First, all banks throughout the state would be eligible for a mathematically computed portion of the state's funds provided they maintained a certain ratio of loans to assets. Secondly, banks could "earn" additional deposits by demonstrating (initially just by indicating) that they were participating in the financing of a number of "public goods". These goods included participation in the interim financing of publicly supported housing; participating in the economic rebuilding of a disaster area; participating in the financing of a variety of community service programs such as student and small business loans. Stevenson, in initiating this policy, did so under a broad authority for the placement of state depository funds. A major success of this policy was the underwriting of $90 million in housing construction funds for rental units for middle-income families under the Federal 221d (3) below market interest rate subsidy program.

The efforts in Illinois led the Ford Foundation, already interested in overcoming the dichotomy between their investment policies and the social goals for which their earnings on these investments were used, to authorize a study of the Stevenson effort. While the Ford Report emphasized the multiplier effects rather than the redistributive effects of such a linked deposits program, its main thesis was that this is a way to further public goals without further cost since the small loss in return on investment will be made up in the long run from increased taxes (on newly built property, via newly employed people, residents with improved educational levels and hence earning power, etc.).

The report also concluded that state governments in the aggregate possess large quantities of funds that are potentially available for use as linked deposits. In 1967, for instance, total cash and security holdings were almost $64 billion. Almost $40 billion of that was in insurance and trust systems, some of which are bound by law not to invest directly in mortgages. Since the goal of most of these funds is to maximize returns in order to increase payments to contributing members, the likelihood of a linked deposit or a harnessed investment program with these funds is probably dimmer. It seems clear, nevertheless, that opportunities exist for access to substantial amounts of public monies.

The Illinois program did not involve pension fund investments, but we think it is easily adaptable to such investments, as well as to cash balances. Above all, this program was a concrete example of something that we think is long past due in the state of Michigan and elsewhere: development of policies to channel public investments into socially-useful programs. Illinois now follows such policies, and while doing so earns the highest rate of interest in that State's history. Michigan and other states could well do the same.

Policy Proposal I: Government should stop paying unrestricted subsidies to banks. The notion that all banks are performing useful public services simply by being banks may be valid in some extraordinarily vague sense, but as a justification for public subsidy, it is indefensible. Grocery stores perform a public service in precisely the same sense, yet they receive no special state payments, nor do drugstores, laundromats or any of a hundred other commercial establishments involved in servicing the needs of the public for private profit. Since such payments serve no visible public ends, and are costly to boot, taxpayers are being shortchanged with every dollar that goes into such subsidies. They should be stopped and soon.

Policy Proposal II: States and municipalities should develop explicit public service criteria to determine bank eligibility for public cash deposits. We have pointed out that state and city investors frequently make cash deposits for reasons that have little or nothing to do with "maximum return." We believe that these practices are perfectly appropriate, for government has a responsibility for and an interest in, a wide variety of social goods that cannot be measured by interest rates. A well-educated citizenry, for example, is a strong government interest and, at a time when education loans are in short supply, public funds might be channeled into banks willing to make such loans. Michigan investment officials have supported such "social goods" in the past, but in a non-rationalized, sporadic and *ad hoc* way. We believe that the time has come to declare the social goods worthy of public financial support in some detail, to develop criteria for relative public investment in each of them, and to require bank support for such social goods as a condition for deposit of state funds.

Note that such a policy would do no harm to bank ability to earn interest on socially-useful loans. Interest, at appropriate rates, would still be earned, but from loans made to achieve social as well as financial profit.

Policy Proposal III: States and municipalities should use their idle cash to encourage greater bank participation in low-income housing. Decent low-cost housing is the social good we are most concerned with here and one that deserves special attention from public investors. Banks willing to provide mortgages for low-income housing should receive preference in the deposit of idle public cash and on a schedule that would permit them to plan their mortgage activities. Similarly, banks willing to provide short-term loans to builders of such housing should receive special preference from public cash investors. The state, in particular, should investigate the possibility of absorbing a portion of the interest cost involved in low-income housing, coordinating its efforts with banks engaged in financing such projects.

The above proposals deal primarily with investment of public cash funds. We now offer suggestions for improving the social returns on pension fund investments:

Policy Proposal IV: State and city investment funds should devote more of their resources to the support of low-income housing. With mortgage money difficult to find, pension funds provide an important source of support for low-income housing. State and city funds already invest in mortgages, though the city funds especially are in a position to do far more than they have. More significantly, these funds, we think, are in a position to change their pattern of mortgage purchasing from one which slights so-called high risk areas and imposes penalties on FHA loans, to one which emphasizes such investments. We think this can be done with no loss of income to the funds, and, perhaps through some additional federal assistance, with no loss of security of investment. Surely, the resident of the ghetto and slum has as great a claim on these monies as the wealthy suburbanite.

Policy Proposal V: State and city investment funds should re-evaluate the geographical distribution of their mortgage investments. It seems odd to us that officials responsible for the welfare of state and city populations, who talk a great deal about the need to restore vitality to the city, and who criticize other governments for practices harmful to the city, should nevertheless allow local money to flow out into other areas of the country. We are fully aware that the security provided by geographic diversification is a powerful incentive for official investors, but we wonder whether in the long run that security may not be more fancied than real. Indeed, it may be that the rate of city decay has already increased to a point where there will shortly be very little left in the city to secure, largely because of a lack of resources. Surely it is time to ask these hard questions and consider whether locally-raised money might not better serve local residents. If our own public officials do not have enough confidence in the future of our large cities to invest in them, why should anyone else?

Policy Proposal VI: Managers of state and city pension funds should take steps to distribute information about their activities more widely and should invite wide-spread applications for financial support from needy groups or organizations. As matters now stand, few people know much about the operations of the funds discussed here, yet as we have argued, their actions are of extraordinary significance. We believe that the public in general and needy groups in particular have as much right to such knowledge and as much right to access to financial support as the brokers and bankers who now interact with a tiny group of official investors. To encourage the access, the funds themselves should publicize their activities and should invite any needy organization to apply for their support.

Policy Proposal VII: Finally, in any state concerned with the issues, the Governor should establish a commission to investigate the possibilities of securing greater public benefits from the investment of idle cash and public employee pension funds. Given present conditions of stringency in public budgets and extraordinarily high interest rates, we think it important that such a commission be created as soon as possible. For today, as never before, a day saved may amount to a good many dollars earned.

Conclusion

We have tried here to sketch out the nature, structure, and procedures of the most substantial public funds in the State of Michigan. It is a policy statement easily adaptable for tenants to use and advocate elsewhere. We find that, though these funds and the investors of idle public cash have accomplished much good, there is a great deal that might be done to increase the services they offer.

Above all, what is needed is the development of explicit policies to guide actions that now appear to us to take place in haphazard fashion. It is ironic in the extreme that in a nation which prides itself upon its financial sophistication, so much that is so important to the financial interests of citizens takes place without plan, without purpose, and without significant social utility. If such conditions exist elsewhere, no citizen—tenant or otherwise—can be content with the situation if only because it is affecting his pocketbook. Furthermore, if public officials ignore or overlook such alternatives, the initiative to investigate these possibilities may well lie with the citizenry. Perhaps tenant unions can help serve such an advocacy function. In these increasingly troubled times, policy making by default is a luxury we can no longer afford.

Part V

CONCLUSION

CHAPTER 17

Some Final Remarks

Stephen Burghardt

Tenants and their organizations are bound to become increasingly influential throughout our housing community. As implied in numerous legal articles, [1] if all legislative acts pertaining to labor and civil rights activity were extended to applicable tenant law, tenant unions would undoubtedly be in a strong legal position to organize tenants and bargain with landlords for the right to represent them in all future negotiations. Furthermore, well-organized tenant-welfare coalitions, through perseverance and sensitive application of social action and community development strategies, [2] could also secure enough political power at the local and state levels to insure greater tenant influence over certain housing conditions—better housing code enforcement, for example. Such accomplishments would make tenant unions well-known and influential voices in many, many communities, similar to civil rights groups in their legitimacy as advocates for better social conditions. With the rapidly growing National Tenants' Organization serving similar functions at a national level, tenants can expect to rapidly increase their influence in future housing policy.

But housing policy must be imaginative enough to encompass the depth of the housing problem. Anywhere one turns the picture is bleak: the building trades have priced themselves out of work; land costs soar in marginally urban areas so that farmers can no longer farm; construction costs are so high that inexpensive public housing becomes an impossibility; speculators continue to tread on the fears of homeowners and tenants, driving property values down and racial antagonisms up; landlords find it cheaper to leave apartments vacant than to rent them; our government builds little more than half its yearly housing commitment, and most of that is outside our decaying cities. The list is endless. And the more closely one examines the problem, the more one realizes that Band-aid approaches of yearly commitments to more housing units and showcase projects of concentrated code enforcement will not even begin to attend to the festering illnesses of our urban housing crisis.

Government can begin to seriously attack this problem by assuming total responsibility for building the necessary housing in our country. To suggest something like "total responsibility" is not to be pragmatic; Roosevelt found his limited public construction firm voted out of existence after only two years of activity.[3] The "sensible" approach would be to provide incentive arrangements for successful, rapid completion of construction contracts, or to arrange easily-financed loans for private construction firms to use so they can continue to take on more and more work. This is our present approach.[4] While undeniably sensible, there is at least one basic problem to this method of operation: it doesn't work.[5] Policy makers are some day going to have to realize that private firms are most interested in profits, not social progress. They will build housing units as cheaply as possible, and if that can't be done, they will build housing only afforded by the comfortably middle class.*

This problem is not contained solely to the private housing market. HUD's well-known lack of success in ending the housing shortage suggests that its policies are either disjointed or incomplete—or both. Even though it sets needed goals, and even though some of its planners are attempting to make public housing less stigmatized and more attractive to live in, HUD has no effective mechanism to see that its policies are correctly or expeditiously implemented. Instead, the department puts out contracts for bid, allocates resources or arranges for F.H.A. loans, sends a few public officials to ground breaking ceremonies, and . . . waits.

The results are obvious. For example, some public housing authorities are now claiming that tenant grievance procedures and a model lease—two landmark agreements achieved by the National Tenants' Organization with the Housing and Urban Development agency early in 1971—will force them to either default on their housing bonds or drastically increase rents.[6] To contend, however, that increased tenant rights are the cause of their financial problems misses the mark. A more realistic assessment is that original construction costs were so high and bonding rates concomitantly so inflated that public housing authorities' budgets have few margins for tenant equity.

If HUD actually had control over the quality construction of the housing units needed in our country, such financial problems might be avoided. A public construction firm would have no reason to sacrifice quality for quantity; the "profits" to be made are for the social good, not corporate stockholders. The problem of racism in the construction firms would begin to fade away; a public organization could more expeditiously follow public policy in the civil rights arena than recalcitrant private firms. The hiring of skilled and apprentice minority workers would be axiomatic. And finally, a public construction firm would include urban planners—those men and women who determine the number of units to be built and how they should be placed—so that at last there would be unity to the entire building process. Speed and quality could be combined.

Another, more popular public policy aimed at alleviating some of our

---

*In discussion with housing contractors, they admitted their disgust over the plethora of government regulations on federally-funded housing (the wall board had to be too thick, the piping was too costly, on and on). They all hoped they'd never have to get involved with the government again. One was frank enough to admit the underlying truth: "Quantity makes us money—quality is for the drawing boards."

housing ills is rent control. There is little doubt that rent control, if uniformly applied and enforced, would be of benefit to tenants. In a market where there is adequate competition, rent control could go far in helping tenants enjoy their housing. If nothing else, they would at least have the slight satisfaction in paying moderate prices for their apartments.

But in the real world of an imperfect, seller's market now found in our crowded central cities, rent control stands dangerously close to being a privilege of the upper middle class. The only landlords who can maintain adequate profit margins under rent control are those with holdings in choice areas where land values will continue to go up. While losing money on rents, the positive interactive effects of capital gains write-offs, depreciation allowances, and increasingly inflated land prices on this group of landlords' profit margins will make them indifferent to whatever minor economic favors are accruing to tenants.[7]

Thus, for example, professionals, out-of-town students, and middle class housewives could enjoy the extra margin of their monthly income in the area, shopping at expensive boutiques, attending local art theaters, and eating at fine neighborhood restaurants. A happy cycle would be completed; extra money, once used for rent, spent locally by already affluent residents, would attract more commercial interests and thus add further to the worth of the landlord's holdings. This pattern actually did hold for a number of years on the upper East Side of Manhatten in New York City.

However, things on the Lower East Side of the same city were not going quite as well. In this area, most of the tenants are poor; they have been for decades. They are living in neighborhoods where the above-mentioned factors on profit margins are no longer present. Many are found in buildings where the present landlord's sole profit is in rents.[8] In this case, rent control can only lead to markedly less maintenance and/or abandonment. The only cycle that presents itself here is one of little benefit to tenant or landlord.

The mistaken assumption of many middle class rent control advocates is the belief that most urban landlords in poor neighborhoods make their profits in other ways than rents. The majority do not.[9] It would be equally fallacious to think that any landlord will remain in business for any other reason than adequate profit. Social concern rarely begins before the ten percent profit margin.

This is not to say that rent control should not be attempted. In the short run (one or two years at least), it would help all tenants merely because rents weren't increased. In the longer run, if legislation can be adopted which safeguards all tenants (middle class and poor alike) from the horrors of abandonment and also maintains rent control, then rent control would be even better. One shouldn't forget, however, that New York City in theory lived under such a legislative package for years: rent control over vast numbers of buildings was coupled with a highly demanding housing code throughout the city. It looked great on paper, but it obviously didn't work.

Policies are needed that go beyond questions of construction and rentals. America needs policies that will attack the roots of its urban housing crisis, not just its manifestations. The Kaiser Commission's Report on Housing put the blame on existing urban housing conditions on "unseen forces" or "poverty." [10] It is an attractive analysis, one that neatly slips by the underlying economic problems, problems which the poor have little to do with except suffer. "Poverty" did not invite speculators into a neighborhood to lower land values and force frightened tenants and homeowners to the suburbs or to more crowded housing. "Poverty" had little to do with skimping on original construction costs or ignoring existing housing codes when apartments' pipes first sprung leaks. It didn't pay off building inspectors. Many of the real causes of housing blight in our cities lie with the opposing interests of tenants and landlords. The former wants quality at minimum expense; the latter perfers optimal profit margins. To undo such conflicting relations would go far in alleviating our housing problems. Any policy that effective, however, would necessitate impinging on some of the underlying values of our American society.

The Need for Urban Homesteading

Yet Americans need not forge new traditions to develop effective housing policy. They could instead demand the updating of an old one—homesteading. Homesteading is as traditional as the Old West, and its application, while limited in the days of land robber barons, was one of the most progressive of the 19th century. [11] While homesteading was in practice, settlers would find some unused land that was adequate to run some cattle and grow some crops—a few fence posts and a bale of wire and they were property owners. As recently as the 1940's, Americans have taken over land in the homesteader tradition, and without governmental retaliation. [12]

There have been a few urban homesteaders today, but they do not put up fence posts around untilled land; they take part in "squat-ins" in unused buildings. [13] Their reception by the public has been mixed at best. The settler on today's unused property is usually a welfare mother with children or an unemployed father and his family in need of a home. While they don't fit the image of the tradition, they are like their predecessors in their vision to see and use what is overlooked by others. To them, common sense dictates that unused housing in our crowded cities is no different from vacant grass lands in the rural west of a century ago.

And common sense may dictate that it is now time for the American people to demand urban homesteading. In the past, homestead acts were passed for brief periods of time giving land to settlers with the provision that they use the land productively. While the problem today is somewhat the reverse—too little land and too many settlers—urban homestead legislation would have the same contingency on a permanent basis. If the land is not used effectively, it would have to be forfeited to new settlers. Thus, when apartment buildings remain abandoned or are allowed to deteriorate for further speculation, the government must take the responsibility for turning over the "untilled" area to the tenants or their unions.

Abandoned apartments could most easily be turned into homesteaders' homes by redesigning the provisions of the 1968 National Housing Act which deal with both rehabilitation projects and condominiums and cooperatives.[14] If rehabilitated housing could be directly subsidized by the government to allow individuals or tenant unions to make necessary repairs—rather than continuing to demand that such projects be maintained by corporations with relatively large resource bases[15]—the occupants would be provided with the rights and responsibilities of the propertied. Perhaps the best way to think of these subsidies is to imagine that they are the reverse of what some large farmowners now get. Rather than receiving money to not grow crops, tenants as homesteaders would receive funds so long as they produced better apartment buildings, at least up to some maximum level. If it sounds far-fetched, it is no more so than the idea that some corporate farmers make over $200,000 a year to let their land lie fallow while others in our nation are starving.[16]

If one prefers a more direct comparison, consider the urban homesteading subsidies as direct, categorical housing grants. Such grants could have been used to avoid the projected $2.4 billion losses in F.H.A. mortgages throughout our nation's cities.[17] Such losses have been administered through our Section 235 and Section 236 programs, the officially-suggested answers to our cities' housing problems.[18] Rather than directly focusing on the homeowner and tenant, the programs concentrated on mortgage guarantees and large rehabilitation subsidies of great profit for real estate speculators and finance corporations. Through scare tactics, intimidation, and graft, the speculators bought up housing cheaply, proceeded to do the minimal patchwork renovation necessary for F.H.A. mortgages, and then sold the property for a high (and guaranteed) profit. The new homeowners, most of them poor minorities, soon found themselves unable to keep their quickly-dissipating buildings in repair; most banks eventually foreclosed.[19] In short, our most recent federal housing policy helped increase the rate of abandonment in our cities, all at a monumental expense to the taxpayer. As H.U.D. Secretary Romney himself stated: "Our housing policy has been a mistake."[20] Direct grants to homesteaders would appear to be both a cheaper and more productive alternative.

If tenants are now homesteaders actively improving their buildings, rent—rather than going to a landlord or some disinterested city bureaucracy—will pay for maintenance and repairs. Once those are completed, each building's rental income can start to pay off the now-subsidized mortgage. The urban homesteading envisioned here is similar to the "core housing" projects used successfully in other countries. In Colombia, for example, former tenants and squatters are given the basic superstructure of a house by Instituto de Credito Teritorial, the national housing agency.[21] In turn, the tenants are helped to finish the work necessary to turn the skeletal house into a comfortable and habital home. As the housing structures in American cities are often very large and usually demand highly-skilled labor to be remodelled, government assistance would be needed. With many small but worthwhile projects to work on, labor could be provided to a large number of minority employees working through their apprenticeships in the construction trades. A public construction firm, of course, would help facilitate these activities greatly.

This type of urban homesteading would first help decrease the housing shortage in a much less expensive way by using all the units available in the city. By concentrating on these units first, the problem of land acquisition, while not forgotten, is at least diminished in importance. Secondly, the social and economic costs in relocation are greatly reduced by concentrating on buildings already inhabited by tenants. If they are actively involved in the construction—or at least know what is being done and that they will directly benefit from it—the secondary costs of vandalism and petty theft so common in most rehabilitation projects might also be reduced.

If direct aid were given to remodel crumbling structures (and not spent instead on some of the worst landlords of all, city housing bureaucracies)[22], the rapid pace to the suburbs by urbanites (including the poor) might decelerate as they saw some visible reason for staying. And finally, *if continuously applied and enforced,* urban homesteading legislation over time would do away with the insoluble tension in tenant-landlord relations because it would do away with the relationship itself. With no landlords present, there can be no tenants, only homesteaders.

The real difficulty with this plan is not with the intricacies of its implementation. Urban homesteading would meet active resistance mainly because it infringes upon present assumptions concerning the rights of the propertied.** Urban homesteading is not akin to a five-year plan involving the state annexation of land. It is a proposal based on what has become increasingly evident within our urban housing community over the past twenty years; the continued and increasing harassment, discomfort and ill health that the many have to bear on account of the prerogatives of the few. There is something frightfully wrong when a landlord is able to charge high rents to his tenants, decrease his maintenance costs within his buildings so that they begin to fall into major disrepair, and tenants can do nothing about it.

Few object to the rights of private property when those rights do not lead to the harm or harassment of others. The concept of private property, and the laws reflecting it, work rather well under the somewhat bucolic conditions of well-tilled farms and attractive summer homes. But what about our urban areas? As cities are continuously pressed for land, the only available space for

---

**Or, perhaps more exactly, the "large-propertied." As Charles Reich has pointed out in "The Law and Planned Society (*Yale Law Journal,* Vol. 75, No. 8, July, 1966, pp. 1227-1270) and in "The New Property," (*The Public Interest,* Winter 1966, pp. 57-89), the legal precedent for public expropriation of property has been firmly established since at least the 1930's. Almost all of the so-called regulatory agencies—PPC, CAB, ICC—have expropriated land from small property owners on behalf of urban renewal, highway development, airport construction. The beneficiaries have been port authorities, large construction and development firms; small homeowners have been easily and legally pushed out of the way. If the precedent exists, shouldn't it more rationally be extended in the public interest to include those areas in our central cities where tenants and others are being exploited due to the privileges of a few? If logic and precedent were strong enough political weapons (they obviously are not), then urban homesteading could become a rather simple reality in our future.

building is up, in the air. "Land" becomes a luxury enjoyed by few. In place of a suburbanite's home, complete with grass plot and outdoor barbecue pit, what does an urban tenant receive? The cultural enjoyment of the city, of course. Many, however, would say that the enjoyment is offered *in spite of* his housing, not because of it. What is offered in return for his rent? If he receives none of the usual rights enjoyed by those with property, he should be guaranteed the right to adequate services; not only a decent apartment, but a well-kept building, safe and secure redress of grievances, adequate maintenance.

The rights of the urban propertied have become prerogatives because none of the above services are legally guaranteed a tenant; a landlord can ignore any and all of them without fear of legal redress. Urban homesteading, made permanent under the law as an alternative to the irresponsibility of some of the propertied, would attempt to end such injustices. Americans and their government must come to recognize that rights to land in our modern urban, congested communities are contingent upon the responsibility of respecting others' rights to a safe and healthy home. If landlords fail to keep that responsibility—if they turn their rights into prerogatives leading to the exploitation of others—then there is little logical reason why those prerogatives should not be terminated.

Americans must also realize that our present housing policies orient away from the improvement of our cities. By placing top priority on rehabilitation funds for racially integrated areas and by enforcing rules that preclude substantive repairs in neighborhoods already heavily blighted,[23] our housing policy flatly states that it has given up on our central cities. The intricate plans stemming from the Kaiser Commission, instead of being innovative, really function like decentralized urban renewal projects of the 1950's. The orientation is still the same; rather than rebuilding slums, they attempt to ignore them. Urban homesteading, by admitting to realities of our urban areas (widespread urban blight and segregation) could help reverse this policy orientation. If it is not reversed, people in our cities will continue to leave for the suburbs because there will simply be nowhere else to go.

If the above proposals are at all startling, it is because they are based on two major assumptions: (1) that the rights of private property should be equated with the rights of adequate service; (2) that the relationship between tenant and landlord should be redefined and made equitable. These are obviously two large assumptions, ones that many people are going to find untenable even though our cities continue to decay and more and more people seek refuge in suburban tracts of ticky-tack. It would be naive to expect such substantive change to become an immediate reality; there are too many vested interests in present property relations, too much influence among realtors and too little among tenants and their organizations to allow such radical reform.

This is unfortunate, for the housing problems of the cities will eventually be those of the suburbs. Multi-unit construction is proceeding throughout suburban communities, and while the housing may look quite attractive now, the same inequities found in our urban housing communities are still present. Unless checked, these inequities over time will breed the same housing blight as in the past.

All of these changes will take money, lots of it. The political cartoonist who suggested that our cities declare they've lost the war in hopes of an urban Marshall Plan was on target as to the kind of financial effort needed to end our cities' housing problems. The pathetic question, however, is whether we must wait until our cities are hollow shells containing the remnants of a once dynamic urban community before housing policy is adopted that can meet the actual dimensions of our urban housing crisis.

---

1. For example, Myron Moskovitz and Peter Honigsberg, "A Model Landlord-Tenant Act," *Georgetown Law Review,* June, 1970; and Paul G. Garrity, "Redesigning Landlord-Tenant Concepts for an Urban Society," *Journal of Urban Law,* Vol. 46, No. 4, are probably the best two reviews of the problems and potential of legal tenant action.

2. Some of the best applicable organizing strategies in the literature come from Warren Hagstrom. For example, see his "Can the Poor Transform the World?" in Kramer and Specht (eds) *Readers in Community Organization,* Prentice-Hall, 1969. For a more theoretical analysis of strategy formation, see Eugene Litwak, Earl Shiroi, Libby Zimmerman, and Jesse Bernstein's "Community Participation in Bureaucratic Organizations: Principles and Strategies," *Interchange,* Vol. 1, No. 4, January 1970.

3. The Report of the President's Committee on Urban Housing, *A Decent Home,* Government Printing Office, 1969, p. 56.

4. This was much of the approach suggested by the Kaiser Commission in *A Decent Home,* pp. 7-36 and Section IV, particularly pp. 113-215.

5. As of August 1971, HUD statistics report that the last three years have averaged little more than 1.6 million units—far less than is necessary to reach the Kaiser Commission's goal of 2.5 million by the year 1978.

6. New York *Times,* July 24, 1971, p. 46.

7. See generally Frank Grad, *Legal Remedies for Housing Code Violations,* Research Report No. 14, Douglas Commission, 1968.

8. George Sternlieb, *The Tenement Landlord,* Rutgers University Press, 1966, p. 119.

9. Ibid.

10. President's Urban Housing Committee, op. cit., p. 45.

11. Peter Barnes, "The Great Land Robbery," *The New Republic,* June 7, 1971.

12. Charles Abrams, *Man's Struggle for Shelter in an Urbanizing World,* M.I.T. Press, Cambridge, Mass., 1964, p. 12.

13. For example, New York *Times,* May 24, 1971, p. 27.

14. For cooperatives, one would revise Section 236; for condominiums, the homeownership program under Section 235 could be applied. See 12 U.S.C. § 1715z-1(j)(6).

15. A rare example of where such a program has worked can be found in New York City. See The New York *Times,* May 14, 1971 concerning a Model Cities low-income cooperative project.

16. Roger Beadwood, "The Southern Roots of Urban Change," (*Fortune,* August, 1968), as quoted in Piven and Cloward, *Regulating the Poor—The Function of Social Welfare,* Pantheon Books, New York, 1971, p. 203.

17. Testimony received at U.S. Senate Anti-Trust and Monopoly Subcommittee, 5/2/72. See the Detroit *Free Press,* May 3, 1972, p. 3. Losses in Detroit alone may reach anywhere between $70,000,000 and $250,000,000. See Detroit *News,* May 3, 1972, and May 8, 1972.

18. See the explanation of this approach in *A Decent Home, op. cit.,* pp. 7-36 and Section IV, particularly pp. 113-215.

19. H. Erich Heinemann, "F.H.A.—From Suburb to Ghetto," New York *Times,* May 7, 1972, Section III, p. 1.

20. Quoted in Heinemann, "Ibid.," and in *Newsweek,* April 10, 1972, p. 61.

21. Abrams, *op. cit.,* p. 173.

22. New York *Times,* April 25, 1971, p. 1.

23. See the *U.S. Federal Register,* Vol. 37, No. 23 (February 7, 1972) for the criteria underlying all federal housing priorities. The central cities, due to segregation and deteriorating conditions, must necessarily rank lower than in the past.